# BEHIND THE MASK

ALFREDO MIRANDÉ

# BEHIND
# THE MASK

*Gender Hybridity in a Zapotec Community*

THE UNIVERSITY OF
ARIZONA PRESS
TUCSON

The University of Arizona Press
www.uapress.arizona.edu

ISBN-13: 978-0-8165-3544-6 (cloth)
ISBN-13: 978-0-8165-3955-0 (paper)

Cover design by Leigh McDonald
Cover photograph courtesy of Naomy Méndez Romero and photographer Andrea Cinta Robles

Publication of this book is made possible in part by the proceeds of a permanent endowment created with the assistance of a Challenge Grant from the National Endowment for the Humanities, a federal agency.

Library of Congress Cataloging-in-Publication Data
Names: Mirandé, Alfredo, author.
Title: Behind the mask : gender hybridity in a Zapotec community / Alfredo Mirandé.
Description: Tucson : The University of Arizona Press, 2017. | Includes bibliographical references and index.
Identifiers: LCCN 2016039134 | ISBN 9780816535446 (cloth : alk. paper)
Subjects: LCSH: Zapotec Indians—Mexico—Juchitán de Zaragoza. | Two-spirit people—Mexico—Juchitán de Zaragoza. | Gender identity. | Sex role.
Classification: LCC F1221.Z3 M57 2017 | DDC 972/.74—dc23 LC record available at https://lccn.loc.gov/2016039134

Printed in the United States of America
⊚ This paper meets the requirements of ANSI/NISO Z39.48-1992 (Permanence of Paper).

*Para Pilar, la Oaxaqueña*

# CONTENTS

# ILLUSTRATIONS

# PREFACE

BEHIND THE MASK is a study of *los muxes* (or los muxe') of Juchitán, a group of indigenous biological males who constitute a third gender in the Isthmus of Tehuantepec.[1] One might wonder why a heterosexual Mexican native living in California, who is neither Zapoteco nor muxe, would undertake such a study. The short and obvious answer is that, as a sociologist who has a long-standing interest in gender and masculinity, this project is a natural extension and continuation of my academic interest in these areas. On a more personal level, I was introduced to the topic by my daughter and her husband, who were living in Oaxaca at the time.

During my visits, we chatted about the muxes; I had read several articles and books on them. Aware of my interest in the topic, my daughter and son-in-law attended a muxe *vela*, or festival, in Oaxaca city to get a bird's eye view of the event and made a video, which they forwarded to me. In the video I saw a large number of indigenous men dancing while dressed in traditional women's Zapotec, or Juchiteca, attire. This image stood in sharp contrast to the prevailing hegemonic view of México as the land of charros, tequila, machismo, and unbridled traditional ranchero masculinity.[2] I was intrigued by the contradiction and wanted to get behind the mask of machismo and traditional Mexican masculinity.

Though my daughter and her husband were outsiders, they had a great time at the vela and were fortunate enough to meet a very friendly and gracious muxe from Juchitán, named Biiniza. Although many of these men were dressed in women's traditional Zapotec attire, and the event was billed as a muxe vela, my daughter and *yerno* were surprised when Biiniza remarked that in fact only a handful of muxes were in attendance. She added that while they may have looked like muxes to the unsuspecting eye, most were not. Presumably, the majority of persons were gay men in drag or "pretenders" rather than authentic muxes. A gay man in drag impersonating a muxe is an intriguing image I address later in the book.

Biiniza gave them a colorful printed invitation to the forthcoming annual Intrépida Vela in Juchitán that November, which they promptly sent to me. Biiniza also shared her e-mail address, invited me to the vela, and told them to have me contact her when I arrived in Juchitán. Before embarking on the research and making the first research trip, I visited my daughter once again and had the opportunity to meet "Julie," a hair stylist in her neighborhood. My daughter's husband is an Oaxacan native, and Julie is both a friend and his hairdresser. Julie is not muxe, but I understood that she knew quite a bit about muxes and had friends who were muxe. I wanted to get the perspective of an openly gay Oaxacan man on the muxes.

Julie graciously invited me to come to her hair salon at about 5:00 p.m., when she took a dinner break. The interview was informative, as she sat in a barber's chair talking while intermittently chewing on a *tlayuda* (a Oaxacan open-face burrito made on a large tortilla) and sipping a super-sized *refresco* (soda). She explained, "We are all technically 'gay' because we have sex with men, but the muxes distinguish themselves from other gays because they consider themselves to be a sort of third sex." Most also live the muxe lifestyle 24/7, dress in traditional Zapotec feminine attire, and are always out of the closet. Julie added that their origins are in Zapotec culture, that most spoke Zapoteco, and that they were generally accepted in their community and culture, whereas gays were not generally accepted in Oaxaca or in México as a whole.

Muxes of the Isthmus are a popular and public group, the subject of many international documentaries as well as articles and books. Many use pseudonyms or "artistic" names. The Intrépida organization to which a number of muxes belong even maintains a website with posted names. In this sense, many muxes are public figures with public personas.

Because most have adopted feminized names, I generally use the feminine pronoun when referring to persons like Biiniza or Felina, who have clearly assumed a feminized public identity and persona, and the masculine pronoun for those who have not adopted a feminized name. When uncertain as to whether the person has assumed a feminized identity, I refer to them as "he," "s/he," and occasionally "hir."[3] For muxes who have not adopted muxe or artistic names, I use pseudonyms. I also use pseudonyms for other persons I interviewed.

Some muxes alternate between a masculine and a feminine identity. An example is Kike, a well-known *travestí* and self-proclaimed performance artist, who uses Kike in his daily life as a hair stylist and Kika when he metamorphoses into a woman. He even refers to himself in the third person as La Kika. Anibal, an accountant and one of the older muxes, has also adopted a feminine name, Anilú. When I asked whether I should refer to a particular muxe as "he" or "she," Anilú said, "It doesn't matter really, because we know it's the same person." I found that they often referred to a person as "he" when referring to his total persona, including childhood, and "she" when talking about the current person as muxe.

After interviewing Julie, I e-mailed Biiniza several times before and after I got to Oaxaca. As it turned out, she had given me the number of the salon where she and other muxes hang out. The owner, Felina, answered the telephone and told me that Biiniza was in Oaxaca city and had not returned. This was ironic because I had just come from the city and could have interviewed her there. The day after I arrived in Juchitán, I sent Biiniza another e-mail message, giving her my e-mail address and telephone number, and telling her that I was staying at a hotel downtown. She wrote back, "I will communicate with you today, okay?"[4] I would later learn that people in El Istmo often self-describe as "informal" and are prone to miss or be late for appointments.

Unfortunately, Biiniza never contacted me, but I attended my first vela that November. I had read about Juchitán's reputation as an insulated place, where residents are leery of strangers. As an outsider, I expected it would be difficult for me to gain access to the Intrépida organization, but at the onset and during the course of the study, I found members of the group and other Juchitecos to be surprisingly friendly, engaging, and willing to talk and share their experiences.

I saw Biiniza in person for the first time at the grand muxe vela, when she appeared on stage in a fancy red evening gown, surrounded by people and greeted with a warm round of applause. I admired her from afar as she was introduced as a former muxe queen and walked down the red carpet. I met and interviewed her on two subsequent trips in 2011 and 2013. She proved to be as gracious with me as she had been with my daughter and her husband and extremely helpful in putting me in contact with other muxes. I feel a special bond with Biiniza because she was literally my initial contact with the muxes of Juchitán and my entrée into the field.

I made other contacts in Juchitán through key informants (Warren and Karner 2015, 71–73), or more accurately "social notables," a term employed by Wayne Cornelius (1982) and Cecilia Menjívar (2000) for people such as Biiniza and Felina. Felina is the owner of the salon that bears her name and a past president of the local muxe organization Las Auténticas Intrépidas Buscadoras del Peligro (The Authentic, Fearless Seekers of Danger). Felina's *estética* (salon) became a place I frequented often and where I met a number of contacts and conducted several of the interviews with Intrépidas and community members. It was also a communication center, where people could leave messages and meet with me.

## THE STUDY AND SAMPLE

Over the past eight years, I have carried out field research in Juchitán and made five research trips to the area, engaging in participant observation, attending muxe velas and other events, and carrying out in-depth qualitative interviews with muxes and other community members. During most of the research I conducted for this book, I worked alone, but in the early phases of the study, I benefited greatly from the help and support I received from muxes such as Felina, Anilú, Gabriel, and Roque, a stylist at Felina's estética who helped me make contacts and schedule interviews.[5]

In addition to attending muxe velas, I used a wide range of qualitative research methods, including archival research, participant observation, and open-ended interviews with a purposive sample of approximately 115 people. I conducted all interviews in Spanish, then transcribed and translated them into English. The formal muxe interviews were open ended, lasted approximately sixty minutes, and covered several broad topics, including where the persons were born and grew up; what their parents did for a living; when the interviewees first realized they were muxe; how their families responded to their gender and sexual identity and lifestyle; whether they were teased, harassed, or bullied as children and as adolescents; how muxes are distinct from gay men; whether they were in or had been in a stable relationship with a man; as well as how they viewed the accomplishments and challenges of Las Intrépidas as an organization and their societal acceptance in the community at large.

In addition to interviews with fifty-two muxes, I interviewed a number of other social notables and key community members, including two priests at the San Vicente Ferrer Parish; the assistant to the municipal president; the assistant principal of the local CONALEP, a government-supported vocational high school and trade school; the director of Casa de la Cultura; several teachers; and a public health nurse.

To gather information from ordinary citizens and assess their views of muxes, I used what I term *encuentros*, or spontaneous encounters, enabling me to engage in informal conversations, which were considerably shorter and more spontaneous than the other interviews. This group of informal interviewees included food vendors, cab drivers, service workers, students, and visitors. In total, I interviewed more than fifty community respondents at velas, parades, parks, restaurants, homes, and other locales.

Although the focus of the study was on los muxes, as the research progressed, I encountered seven men like Julie who identified as gay, distinguished themselves from muxes, and provided a unique perspective on the latter. I also learned that muxes have sex with hombres rather than with other muxes, and that their partners are called *mayates*, so I arranged interviews with five mayates who have sex for money. I also learned that Las Intrépidas had reached out to women, and I was able to interview three *lesbianas*, including one who belonged to, and was president of, the *mesa directiva*, or governing board, of the Intrépidas organization.

## METHOD AND THEORY

Although I conducted ethnographic field research and employed mixed qualitative methods, this is not an ethnography in the traditional anthropological sense of the word, as reflected in the work of pioneer ethnographers like Bronislaw Malinowski and Franz Boas. The model of anthropological fieldwork as a mechanism of sustained observation in the life of a group studied over a prolonged period was first proclaimed and promoted by Malinowski (1922; Kemper and

Royce 2002, xiii). Boas similarly stressed the importance of rigorous anthropological theories derived from systematic observation obtained through ethnographic fieldwork (Emerson 2001, 4).

While fieldwork conducted as outlined by Malinowski and Boas became
the signature method in anthropology, ethnographic field research developed
differently in sociology. It emerged not from the study of "primitive" people in
exotic places but from nineteenth-century reform movements, which sought to
study and to change the life conditions of the urban poor (Emerson 2001, 9).
One of the most important developments in sociological fieldwork was the social survey method, through which researchers attempt to understand the lives
and conditions of the urban poor. The method was developed first by Charles
Booth (1902), in his study of the London poor, and then by the University of
Chicago School of Sociology, which introduced distinctive sociological methods, such as the eclectic case study method, interviewing, direct observation
combined with informal interviewing, and participant observation (Emerson
2001, 12).

This qualitative sociological analysis of the muxe experience employs not
only mixed methods, including interviews, case studies, archival research, and
participant observation, but also what Geertz describes as "thick description,"
which is primarily an attempt to describe how members of the studied group
portray, understand, and interpret the events that make up their lives (Geertz
1973, introduction). Finally, rather than entering the field seeking to test pre-
conceived formal theories or hypotheses, I anchored the study in what sociologists describe as grounded theory, which endeavors to produce a general theory
from empirical data and to base such study on the careful observation of particular groups and settings. Grounded theory posits that "it is necessary to do
detailed, intensive, microscopic examination of the data in order to bring out
the amazing complexity of what lies in, behind and beyond these data" (Strauss
1987, 10).

During most of my visits to Juchitán, I stayed at the Hotel Central in downtown Juchitán. I would like to thank the owner and staff for their hospitality,
help, and support in carrying out the research. I also had the opportunity to
meet a personable young man, Davíd, who not only was my workout coach at
the local gym but also shared much information and insight about Juchitán
and its local attitudes and customs, introduced me to several key participants in
this study, and provided the perspective of youth on the muxes. Finally, *muchas
gracias* to all the people from Juchitán, especially the muxes, *que compartieron sus*

*vidas e historias familiares conmigo* (who shared their lives and family histories with me) and who ultimately made the study and this book possible. I would also like to acknowledge two muxes, Mandis and Roque, who, sadly, passed away during the course of the study. Mandis was one of the founding members of Las Intrépidas and was greatly respected by muxes and the larger community. Roque was extremely gracious, helpful, and someone I considered a friend. While acknowledging the assistance of the people of Juchitán and those from surrounding communities, I am ultimately responsible for any errors, misinterpretations, or omissions.

# BEHIND THE MASK

# INTRODUCTION

*God entrusted San Vicente with three sacks: one with women, one with men, and one with a third mixed gender. Vicente was supposed to distribute all three around the world. But when he got to Juchitán, the sack containing the third gender ripped open, and Juchitán received many more than its allotment as third-gender people got out.*

MICKEY WEEMS (2011)

T HIS CHAPTER'S EPIGRAPH is a variation of a popular Juchitán myth that links the prevalence and local acceptance of muxes to the patron saint of Juchitán, San Vicente Ferrer. Other variations are that San Vicente had only one sack with the third gender; that he had three sacks, and each contained the seeds for women, men, and a third gender; or that the sack with the third gender was damaged because the muxes inside were so boisterous that they caused it to rip open over Juchitán (Weems 2011).

## SAN VICENTE: PATRON SAINT OF JUCHITÁN AND THE MUXES

The isolated, hot, and inhospitable landscape and climate of Juchitán appears linked to the history and characteristics of its people, who are generally described as hardy and hardworking. According to local legend, after the death of Santa Teresa, the city in which God sought to bring together dispersed men had not yet been constructed. The Lord persisted in his plan to build the city and ordered his emissaries to summon Vicente Ferrer, who was already a saint despite his youth (Henestrosa 1993b, 39). San Vicente returned to earth to carry out the Lord's wishes and discovered an idyllic location nearby, where the air was "fine and clear," the land fertile, water plentiful, and the jungle filled with fruit (39). But San Vicente was not satisfied, and he decided that this would *not* be the place where he would build his city because "the residents would have no obstacles or dangers, and they would become indolent and dispirited; I want children who are hardworking and swift. He abandoned the region which the following morning became Tehuantepec and looked for an area where the air was thick and dirty, the land arid, the water deep, the rain unruly, and where the jungle extended from the foot of the horizon" (39–40). When he found such an area, San Vicente rejoiced and proceeded to gather the first inhabitants to build the first house and dig the first well. He reputedly built Juchitán in an area where the wells were seven fathoms deep, and settlers would have to "rip the chest of the earth after scarce rains to obtain its fruits" (40).

San Vicente Ferrer not only is the patron saint of Juchitán but also has emerged as the spiritual saint of the muxes and been adopted by the LGBTQ community in the region. He is a popular saint in Spain and in Latinoamérica, as well as being the patron saint of construction workers and people who suffer from headaches.

Excitement foreshadowed Vicente's birth in Valencia on January 23, 1350, as his mother, Constance, was said to have experienced only joy and painlessness during her pregnancy.[1] His father had a prophetic dream in which an unknown Dominican preacher appeared to him, saying that he would have a son who would be world renowned. In addition, a poor blind woman predicted that the child would be an "angel who would one day restore her sight"—which he did, several years later. As a child, Vicente was a happy boy with a disposition for learning and piety. He subdued his passions by fasting rigorously every Wednesday and Friday. Vicente saw the poor as the children of Christ and treated them with such great affection and charity that it led his parents to make him a dispenser of their bountiful alms. Rather than pursuing a secular vocation, Vicente decided to devote himself to the service of God and entered the order of Saint Dominic in 1368, at the age of eighteen.

He made rapid progress on the paths to perfection and took Saint Dominic as his model. In addition to prayer and penance, he enjoyed the study and meditation of the Holy Scriptures and the readings of the fathers. For three years, he read only the scriptures and learned the entire Bible by heart. Vicente studied philosophy and published a treatise on dialectic suppositions before the age of twenty-four. He was then sent to Barcelona to continue his studies, and he preached the word of God with much success, especially during a great famine, when he prophesized the arrival of two vessels loaded with corn to relieve hunger in the city. He later attended Lerida, the most renowned university of Catalonia. There, he continued his education and apostolic function and was awarded his doctorate at the age of twenty-eight.

Vicente was a devout child with an unusual intellect, an intellect that won him a post as a professor of philosophy, and he was known for his oratory skills, gift of tongues, and missionary zeal, which led him to travel extensively and to preach to many nations (Reinhart 1912). Vicente died in 1410 and was canonized several decades later.

Two principal images of San Vicente are venerated in Juchitán. Both are located in the Parroquia de San Vicente Ferrer (Parish of Saint Vincent Ferrer), near downtown. The larger figure is San Vicente *gola* ("old" or "large" in Zapoteco) and the smaller, San Vicente *huini* ("small" or "young"). Among the numerous velas held annually in Juchitán is an annual vela, a major festival, in May dedicated to each of the images.

## IN SEARCH OF THE AMAZONS AND MATRIARCHY

Juchitán is also known in popular culture for the mythical Amazon women, and many observers have commented on the extraordinary strength and independence of Juchitecas. Descriptions of gender in Juchitán also defy the patriarchal ideal found in hegemonic ranchero masculinity and femininity, where men have power and authority while women defer and obey.

Writer Elena Poniatowska described Juchitecas as almost Amazon-like: "huge women, mountain women, rattle women, women whom nothing can hurt" (cited in Keller 2007, 3). In Juchitán everything is different, as "women like to walk embracing each other, and here they come to the marches, overpowering, with their iron calves. Man is a kitten between their legs, a puppy they have to admonish" (Poniatowska 1993, 133). She adds that women in El Istmo like to laugh and joke with each other, and their jokes always have sexual connotations: "Zapotec women have always been openly erotic, and they wear their sensuality on their shirtsleeves. Sex is a little clay toy; they take it in their hands, mold it as they please, shake it, knead it together with the corn of their *totopos* [tortillas]" (135).

Others have similarly observed that the women of Juchitán generally have *presencia*, or a presence that commands respect and self-esteem (Giebeler

1997, 255). Juchitecas (Tecas) are recognizable anywhere in México because of their long *enaguas* (skirts or underskirts), multicolored huipiles (loose-fitting blouses), and a long kerchief that is attached to the skirt (254). The most important moment for demonstrating presencia is when a woman enters a social gathering with a firm, almost heavy step, her skirt swirling against her petticoats, and the hem touching the floor (255).

> La mujer Juchiteca se pone en escena en una fiesta, entrando al recinto, detenié-ndose en el centro y mirando el rededor hasta que la anfitriona se acerca a salu-darla, le indica un puesto y le ofrece comida y la inevitable cerveza. (256)
> [The Juchitecan woman commands attention as she enters a social gathering, stands in the doorway and stops and glances around the room until the hostess approaches to greet her, indicate where to sit, and offers her food and the predict-able beer.]

Giebeler adds that the woman's posture is always erect and that she has never known a Juchiteca who enters a space with stooped shoulders, eyes lowered, or head bowed (256).

Because of the strength and independence of Juchitecas, a number of researchers have described Juchitán as a matriarchal society (Bennholdt-Thomsen 1997, 22). However, given substantial differences between the Valley of Oaxaca and El Istmo de Tehuantepec in the social organization of Zapotec society, the matriarchal nature of Juchitán society appears to have had pre-Columbian origins, likely predating the arrival of the Zapotecs in the area (45). Zapotec society in the Valley of Oaxaca was, after all, militaristic and patriarchal, whereas the Istmo was agricultural and matriarchal.

> Sólo entre los zapotecos del Istmo las mujeres tienen esa posición social tan ex-traordinariamente fuerte, que parece emanar de una estructura social antigua. Es muy probable que provenga de una tradición específicamente ístmica, anterior de la Zapoteca. (45)
> [Only among the Zapotecs of the Isthmus do women have a social position that is so extraordinarily strong that it appears to emanate from an ancient social structure. It is quite probable that it emerged from a tradition that was specifi-cally Isthmic, predating the Zapotecs.]

In discussing the so-called matriarchy in El Istmo de Tehuantepec, it is often difficult to separate fact from fiction, but clearly by the beginning of the twentieth century, the myth of the Isthmus of Tehuantepec as the land of liberated Amazon women had taken hold. As early as 1859, French traveler and historian Charles Étienne Brasseur de Bourbourg described the marketplace in Tehuantepec as dominated exclusively by women and found them to be the least reserved women in the Américas. "[They] chattered, laughed, conversed, screamed, and argued with an incredible animation. They openly made fun of their men, who they provoked in Spanish and Zapotec with a shamelessness hardly equaled" (quoted in DeMott 2006, 18).

At the urging of José Vasconcelos, a native of the city of Oaxaca and México's minister of education, the young Diego Rivera returned from Europe in 1922 and, wishing to shed European influences in his work, went to El Istmo, where he sketched Isthmus women, festivals, and landscapes. He observed Isthmus women bathing in the Tehuantepec River and painted *The Bather of Tehuantepec*. This painting became a turning point in his career, with the creation of a style that was free of European influences (DeMott 2006, 19). By the late 1920s, the Isthmus had become a popular destination point and center for many artists and intellectuals, including Rivera, Frida Kahlo, Sergei Eisenstein, and Langston Hughes. Whether because of bathing in the Tehuantepec River without shame or regret or because of the bluntness of the Zapotec language, which is said to be free of forbidden words, "The Women of the Isthmus soon had a reputation as sexually liberated women," who assumed a dominant role in a matriarchal society (21).[2]

More recent visits from anthropologists like American Beverly Newbold Chiñas, however, have led to dismissing the Isthmus matriarchy as a myth. Chiñas remarks that anthropologists have never actually documented the existence of matriarchal society anywhere in the world (2002, 87). Italian anthropologist Marinella Miano Borruso also rejects the existence of a matriarchy: "Zapotec society can be defined as a mercantile society in classic Marxist terms. In particular, women are able to produce a sufficient surplus that allows them to be economically autonomous but also to support a good portion of the festival structure of the community and to invest in their businesses and in gold" (Miano Borruso 2002, 60).[3]

The recurring debate about whether Isthmus Zapotec society is or is not a true matriarchy may turn on how matriarchal societies are defined. Chiñas contends that Isthmus Zapotec society is best described as a patriarchy with a matrifocal emphasis. "Matrifocality (in contrast to matriarchy) can function perfectly well along with a patriarchal superstructure because matrifocality often operates at the informal level and in separate arenas from the patriarchal overlay of male roles" (2002, 87). She likens matrifocality to an iceberg, with a tip that is as visible as the formal patriarchal system, while the informal matrifocal system lies beneath the surface and is not readily visible. A good part of the Isthmus social system is thus submerged and invisible.

Regardless of whether Isthmus Zapotec society is a true matriarchy, the blend of Isthmus Zapotec gender roles clearly results in a balanced equality between the sexes (Chiñas 2002, 87) and stands in stark contrast to gender roles in México at large, which may be unparalleled.[4] Although relatively rare, matrifocality has been found in a number of societies throughout the world, including West Africa, Java (bilateral kinship and neolocal residence), and Belize.

> Gender roles in Isthmus Zapotec society are relatively egalitarian as Zapotec women hold strong roles economically, socially, and in the kinship system. The father is almost always living in the Zapotec matrifocal household, and relations between husband and wife tend to be highly egalitarian. It is not only *acceptable* for women to exercise power and authority in their everyday lives, it is culturally expected and encouraged. (Chiñas 2002, 87)

Veronika Bennholdt-Thomsen similarly observes that the women of Juchitán control commerce and the public market:

> Todo lo que hacen las mujeres en Juchitán es considerado de importancia, no *a pesar* de que ellas lo hacen, sino *porque* ellas lo hacen. La diferencia entre el trabajo que vale porque es pagado con dinero, definido como masculino en nuestra sociedad, y el trabajo femenino menos valorado no se conoce allí. (1997, 22)
> [Everything that women do in Juchitán is considered important, not *in spite of* the fact that they do it, but *because* they do it. The distinction between work that is valued because it is salaried, defined as masculine in our society, and female work, which is less valued, is unknown there.]

Interestingly, the role of housewife as such is unknown in Juchitán. A more common role is as housewife-artisan-merchant.

The market in Juchitán is controlled by women, and on any given day, fifteen to twenty thousand persons pass through the market, most of them women (Bennholdt-Thomsen 1997, 67). Of the 1,150 stands that Bennholdt-Thomsen and her associates counted, 797 were inside the market, and the remainder were on surrounding streets. Between 8:00 a.m. and 10:00 p.m., they counted 1,704 women and 87 men in the market. Most of the men were *cargadores* (loaders of goods, or porters), family members helping merchants, or mobile sellers of goods.

In this society, going to the market plays an important social function, as one of every two adult women goes to the market at least once per day to buy or sell goods. It is a place to exchange not only goods but also news, gossip, and commentary on any and all existing social issues. But perhaps the market's most important function is that it reinforces interpersonal relations. The custom is to shop at stands of one's friends, relatives, neighbors, and acquaintances, where prices are negotiated and determined by the relationship that exists between buyer and seller (Bennholdt-Thomsen 1997, 69).

## HOMBRE, MUJER, Y MUXE:
## A GENDERED INSTITUTIONS PERSPECTIVE

Juchitán is also widely renowned as a "gay paradise," where gay and transgender persons are readily accepted. Women's work patterns and overall status in Juchitán reveal a great deal about muxes in the community. Although Juchitán is not a matriarchal society, its institutions are distinctly patterned by gender. The fact that women control the market and manage the household also means that los muxes are accepted and integrated into the economy and society.

According to Marinella Miano and Águeda Gómez Suárez (2009, 1), Isthmus Zapotec society recognizes three elements that make up the gender order: *los hombres, las mujeres, y los muxe*. Rather than being considered an exceptional figure outside the norm, muxes assume an important economic role in the family and in the community at large (3). They are actively involved in the festival system, as artisans who create the colorful regional feminine dresses worn at fiestas and who make decorations for the velas and floats for parades. The road muxes follow to gain the same societal acceptance that women enjoy is described by Miano and Suárez as un largo camino de producción de méritos para consolidar un prestigio familiar y social: ocuparse en la casa de la reproducción de las condiciones básicas de la vida, desde la comida a los cuidados de niños, ancianos y enfermos, contribuir y acrecentar el patrimonio familiar, participar activamente en el compulsivo festivo y ceremonial. (4)

[a long road of accomplishments to gain social and familial status and prestige: reproduce basic needs in the home, from food to the care of children, the elderly and the sick, manage and contribute to family finances, actively participate in the mandatory festive and ceremonial life of the community].

Traditionally, having a muxe son is seen as a blessing from God, because muxes provide "an extra set of hands" for Zapotec women. Muxes are also the children who support the family in adulthood, take care of elderly parents, and, in some cases, become heads of households. Like women, muxes have a well-deserved reputation for being hard workers, skilled artisans, and successful merchants.

In addition to the market, the economy, and the family, other institutions, like the Church and the polity, play equally important roles in the acceptance of muxes. Velas, for example, are festivals organized by hermandades (brother-hoods) or societies dedicated to a saint, a location or *sección* (neighborhood), an occupation, or a family.[5] These associations, or societies, are sanctioned by the Church and work for an entire year to organize a four-day event, which includes a Mass; Regada de Frutas (Tossing of Fruit); the vela, or all-night dance; and the Lavada de Ollas (Washing the Pots), an afternoon event held the day after the vela.

The major vela season starts in April and culminates with the Velas Grandes in the last two weeks of May, concluding with the two for San Vicente. The Gran Intrépida Vela, celebrated in the third week of November, is one of many annual velas and an extension of a much larger cultural tradition. Muxes also participate in and support other velas, serving in various capacities and some-times assuming the mayordomo role in velas tradicionales, such as the Vela San Antonio, Vela San Jacinto, and the August Vela de la Virgen de la Asunción (Virgin of the Assumption; Miano and Suárez 2009, 4).

The Intrépida Vela is important because it provides an economic boost for Juchitán and is a major tourist attraction, with the crowning of a queen. The vela also has a political base since it is supported by the national political system, primarily by the PRI (Partido Revolucionario Institucional) and the municipal government. Class differences are evident, as the mayordomo in most velas is typically a person from the higher economic classes who has earned the right to sponsor it.

Although muxes are found in all economic strata, most come from modest working-class backgrounds, many from the more indigenous and poorest sections of the city. The Intrépida organization has been criticized by smaller muxe groups for increasing the entrance fee and cost for a *puesto*, or space for hosting guests, at the vela to the point that it is prohibitive and excludes many muxes. While the "muxe" label is applied to poorer and less educated persons, the term "gay" is generally reserved for the middle and upper classes. One respondent said flippantly that the difference was that "if you didn't have a car, you were muxe, not gay."

Economic divisions in the community are further reflected in the structure and organization of the vela system, as some are held in honor of the oldest and most successful families in the community. In Unión Hidalgo, a nearby historic community, separate velas are sponsored by the elite and by poor members of the community, although the one sponsored by the poor is said to be better organized and more successful. In El Espinal, another neighboring town, the community vela is sponsored by *los más finos*, or wealthier classes.

The economic boost the velas provide is part of what Bennholdt-Thomsen refers to as a "prestige economy," in which the highest esteem is accorded to not "the one who owns most, but the one who gives most" in the community. More specifically, "one earns one's merits in the community through the festivals" (2005, n.p.) and through one's generosity in hosting these events. To assume the sponsorship or patronage of a vela is the dream of each Teca, since velas largely fall within the sphere of women. It is through sponsorship that they gain prestige, not only for themselves but also for their families.

## JUCHITÁN: A CITY OF MANY NAMES

Juchitán is known by a variety of names.[6] In addition to Ciudad de Las Mujeres (City of Women), it is also known as Ciudad de Las Flores (City of Flowers). Its official name is Juchitán de Zaragoza, while its indigenous name is Ixtaxochitlán, or *lugar de las flores blancas* (land of the white flowers; Jiménez López 2005, 15).

An indigenous community of 71,714 persons, according to the 2005 census, located in the southeast section of the Mexican state of Oaxaca, Juchitán de Zaragoza is the seat of the municipal district of Juchitán, in the western section of the Isthmus of Tehuantepec. Juchitán is the fourth largest city in the state, only slightly smaller than Salina Cruz, and the third largest in El Istmo. The municipal district has a population of 85,869, estimated to be over 100,000 today, and encompasses an area of 414.64 square kilometers, or 160.1 square miles. The majority of inhabitants are indigenous Zapotecs and Huaves. Zapotec king Cosijopíi founded the city in an unknown year, possibly 1486.

Located some twenty-six kilometers northeast of the city of Tehuantepec and five miles inland from the Pacific Ocean (Binford and Campbell 1993, 4), Juchitán de Zaragoza's *palacio municipal* (municipal palace) dates back to the middle of the nineteenth century and is perhaps the widest "palace" in México, with thirty-one arches in its front portal. The city's main church is the Parroquia de San Vicente Ferrer, dating from the seventeenth century, about three blocks from the main plaza. Next to the palacio is the large market, where local products are sold and a local variant of the Zapotec language can be heard.

Geographically, Juchitán is located in the southernmost section of North America between the Atlantic Ocean (Gulf of Mexico) and the Pacific Ocean. Its strategic location as the gateway to Central America and an alternative route to the Panama Canal has made it a center of communication. According to Bennholdt-Thomsen,

> Por su realidad geográfica la gente de la región está abierta al mundo, pero combinado esta característica con su capacidad étnico-cultural de perseverar en sus propias costumbres. (1997, 40)
> [Because of its ideal geographical location, the people of the region are open to the world, but this is coupled with its ethnic and cultural capacity to preserve its native customs.]

El Istmo spans from the state of Veracruz in the north to the Pacific Ocean in the south, is bounded by the Sierra Madre del Sur on the west and Chiapas on the east, and is surrounded by ample coast and the Sierra Madre ranges, which traverse México from north to south (Binford and Campbell 1993, 6). The Isthmus is a mountainous and sparsely populated region, where the majority of residents are poor, even by rural Mexican standards (6).

Juchitán is also one of the most culturally, ethnically, and linguistically diverse regions of México (Binford and Campbell 1993, 4). Some 73 percent of the population speaks Zapoteco, and about 85 percent also speaks Spanish (Bennholdt-Thomsen 1997, 40), indicating that most Juchitecos are bilingual. In comparison, only 9 percent of the Mexican population speaks an indigenous language, whereas in Oaxaca, the figure is 44 percent, with 71 percent who also speak Spanish. Although there are fifteen or sixteen different dialects in Oaxaca, most people who speak a dialect cannot understand those who speak a different one, making such dialects mutually unintelligible (Chiñas 2002, 6). This is the case for residents of the Valley of Oaxaca and people who live in El Istmo de Tehuantepec (Bennholdt-Thomsen 1997, 40). In addition to the linguistic barrier, "since pre-contact times, 150 miles of rugged mountains have formed a barrier between the Isthmus Zapotecs and their linguistic cousins in the valley of Oaxaca" (Chiñas 2002, 6). Of Oaxaca's 2.5 million inhabitants, some 900,000 speak at least one indigenous language.

Today at least sixteen distinctive languages are spoken in Oaxaca, and of these, eleven belong to the Otomanguean family: Amuzgo, Chatino, Zapoteco, Chinantec, Chocho, Ixcatec, Mazatec, Popoloco, Mixtec, Cuicatec, and Trique (Joyce 2010, 43). The two most common languages are Zapoteco and Mixtec (33).

While the climate in Juchitán has been described as tropical, it is hardly an idyllic paradise. Tom DeMott, a San Francisco–based travel writer who wrote an interesting travelogue account of his experiences in Juchitán, describes it as a "dusty windblown town deep in the flatlands that lie along Oaxaca's Pacific coast" (2006, 6). Although DeMott arrived at the beginning of the rainy season, he noted that the first rain had not yet arrived, and "from my seat on the bus the only signs of life on the desert flats were gray shrubs and leafless trees" (3). Bruce Stores writes in a fictional historical account of the Isthmus, "The intense heat, humidity, wind, and dust seem to conspire to make the area as inhospitable as possible" (2009, xi), adding that it does not have any exotic beaches or other distinguishing sights to draw visitors and is seldom mentioned in travel guides (xi).

California anthropologist Chiñas describes the climate in El Istmo as at once "tropical and semiarid. . . . One gains the impression of severe desert-like aridity or lush verdancy, depending on the season" (2002, 6). The rainy season is brief, lasting from May to October, and is characterized by a great deal of flooding and soil erosion resulting from intermittent torrential storms (6). The coordinator of a team of German anthropologists, Veronika Bennholdt-Thomsen, similarly commented on the heat and difficult conditions in Juchitán:

> Hacía mucho calor en Juchitán, casi siempre más de 30 y hasta 40° C, y había mucho polvo. En invierno, los vientos del norte soplaban tan fuerte que nos llenaban la casa de arena, y también los ojos y los poros. . . . Sufríamos por los mosquitos y nos enfermamos de dengue, hepatitis y disentería amibiana [*sic*]. (1997, 21)
>
> [It was very hot in Juchitán, almost always over 30 and sometimes 40° C, and there was a great deal of dust. In winter, the northern winds blew so strongly that the house would be filled with sand, as would one's eyes and pores. . . . We always suffered from mosquitos and got sick with dengue, hepatitis, and amoebic dysentery.]

Chiñas's description of San Juan Evangelista, a community of approximately twenty-eight thousand inhabitants in the municipal district of Juchitán, is also consistent with the view of the area as being hot, difficult, and inhospitable. Describing her initial fieldwork experience in El Centro, Chiñas notes, "[I]t is doubtful that I could have found a more unpleasant, malodorous marketplace in all of Mexico" (2002, xi). She describes the market as having a cavernous interior with terrible lighting and ventilation and an amazing display of fresh and decaying produce, fish, meat, and poultry, in addition to a wide assortment of clothing, yard goods, and housewares.

> The combination of scents that greeted the unwary market entrant were, at first, so overwhelming as to prove nauseating. But I soon struck upon a game that served to divert my attention as I entered each morning until my nose became familiar with the unfamiliar odors. The "game" was nothing more than trying to distinguish the individual sources of the various intermingled odors, some of which were quite agreeable when considered singly. (xii)

In addition, the Isthmus in general and Juchitán in particular appear to be places where the past is alive and well (Stores 2009, xi). Horse-drawn carriages are not uncommon and are the preferred mode of transportation for many workers and families (xi). And one often sees beasts of burden, rather than trucks, pulling large loads. DeMott similarly observed, "As we approached the outskirts of town, men in wooden carts drawn by oxen returned from the fields along a dirt road that ran parallel to the highway" (2006, 3).

According to Leigh Binford and Howard Campbell, Juchitán and other communities in the narrow Pacific coastal area stand apart from other communities in El Istmo, and they have been separated since before the Spanish Conquest (1993, 6). The relatively flat topography, a large area of fertile land, rivers and springs, and a relatively deep harbor at Salina Cruz have helped to transform the rough triangle formed by Tehuantepec, Tapanatepec, and Matías Romero into a major fishing and agricultural region in the state of Oaxaca (1993, 6).

## JUCHITÁN: A HISTORY OF CONQUEST, RESISTANCE, AND REBELLION

While a history of Juchitán is beyond the scope of this book, it is important to place the muxe experience within a social and historical context. Acceptance of muxes and homosexuality is consistent with the history of resistance in the Isthmus in general, and Juchitán in particular, to both colonial rule and national control. Historian Howard Campbell notes, for example, that

> The Zapotecs of the Isthmus of Tehuantepec, and especially, the town of Juchi-tán, are intensely proud of their history, control local political offices, run most of the local commerce, and have a lively cultural movement that produces fine works of poetry, painting, and music. Moreover, women in Zapotec society are said (by outsiders and local people) to enjoy equality with men, and homosexuality is accepted to an unusual degree. (Campbell 1994, xv–xvi)

John Tutino and other observers have similarly commented on the uniqueness of Juchitán, noting that the contrast with most Mexican communities is striking (1993, 41). He suggests that Juchitecos have maintained a community that is proudly Zapotec, from local elites to the ruling majority, and that has resisted the centralizing Mexican state and national culture.

In 1981 Juchitán gained national and international attention when the COCEI (Coalición Obrera, Campesina, Estudiantil del Istmo) won municipal elections, and Juchitán became the first city in México to be controlled by the political left since the Mexican Revolution (Binford and Campbell 1993, 1). After the government removed COCEI from office in 1983 and imprisoned its members, Juchitán became a symbol of indigenous resistance to political control (Campbell 1994, xvi). The town gained notoriety once again in 1989 and in 1992 when COCEI won new municipal elections.

These victories were perhaps not surprising given Juchitán's history from colonial times to the present, which has been characterized by rebellion and resistance to external control. Isthmus mythology describes the origins of the ancient Zapotecs, or Binnigula'sa', as coming down to earth from clouds shaped like beautiful birds, emerging from tree roots, or descending from large rocks or wild beasts (Burgoa [1674] 1934, 1:412). There is considerable Isthmus folklore surrounding the Binnigula'sa' and *binni guenda* (spirits), as well as an ideological nexus between the current political movement and the mythical great Zapotec past, which, according to Campbell, "appeals to existing notions of antiquity and an ancestor worship in Zapotec culture" (1994, 5).

Throughout the ages and long before the Spanish invasion, "the ancient ones," or Natives of the land, vigorously resisted colonization, defending their uniqueness as an extremely proud people (Stores 2009, xii). Although this mythology is familiar to every Zapotec resident of the Isthmus, who their ancestors actually were is a question not even archaeologists can answer unequivocally, since a great many people have inhabited or passed through the area (Jiménez López 2015, 15).[7]

According to Victor de la Cruz, one of the problems in documenting the ancestors of the Binizá, or Zapotecs, that is to say, of the Binnigula'sa', or the ancient Zapotecs, is that the Spaniards tended to interpret Native myths from within a colonizing and condescending framework. The colonizing missionaries' work "was to invalidate the record that the indigenous people kept of their past by characterizing it as foolishness, lies, and nonsense that the devil has put in their head" (de la Cruz 1993, 32), and to replace the ancient myths with new myths based on Judeo-Christian religions. The primary Spanish chronicler of the history of the ancient Zapotecs, friar Francisco de Burgoa, negated and distorted their indigenous past and replaced it with new myths brought by the colonizer (32). Unfortunately, Burgoa failed to grasp the nuance of the Zapotec language and its metaphorical use by the Zapotecs in narrating their myths. When the Binizá wanted to characterize themselves as valiant, for example, they would say that they were "the children of lions and wild beasts" (33). Burgoa's response to these ancient myths was to say, "[T]here is so much nonsense in their histories and paintings instilled in them by the devil that it is indecent to refer to them" (Burgoa [1674] 1934, 1:412; de la Cruz 1993, 33)

Unlike Fray Bernardino Sahagún, who chronicled the history of the Nahuatl culture shortly after the Conquest, Burgoa's work was produced in the second half of the seventeenth century. An additional difficulty in interpreting Zapotec history is that in chronicling their history, the Zapotecs sought to exaggerate and to embellish their deeds and accomplishments (de la Cruz 1993, 33).

Although the exact date of the founding of Juchitán cannot be clearly ascertained from either oral or written records (Burgoa [1674] 1934, 1:412; Jiménez López 2005, 15), prior to the Spanish Conquest, Aztec merchants, or *pochteca* caravans, made incursions into remote lands in the Soconusco (now in Chiapas bordering Guatemala), bringing back coveted chocolate on their return (Jiménez López 2005, 15). The Aztecs also undertook a number of military campaigns in order to expand their territory and increase the number of towns that would pay tribute to them (Flannery and Marcus 1983, 314). According to Burgoa, the Zapotec account was that the king of Zaachila was motivated to occupy the land because he objected to the ease with which the local Huaves granted access to the powerful Mexica (Aztec) armies en route to the cacao groves (Burgoa [1674] 1989, 2:340–42).

The Mexica armies traveled through the area and camped along the banks of the Guigu' Bicunisa River, which was known for its crystalline water and abundant nutria, or marsh dogs. This led to its misnomer, Río de los Perros, or Dog River (Jiménez López 2005, 15). The Mexicas and people of southern and southeastern portions of Mesoamerica knew Juchitán by its Nahuatl name, Ixtaxochitlán. The name was later modified to Xochitlán, Huchitlán, and Juchitlán. It was changed during the colonial period to San Vicente Juchitán, and later it became known simply as Juchitán (Jiménez López 2015, 19).

The first archaeological signs of Juchitán date back to about 1500 BC. The archaeological site Laguna Zope, two kilometers west of its present location, was one of the principal sites of the Isthmus region during the middle of the preclassic period (González Licón 1990, 204; Jiménez López 2015, 16) and dates to at least 1100 BC if not 1500 BC (Jiménez López 2015, 15). It maintained extensive commercial, political, and cultural ties with surrounding sites and lasted until about AD 250 (González Licón 1990, 204).

According to Campbell (1994, 6), Zapotec colonization of the region took place during a period described by Flannery and Marcus (1983, 217) as the "Postclassic Balkanization of Oaxaca." Historical records indicate that by the middle of the fourteenth century, the Zapotecs from the Valley of Oaxaca had not only occupied the Isthmus but also appropriated the best land, salt pans, and settlement sites from the Huaves and the Zoques (Binford and Campbell 1993, 6; Zeitlin 2005, 32–33). Indeed, there is evidence that the royal house of the Zapotecs had moved to the Istmo de Tehuantepec by the end of the fifteenth century to avoid military incursions by the Aztecs.

Research from the southern Isthmus of Tehuantepec shows the movement of Zapotecs into the region as illustrated in ethnohistorical records (Zeitlin 2005, 32–34). The data indicate that in the early colonial period, the Río de los Perros, which runs north and south through Juchitán, marked the boundary between Zapoteco-speaking communities in the western coastal plain and the Zoque villages to the east (Joyce 2010, 277; Zeitlin 2005, 32).

In 1496 Zapotec-Mixtec troops defended the Isthmus, from an invulnerable fortress at Guiengola, against a Mexica invasion in a siege that lasted seven months, when, it is said, the Mexicas were defeated and finally gave up (González Licón 1990, 206).[8] From their fortress, Zapotec warriors would attack groups of unsuspecting Aztecs at night and, after killing them, would take them, along with their weapons, back into the fortress, where they would salt and eat the bodies (Burgoa [1674] 1934, 2:342).

Conflict with the Aztecs was temporarily resolved when a wedding was arranged between the Zapotec king Cocijoeza and Coyolicatzin, daughter of the Aztec emperor Ahuizotl and known among the Zapotecs as Pelaxilla (Jiménez López 2005, 15; Burgoa [1674] 1934, 2:343). Out of their union was born Cosijopíi, the successor to the throne. Despite the marriage, war continued with the Aztecs, who were ruled by Moctezuma II.

After the Spanish invasion, Hernán Cortés directed Captain Pedro de Alvarado to explore the region that is now Guatemala in efforts to expand New Spain. Alvarado traveled through the Isthmus in 1522, when there were probably more than one million Mixtec, Zapoteco, and Chatino speakers residing in the area (Joyce 2010, 42). The major population centers were the highland valleys, the lower Río Verde valley, and the southern section of El Istmo de Tehuantepec (2010, 42–43). Because there are limited records on the early Chatino communities, most ethnohistorians have focused on the Mixtec and Zapotec peoples (2010, 43). Some historians, however, maintain that the Zapotecs were the oldest inhabitants of the area (Barrios and López Matus 1987, 51).

The first Spanish description of the Isthmus of Tehuantepec came from Fray Juan de Areyzaga, a member of the ill-fated Loaysa expedition to the Spice Islands (Zeitlin 2005, 40). Areyzaga's boat was separated from the other ships after passing through the Strait of Magellan, and it sailed two thousand leagues before landing near Tehuantepec on July 25, 1526 (Zeitlin 2005, 41).[9] When the Spaniards finally arrived in 1523, the Isthmus was governed by Cosijopíi, the founder of Juchitán. Cosijopíi initially aligned himself with them in a strategic move to protect Zapotecs from the troublesome Mixtecs and Central Americans (González Licón 1990, 206; Campbell 1994, 9). The Zapotecs offered little resistance to the Spanish, and Cosijopíi was even baptized, changing his name to Don Juan Cortés (Tutino 1993, 45; Zeitlin 2005, 8). He donned Spanish clothes, exchanged his jaguar throne for a European chair, rode horseback, and was afforded the opportunity to adopt Spanish patterns of consumption (Campbell 1994, 10).

## ZAPOTEC REBELLION

Despite the cultural similarities between the Zapotecs and the Aztecs, there were also important differences in their social and political organization. While the Aztec state was large and hegemonic, Zapotec society in the pre-Conquest era comprised a set of loosely linked major towns and surrounding villages in what is today the state of Oaxaca (Campbell 1994, 7). Zapotec nobles like Cosijopíi and their representatives lived in and governed the major towns and surrounding communities. They also wielded a great deal of power over ordinary citizens. Zapotec society consisted of four major groups: nobles (who were subdivided into caciques and lesser nobility, or *principales*), commoners, slaves, and serfs. In the pre-Hispanic Isthmus and during the early colonial period, Tehuantepec was the principal Zapotec city, a significant regional market, and a cultural center (7).

The Spanish initially encountered little resistance in the Isthmus because the Zapotecs were seeking allies, not only to protect themselves against Aztec invasions but also to eliminate the troublesome Mixtecs and solidify their control over other groups, like the Huaves and the Zoques (Binford and Campbell 1993, 7). But once the Spaniards established themselves, seized major tracts of Indian land, and imposed colonial rule by exacting large tribute, the Zapotecs resisted vigorously (7).

Victor de la Cruz (1993, 29), a leading Zapotec intellectual, argues that the much greater number of documents produced by the Aztecs and their chroniclers compared to the paucity of materials written by the Zapotecs themselves (and representing their view) has biased the history of Aztec/Zapotec relations. De la Cruz notes that because history has been written from the perspective of the colonizer, "[t]he idea that indigenous people have history is now a scandal" (29). He therefore seeks to emphasize the success of the Zapotecs on the battlefield, particularly at Guiengola, which became a symbol of their military prowess (Campbell 1994, 7).

Like Guiengola, the colonial history of the Isthmus is filled with periodic Zapotec armed rebellions, resistance, and creative adaptation to colonial control. Despite the political control of the Spanish overlords, the Zapotecs were able to maintain a fairly robust economy, which centered on the production and trade of locally produced cloth, fish, and other products (Binford and Campbell 1993, 6). They also clung steadfastly to their language and culture, and remained the dominant ethnic group in the Isthmus of Tehuantepec in the colonial and postcolonial periods (6).

Isthmus colonial history was marked by numerous armed rebellions and resistance to colonial rule, with some of the most prominent of these occurring in 1550, 1660, and 1715 (Binford and Campbell 1993, 7). Resistance to colonial and state rule has been so extensive in Juchitán that, according to John Tutino, Juchitecos "have stood staunchly against the mainstream of modern Mexican history" (Tutino 1993, 41).

After the Conquest, the peoples of the Isthmus engaged in what has been described as a creative adaptation to colonial rule as well as developing a culture of resistance. According to Tutino, "The decades of respite that followed the first colonial incursion had allowed the Isthmus Zapotecos to adapt and consolidate a colonial culture of resistance, adamantly Zapotec, that enabled them to face the livestock and commercial developments of the decades around 1600 with some strength, despite declining numbers" (Tutino 1993, 49).

Among the many rebellions that took place in the region, at least three stand out in Juchiteco consciousness, in addition to the defeat of French forces on September 5, 1866 (Campbell et al. 1993, 25; Martínez López 1966). These were the Tehuantepec Rebellion of 1660, the Che Gorio Melendre rebellions in the 1840s, and the Che Gómez revolt during the Mexican Revolution.

## THE TEHUANTEPEC REBELLION, 1660

The 1660 Tehuantepec Rebellion was triggered by the demands of a newly appointed colonial justice, Don Juan de Abellán, who, believing that the people of

Tehuantepec were taxed too little, doubled tribute demands (Rojas 1964, 21–22; Tutino 1993, 49; Archivo General de Indias [AGI] 1660).[10] Specifically, a major cause of the rebellion was the forced purchase of Spanish products at higher prices and the coerced sale of indigenous goods, such as vanilla, cochineal, and cotton cloth, at lower prices (Manso de Contreras 1987, 15).

In response to the forced disparity of prices, on March 22, 1660, a raucous mob of approximately six thousand Zapotec men and women stoned, looted, and burned the Spanish buildings of Tehuantepec and killed the alcalde, or mayor (Rojas 1964, 24–27; Manso de Contreras 1987, 4). According to reports of the incident, "the boldest and most obstinate stone-throwers were the Zapotec women" (Campbell 1994, 20); the rage of Native women was intensified by their forced production of a large number of mantles for the benefit of Don Juan (Rojas 1964, 25).

Local Zapotec elites, who were expected to collect the suddenly increased taxes, were also quick to resist this incursion (Díaz-Polanco and Manzo 1992, 15). People protested, and the protest blossomed into a riot in which Abellán, two of his servants, and an African were killed with sticks (Manso de Contreras 1987, 4). The rebels also ousted Hispanicized Native officials.

The mutinous Zapotecs elected their own public officials, set up guards to regulate traffic in and out of Tehuantepec, and sent word of the rebellion to nearby communities. The rebels controlled Tehuantepec for one year and one month (Campbell 1994, 21). Once the insurrection was quelled, the rebel leaders were captured and punished. Significantly, of the fifty-three imprisoned rebels, at least seven were women (21). Two women in particular, Magdalena María and Gracia María, were accused of and punished for inciting the riot (Dalton 2010, 78). Magdalena María was reported to have "sat on top of the dead mayor's body hitting him with a rock and swearing at him" (78). Her punishment was to cut off her hair, flog her one hundred times in public, cut off one of her hands, and have her amputated hand hung near the location of her alleged crime (78). The region remained in revolt for more than a year as rebellious Zapotec leaders sought allies from the Oaxacan highlands, thus revealing the existence of a persistent, subterranean resistance that linked Isthmus lords and highland Zapotecs (Tutino 1993, 49).

Knowing that they could not successfully oppose the force of the colonial regime, a group of indigenous leaders wrote to the viceroy in Mexico City, explaining that they were not revolting against colonial rule per se but against the excesses of a particular official (Tutino 1993, 50; Rojas 1964, 275–76). In 1661, an army organized under the direction of the bishop of Oaxaca occupied Tehuan-tepec and captured key leaders of the rebellion (AGI 1662). Several of these leaders were executed, but the people of the Isthmus were granted a general pardon (Rojas 1964, 281).

Whereas Tehuantepec, home of the royal family and of indigenous high culture, was the center of rebellion in the early colonial period, the focus of Isthmus Zapotec resistance shifted from Hispanicized Tehuantepec to Juchi-tán after the mid-eighteenth century (Campbell 1994, 32). Previously viewed as an insignificant village, Juchitán now became the center of resistance to state control in the Isthmus.

## THE CHE GORIO MELENDRE REBELLIONS, 1834–1853

After Mexican Independence from Spain in 1820, another major series of re-bellions took place, led by José Gregorio Meléndez, also known as Che Go-rio Melendre (Jiménez López 2015, 24).[11] Born on March 12, 1793, on a ranch northeast of Juchitán, Meléndez would eventually be known for attempting to recover Juchiteco control over the salt mines, defending communal lands, tak-ing over the Juchitán jail to free partisans, jailing and fining local officials, en-gaging in acts of social banditry, and organizing a separatist movement (Camp-bell 1994, 37; Jiménez López 2015, 26–38). Meléndez's first rebellion (1834–1835) was in defense of communal lands, lagoons, and salinas, which were threatened by creole outsiders (Campbell 1994, 37; Jiménez-López 2015, 26–27).

Between October 1850 and January 1851, Meléndez and his followers issued two manifestos calling for an end to the nine-month revolution between Tehuan-tepec and Juchitán, the elimination of customs offices that limited Juchiteco trade with Guatemala, and secession of the Isthmus from the state of Oaxaca (Campbell 1994, 42). While Juchitecos had great success in mobilizing virtually all sectors of the community against their bitter enemies in Oaxaca, Tehuan-tepec, and Mexico City (Campbell 1994, 40), one of their principal adversaries during this period was Benito Juárez, a highland Zapoteco and liberal who had risen to power and wanted to establish state control over the region.

After the U.S.-Mexican War, Juárez sought to establish central control over the Isthmus (Campbell 1994, 38). Meléndez had somehow been appointed as regional governor of the Isthmus, and seeking to pacify the region, Juárez ap-pointed him as head of the local national guard. Meléndez took this as a demo-tion, and he and his followers joined rebels from San Blas Atempa, a traditional ally of Juchitán, in calling for secession of the Isthmus from the state of Oaxaca (38). According to Campbell, these mobilizations, "strongly shaped their sense of being a people with a distinct ethnic identity and a set of common political interests. A multiclass alliance was possible because, unlike the situation in Tehuantepec, the majority of Juchitecos retained their indigenous ethnic identity" (Campbell et al. 1993, 40).

## THE CHE GÓMEZ REVOLT, 1911

The third major rebellion occurred in 1911, shortly after the outbreak of the Mexican Revolution, and was led by Che Gómez (José Fructuoso Gómez), a lawyer who, after returning from Mexico City to become mayor of Juchitán, led a revolt against the dictatorship of Porfirio Díaz (Campbell et al. 1993, 26; Jiménez León 2015, 205–30). As Meléndez had done, Gómez defended Juchitán's natural resources against exploitation by the federal government and outsiders (Campbell et al. 1993, 26).

Although Gómez was a mestizo elite, he distinguished himself in battle in open rebellion against the state, likely spoke Zapoteco, and was recognized as a Juchiteco. These characteristics were important because, at times, factors such as being born in Juchitán or being from the Isthmus can trump other, traditional ethnic markers (such as skin color, clothing, and language ability), which are generally used to determine whether a person is viewed as an insider or an outsider (Royce 1975, 193–202). Thus, Gómez and his followers gained a great deal of support among Juchitecos because their focus was on local autonomy, rather than national political issues. When Oaxaca governor Benito Juárez Maza attempted to replace Gómez with Enrique León, Juchitecos revolted. "León's military escort sought refuge in the local barracks, where they were promptly besieged by thousands of Juchitecos and pro-Gómez residents of more than a dozen nearby villages armed with machetes, sticks, slingshots, spears, and a few rifles" (Campbell 1994, 64).

As in the Meléndez rebellion, government forces burned down the city. In the interim, from his rural headquarters, Gómez called for Juchiteco independence from Oaxaca and independence for the Isthmus from the nation (Jiménez López 2015, 202). Gómez subsequently led a revolt in support of the Mexican Revolution, joining Revolutionary forces led by Emiliano Zapata and Pancho Villa. Gómez was murdered by government officials during the Revolution (223–25).

## JUCHITECO DEFEAT OF THE FRENCH ARMY,
## SEPTEMBER 5, 1866

Juchitecos also resisted the Franco incursion in a series of bloody battles against the French, who had invaded México under Louis-Napoleon (Rubin 1997, 33; Martínez López 1966). Although not widely recognized outside the Isthmus, September 5, 1866, is a memorable date for Juchitecos. On this day a group of poorly armed indigenous soldiers from Juchitán, Unión Hidalgo, San Blas Atempa, and the surrounding area overcame great odds by defeating the invading French army, at the time one the most renowned armies in the world. The Juchitecos burned and abandoned Juchitán and then seized it again after the French had occupied it (Rubin 1997, 34). They ultimately defeated the French in a swampy area as the latter fled the city. Prior to the fighting, the oldest of the indigenous partisans exhorted his compatriots to fight, invoking the name of Juchitán's patron saint, San Vicente Ferrer: "Ahora, padre Vicente, sobre ellos, o ellos o nosotros, pero de aquí no pasaran" (Now is the time, Father Vicente, let's jump on them, it's either them or us, but they will not pass through here; Martínez López 1966, 72).

Reportedly, the women of Juchitán also emboldened the men. Sensing that the troops were feeling downtrodden on the eve of battle, the Tecas admonished them to fight by asking,

¿Que dicen pues? ¿qué ya no les pegaron en Puebla? Si no pueden sacarlos del centro de nuestro pueblo, ¡hablen! y nos dan a nosotras, las mujeres, las armas que tienen y verán si los sacamos o no. (Martínez López 1966, 82)
[What have you got to say? didn't they already defeat you in Puebla? If you can't get them out of our town, speak up! and give us, the women, your arms and you will see if we get them out or not.]

Although the three rebellions and the September 5 battle are most prominent, Juchitán history is replete with acts of resistance to government control. In addition to resisting Aztec, Spanish, and French incursions, Juchitecos have defended their land and resources, actively resisted the centralizing Mexican state and its national culture, and even threatened secession on several occasions. In more recent times, Juchitán gained notoriety as the first Mexican town to elect a left-wing, prosocialist municipal government when its citizens elected Leopoldo de Gyves as mayor in 1990, defeating the ruling party, the PRI.

## PLAN OF THE BOOK

This introductory chapter is meant to provide an overview of Juchitán—its unique sociogeographical location and climate, linguistic diversity, and gender structure. I have also presented the folklore surrounding the city's founder and patron saint, San Vicente Ferrer; the mythology of the Amazon woman that is often applied to the so-called matriarchy among Zapotec women; and the prevailing belief that Juchitán is a gay paradise, where homosexual and transgender persons are readily accepted.

The introduction also identifies Juchitán as a historical site of resistance and rebellion aimed at maintaining local indigenous culture, language, and traditions. The contrast between Juchitán and other Mexican communities is striking because Juchitecos persist in being proudly Zapotec rather than simply Indian, and they resist the influence of the state while remaining prosperous, providing economically important roles for women and being tolerant of los muxes.

Chapter 1 describes the process of going into the field to carry out the research, including my entry into the community and some of the problems and issues I encountered in conducting the study. I discuss the major local muxe organization, Las Intrépidas; describe Estética Felina, a muxe haven where members of the organization and friends regularly gather and socialize; and conclude with an inside look at the annual Intrépida Vela.

In the next chapter (2), I use the metaphor of the mask to interrogate the relationship between *máscaras*, or "masking," and the macho ideal of manliness, machismo. I ask how one can reconcile acceptance of muxes in the Isthmus of Tehuantepec with cultural conceptions associated with hegemonic Mexican masculinity. A second, related issue is the extent to which acceptance of a third gender may have had pre-Columbian origins and whether acceptance of gender variants can be traced to accounts of cross-dressing Aztec priests and Mayan gods who were at once male and female (Lacey 2008). A social and historical context compares prevailing attitudes toward homosexuality and sodomy held by the Spanish colonizers with those of the precontact indigenous population.

Chapter 3 is a critical examination of an important question and debate in the sociological literature on "doing gender." Specifically, I look at how the muxes go about doing and undoing gender in the workplace and extend the debate beyond Anglophone conceptions by reporting on data from this study. I use interviews with muxes to reveal the wide range and variety in how muxes go about doing and undoing gender, place the findings in a global context, and suggest that muxes are a hybrid third gender category that cannot be understood by using conventional binary conceptions of gender and sexuality. These case studies also reveal how muxes distinguish themselves from gay men and present a rare handful of interviews with mayates, men who have sex with other men for money. The chapter concludes with a brief discussion of lesbianas and their differential treatment in Juchiteco society.

Chapter 4 challenges the popularly held belief that having a muxe child is seen as a blessing from God in Zapotec society. Personal narratives of several muxes focus on their treatment—in the family, among peers, and in society at large. In chapter 5 I take an in-depth look at the larger societal acceptance of los muxes. Beginning with a discussion of how muxes are integrated into Juchiteco society, including their acceptance as a third gender, I then present a brief overview of the forty-nine community respondents included in the study. In particular, this chapter highlights an important interview with two muxes and their families that quickly turned into a spontaneous focus group, providing important insights.

Chapter 6 extends my analysis of the study findings by placing them in a global theoretical context, comparing anthropological writings on the berdache among North American Indian communities with anthropological and journalistic accounts of the muxe experience in Juchitán. I look at how the two-spirit indigenous movement challenges the anthropology of the berdache by displacing anthropological terms and locating two-spirit persons in Native traditions and society, then draw parallels between the experiences of two-spirit peoples in North America and those of the muxe of Juchitán.

Chapter 7 provides a view of muxes through the lens of more recent, nuanced, and fluid literature, revealing a sexuality/gender hybridity that enables muxes to adhere to seemingly contradictory perceptions of sexuality in ways that extend beyond the sexuality/gender hybridity identified by Héctor Carrillo for gay Mexican men. Muxes expand this hybridity because they are simultaneously exposed not only to the traditional Mexican systems of sexuality and gender as well as to the emerging modern gay object choice model, but also to an indigenous two-spirit system of gender classification, which accommodates a third gender consistent with their indigenous roots.

In the concluding chapter I abandon the mantle of objectivity, neutrality, and detachment by presenting a decidedly personal account on the study and my role as a researcher and an outsider in Juchitán. Specifically, the chapter addresses the primary issues, foibles, and concerns that arose in the course of the fieldwork, and the lessons I gleaned from those experiences.

# 1

# LAS INTRÉPIDAS AND THE GREAT MUXE VELA

ANTHROPOLOGIST VERONIKA BENNHOLDT-THOMSEN describes the total respect and deference accorded to a muxe mayordomo at a vela in Juchitán:

> A man approximately 30 years of age, of medium build, tending to be overweight but with a well-proportioned physique, nonetheless, which was accentuated by tailored trousers, a fitted shirt, and the expensive Italian shoes he wore. The only thing that distinguished him from the other men in attendance were the solid gold jewels which he wore around his neck, wrists, and fingers. . . . The young mayordomo was treated with such respect, such courtesy and deference that it appeared effortless and natural. In this society, he obviously had a place of total and unqualified acceptance.[1] (Bennholdt-Thomsen 1997, 280)

Bennholdt-Thomsen wondered whether the young mayordomo was accorded respect because he came from a rich and well-positioned family. Or perhaps the acceptance was simply because, except for the lavish jewelry and expensive clothing, nothing in his demeanor, language, or actions deviated from *el código de la masculinidad*, or "the masculine code of conduct" (1997, 281). In other words, what was significant was that despite being muxe, he carried himself and acted in a dignified and respectful manner.

After carefully observing two young "women" at the *mercado* for several months, Bennholdt-Thomsen became aware that the rules defining gender were different in Juchitán. In a sense, these young men who masqueraded as women hid their identity behind cultural masks. She identified one of them as a muxe only after months of careful study. The "young woman" in the mercado had drawn the anthropologist's attention for some time. Although she wore a Native costume, a Juchiteca skirt and a huipil, when compared to her peers, she was almost deplorably thin, did not wear makeup, and wore her hair long and loose, rather than *trenzada* (braided). When Bennholdt-Thomsen inquired about this person, the response was "Es un muchacho muy trabajador" (He is a very hardworking young man; 1997, 281). His work ethic was what really mattered, rather than his dress or appearance. Women have a reputation for being hard workers, a quality that is recognized and respected even by men (281). Muxes are also recognized for being very hard workers.

The second young "woman" was a *regatona* (reseller) of bread at the market, where s/he also sold pimentos filled with chopped fish, which he had prepared (1997, 281). He wore pants and a T-shirt, an apron, and his long hair pulled back into a ponytail with a multicolored ribbon tied at the end. As is the custom, the regatona was constantly talking with women in adjoining puestos and appeared to be well integrated in his/her social circle. It becomes evident that commerce in the mercado is women's work, and a man who dedicates himself to this activity becomes defined as a muxe and only then is accepted among the merchants (281).

During my field research, I similarly discovered that a young woman I had seen selling huaraches at a *zapatería* (shoe store) next to the market was, in fact, a twenty-one-year-old biological male, Lorenzo Antonio, who went under the muxe name of Tifani (see chapter 3). I had observed this young woman dressed in a sexually indeterminate way for several days before finally getting up the nerve to go up to her and ask discreetly whether she was muxe. She became one of my interviewees.

## "UNINVITED, UNANNOUNCED, AND UNEXPECTED"

I arrived in dusty Juchitán on my first visit with considerable trepidation, not knowing anyone, and fearing that I might not be welcomed or well received. I could certainly relate to Chiñas's observation as she embarked on her first major fieldwork experience after graduate school in El Istmo "uninvited, unannounced, and unexpected" (2002, xi). I also was not announced, invited, or expected and, like Chiñas, was not indigenous and did not speak Zapoteco. Despite being a native of Mexico City, a Mexican citizen, and fully bilingual and bicultural, I was a novice when it came to understanding the local indigenous culture, customs, and language. In short, despite the reading I had done, my academic training and experience as a sociologist, my personal background and cultural repertoire, I was not adequately prepared for this field experience. I was often asked where I was from because I had more of a Mexico City accent in my Spanish than a Zapoteco one. The vendors in the market also affectionately referred to me as *güero*, a generic term for a fair or light-skinned person, used especially by indigenous persons. After spending time in the noisy market and learning a little about the city and its various neighborhoods, or secciones, I encountered an elderly woman in the market who asked me in Spanish, "¿De dónde es usted?" When I said jokingly that I was from Juchitán and from la séptima sección (a local, largely indigenous neighborhood), she smiled and said, "¡No! Una cara como la suya, no se encuentra, aquí." (No! A face like yours is not found here.)[2]

Despite these limitations, my introduction to Juchitán was far more pleasant and much less traumatic than the experiences described by visitors like Chiñas, who also commented on the oppressive climate of El Istmo and its "malodorous" marketplace, or like Bennholdt-Thomsen and her associates, who had to battle with dust, dengue, hepatitis, and dysentery.

The five-and-a-half-hour bus trip I had to take from Oaxaca city to Juchitán, through rugged mountainous terrain and dizzying, seemingly endless winding roads, was at once breathtaking and uneventful. The bus made only one stop, about a ten-minute break, barely enough time for passengers to go to the bathroom, stretch their legs, and get a soda or quick snack before departing once again. The long trips gave me an opportunity to meet and interact with people from the area, including an engaging young man named Sergio, who sat next to me on the bus.[3] He was about twenty-one and was studying law and criminology in Oaxaca city. We had a pleasant conversation and spent several hours talking about law and justice, comparing the Mexican civil court system to the American common law judicial system.

He was from a town about an hour from Juchitán. I brought up the topic of the muxes to get his response. He found it interesting that most people speak Zapoteco in Juchitán. He mentioned another town where they also maintain the language, but in his town, Zapoteco was hardly spoken. The muxes were very well accepted in Juchitán. There were some in his community, but not many. Being muxe is an entire way of life, according to Sergio, and it is different from being gay. Muxes are a third gender, very good workers, and they play an important role in taking care of elderly parents. Heterosexual sons eventually marry and leave home, and women nowadays also get married and leave, but muxes stay and take care of their elderly parents. He added something that reminded me of Bennholdt-Thomsen's description of the young mayordomo, which was that many muxes come from families with a lot of money. I had learned from my reading that although muxes come from all walks of life, many come from working-class or lower-class backgrounds (Bennholdt-Thomsen 1997, 280–82), never that they disproportionately come from wealthy families. In fact, I would later learn that although there are muxes from elite families, most people believe that muxes tend to come from poorer sections of Juchitán, like la séptima, and from indigenous families.

I arrived at the Juchitán bus terminal in the evening, checked into a hotel, and then ventured out into the cool and pleasant evening to make the fifteen-minute walk to downtown. The streets were crowded with people, and the market and the area around the plaza were bustling and full of life. I quickly discovered that it is impossible to enter the mercado without being verbally accosted by the various vendors, most of them Juchitecas, and a number of muxes hawking their wares. The market occupies a large area in the back and west of the two-story palacio municipal. The building has a large patio area in the center and faces the main plaza.

Bennholdt-Thomsen notes that if the Paris market Les Halles is the belly of the French capital, then the market of Juchitán is surely the heart of the city (1997, 67). She describes the market as located in

> un edificio sólido de dos plantas con árcades; en la planta baja se encuentran los puestos del mercado y en la planta alta, por el lado frontal que da hacia la plaza, la presidencia municipal. El simbolismo de este orden habla por sí solo. (67)
>
> [a concrete two-story building with arcades; the shops of the market are found on the lower level, and on the top floor, by the front of the building facing the street houses, the municipal presidential offices. The symbolism of this layout is self-evident.]

The mercado was busy and not particularly hygienic, but no more malodorous than any other open-air market I had visited in other large cities, such as in Mexico City, Guadalajara, or even Oaxaca. In fact, the Juchitán market is much smaller than the principal mercado in Oaxaca city and the Mercado Juárez in Guadalajara, both of which I had recently visited. El mercado had at least three immediately distinguishing features. First, most, if not all, merchants were women dressed in their daily Juchiteca attire of wide skirts and richly embroidered huipiles. Second, the merchants were extremely aggressive and engaging, not letting prospective customers pass without verbally accosting them. Finally, the market included exotic items, like gold, that one would not normally see at other Mexican markets. What immediately caught my eye were the large turtle and iguana eggs for sale, as well as iguana and armadillo meat.

The streets surrounding the main plaza were also crowded with people, which made it difficult to navigate from one part of El Centro to the next. I noticed that the street immediately in front of the palacio municipal had been closed off to traffic, and a very large stage had been set up at the northern end. Several bands played music into the night as people danced in the street, which served as an impromptu dance floor. At the front of the palacio, another makeshift stage was set up, with a microphone for speeches and entertainment. One of the side streets was closed to traffic and had a number of tables with vendors selling a wide assortment of food, including *tlayudas*, mole, tortas, tacos, and chicken. These were not regular restaurants but puestos operated by private parties, largely families, who were allowed to cook on outside grills and sell food on the street on special festive occasions like this. Several flower vendors were also among them. Other vendors throughout the zócalo were selling items like hotcakes, cotton candy, *elotes* (corn on the cob), *helados* (ice cream), jewelry, and toys. Others laid out sarapes (blankets) on the sidewalk and sold jewelry and other items. At the center of the plaza was a concession stand that sold pizza, sodas, and ice cream.

One of the things that immediately impressed me during the festivities was how well integrated muxes were into the community both socially and politically. A number of them were in the crowd, and when the bands started to play, several rushed out onto the dance floor and danced together without drawing any response or fanfare. This is culturally facilitated by how common it is for women to dance together in Juchitán. Bennholdt-Thomsen remarked that she enjoyed going dancing with her female next-door neighbor. Although men sometimes cut in between Bennholdt-Thomsen and her female companion, it was not unusual for women to dance with one another or with muxes—or occasionally, even for a man to dance with a muxe (1997, 290). When Bennholdt-Thomsen observed several straight men dancing at her birthday celebration with Crystal, a muxe, she concluded (290), "En Juchitán realmente no existen reglas que no puedan ser infringidas." (In Juchitán there are really no rules that cannot be violated.)

Earlier in the evening, before the bands had taken the stage, a performance of skits demonstrated the social roles muxes play in Juchitán. This event was actually hosted and organized by muxes. Some of the program themes were AIDS education and ending domestic violence. I learned that the local muxe organization Las Intrépidas worked with youth in the community on relevant and pressing contemporary issues, such as sex education, domestic violence, and AIDS awareness. Staging skits with the youth was part of their outreach efforts. Amaranta, a one-armed muxe and well-known local politician, who had been a progressive candidate for México's house of representatives, also spoke at the event and proved to be an eloquent motivational orator.

The next morning when I called Felina to try to connect with Biiniza for an interview, she suggested that I come down to the salon at 5:00 to see if she dropped by. The name of the salon was Estética Felina, but I initially misunderstood the name and thought she had said "Selena," so I asked various people downtown if they knew where the Estética Selena was located. Fortunately, I eventually figured out the correct name and found the salon, but Biiniza never showed up.

Felina was pleasant and welcoming. It was clear from the way she was dressed that she too was muxe. I introduced myself and told her I was a professor and researcher from California who was interested in the muxes and wanted to know more about them and their lifestyle. She responded by inviting me to an upcoming event at the ecological preserve, near the banks of Río de los Perros. Several muxes would be meeting there with a politician from Mexico City. The politician had been instrumental in passing domestic partner legislation for the city, which legalized or at least formally recognized gay unions, an important issue for the muxes. Mexico City subsequently legalized gay marriages. The meeting would give me a chance to meet and socialize with some of the muxes in an informal setting.

I went to breakfast in the morning at a little restaurant on the corner, where the waiter was a young man, Marcos, around twenty-one or twenty-two years of age. In the course of the conversation, he asked what I was doing in Juchitán. I said I was a researcher and had come to study the muxes. He volunteered that he was gay, not originally from Oaxaca, but not muxe. He also said that he knew a couple of people who were involved in a splinter group of muxes that had separated from the larger Intrépida group. He added that the splinter group had hosted a vela the previous night, noting that the proprietor of a bar down the street was muxe, and that Enrique, the owner of Kike's Hair Salon, would be a good person to talk to about this group. I went to the bar, but the manager told me I had the wrong place. I also went by Kike's Estética on three different occasions, but it was closed, perhaps because it was Dia de la Revolución, a national holiday. I was excited after meeting this young man and about talking to Felina, because I had just started my research and had already made some important connections. I wrote in my field journal:

> I was upbeat after meeting this young man because it seemed like some doors were beginning to open up for me. I always feel lonely and insecure when I start a research project because I don't know anyone. There is nothing worse than sitting in your hotel room waiting for your contacts to call you. I suddenly felt like my contacts were opening up to me.

I no longer felt uninvited or unwelcomed.

## THE MEETING AT THE ECOLOGICAL PRESERVE

I attended the meeting at the ecological preserve scheduled with the female politician who had been instrumental in passing Mexico City's domestic partner legislation. The meeting demonstrated Intrépidas' political involvement and its rivalry with a smaller splinter muxe group. The first person I met was a freelance photographer from Mexico City, who was there to cover the meeting. The photographer requested a photo op, and one of the young muxes proceeded to ham it up, taking cheek-to-cheek pictures with an older man, who struck me as not being muxe but who went along with the joke and posed for the shot. Bystanders were smiling and laughing at the performance. A film crew from Colombia doing a documentary on the muxes was also present. The seven to eight Intrépidas who attended were friendly, and I had a chance to hang out with them and observe their interaction for several hours. People were warm, but there were no formal introductions because almost everyone seemed to know each other.

After we had been waiting for a considerable amount of time, an announcement was made that the politician would not be attending after all but that she had sent one of her aides to represent her. After another substantial delay, and once it became evident that no one was coming, a member of the group formally announced that the meeting was canceled. Everyone was obviously disappointed, yet they seemed to take it in stride. A communal feeling took over as simple, unremarkable tortas on *pan* Bimbo (white bread), prepared by a member, were passed around.

Several Intrépidas were visibly upset, however, because they had reserved the meeting room, and members of a splinter group had arrived first and occupied it. I also noticed that a couple of the people at the event were very young, about sixteen or seventeen years old. While it was evident that the muxe groups were in competition, and there was tension between them, it was also clear that the Intrépida group was the main organization and the other was a smaller one. I walked back downtown with a group of people from the meeting, including the young members, who appeared to be new Intrépida recruits.

## LAS INTRÉPIDAS: "THE AUTHENTIC, FEARLESS SEEKERS OF DANGER"

I had met Felina but hadn't formally interviewed her, and after several prior attempts, I arranged an appointment at 5:00 p.m. at her salon. When I arrived, Felina explained that she had to take another muchacha (an Intrépida) home and then go shopping for the vela the next night. After several more delays, I was finally able to interview her after 11:00 p.m. I told her that I especially appreciated her taking time out of her busy schedule to speak with me.

The interview went well, except that people kept dropping in to chat. This was bad because it interfered with the flow of our conversation, but good because I was able to meet other muxes and their friends as they stopped in to say hello. Felina's salon was a place to prepare for the vela as well as a place where muxes felt comfortable hanging out and socializing. The following day several muxes would be there, frantically doing their hair and makeup.

Felina told me about the Intrépida organization and some very interesting details about muxes, their lifestyles, and their politics. At the time that I interviewed her, Felina was not only one of the leaders of Las Intrépidas but also the outgoing president of the organization. The longevity of the group, nearly forty years, speaks to its public acceptance and the integration of muxes into the community by political and civic leaders as well as by the Catholic Church. Felina explained that members of Las Intrépidas came from all walks of life and included accountants, lawyers, teachers, social workers, and merchants. About ninety muxes were loosely associated with the organization. I would later learn that the group had only about thirty-six *socias* (associates), defined as those who had the funds and resources to sponsor a puesto (place or designated area for muxes and their guests) at the annual vela.

The vela is a very important celebration and the culmination of the group's activities for the year. Given the broad-based membership of the organization, internal conflicts are perhaps not surprising. Felina explained that because of conflicts within the group, a subgroup had splintered off.[4] This reminded me of an observation made by a local priest I had interviewed, Father Luis, who had pointed out that many organizations in the community had more leaders than followers (see chapter 5). The splinter group consisted of fourteen people who were disgruntled and very negative. They subsequently had another internal disagreement and split into two groups, one with about eight members, and the other with six.

Felina said that muxes are different from gays because they do not date one another. You will also not find gay bars or clubs in Juchitán because the muxes are integrated into the entire community. She repeated that they do not date each other, and added that because they are attracted to men, their partners are hombres, or ordinary men. It was apparent that muxes were accepted as long as they did not pair up with one another. In response to a question regarding major problems facing the organization, she said that one problem they had was that they were well aligned with the PRI, the dominant political party in Oaxaca.[5] The PRI had been the ruling party in México for seventy-one years prior to the 2000 presidential election, which resulted in the election of Vicente Fox, the PAN (Partido Acción Nacional) candidate. The PRI was recently returned to power with a newly elected president, Enrique Peña Nieto. The fact that the muxe organization is supported by the PRI and that a lot of members are not very progressive is politically frustrating, according to Felina.

In the middle of the interview, the muxe politician who had spoken at the municipal palace the first night I had arrived came in to say hello. Amaranta is an HIV/AIDS progressive activist who lost her arm in an automobile accident.

She was extremely political, and I was impressed with her public-speaking skills and with how articulate she was in person, even though she appeared to be a bit tipsy. I should add that she always dresses in traditional Zapotec attire.

I stopped the tape when she entered, but she wanted to say something, pointed to the recorder, and ordered me to turn it back on. It appears that a politician never misses an opportunity to comment on the record. One of the problems with the Intrépidas, she said, is that they would not accept people like her because she was too much of a leftist and too progressive. She reiterated that most of the members of the group belonged to the PRI rather than to the COCEI, the left-wing alliance, and that the PRI supported the organization. As a result, she concluded, most members were not progressive and were reluctant to speak out on important and controversial community issues. In 2003, at age twenty-five, Amaranta had been a candidate for the Cámara de Diputados, the lower house of México's congress, and was recognized in the international media as the first third-gender Mexican political candidate.

As I sat on a sofa across from Felina in her office, I noticed the many posters on the wall providing information about contraceptives as well as promoting safe sex and AIDS awareness. The posters reinforced the idea that she and other members of the organization were quite involved in health issues. I later learned that at the time, Felina had been the director of sexual diversity for the Municipio de Juchitán.

## THE IMPORTANCE OF THE VELA
## IN ZAPOTEC CULTURE

Velas are an important tradition in Zapotec culture. The Intrépida Vela and other muxe velas are relatively recent additions to a year-round tradition of velas in Juchitán and in Isthmus Zapotec society.[6] When I interviewed the director of Casa de la Cultura, Lidxi Guendabianni, she described the underlying structure of la vela:

> The traditional vela is organized and sponsored by an association with members, or associates. The organizational structure of the vela includes the president, treasurer, secretary, elderly deputy, and a female deputy. The association seeks out and appoints the incoming mayordomos. The board of directors is renewed yearly.

The mayordomos may be incoming or outgoing. The outgoing is the current or existing mayordomo. The board selects the captains, the queen, and the princesses. The mayordomo is in charge of organizing the fiesta in conjunction with the board. The mayordomo assumes about 50 percent of the costs, and the association, the other 50 percent. The queen has her puesto, selects her band, buys her dress. She orders her standard.[7]

The Intrépida Vela is held in the third week of November. The creation of the Intrépida-sponsored vela and other muxe velas are therefore an extension of a much larger tradition. Muxes also participate in and support other velas, as well as serving in various capacities, sometimes assuming the mayordomo role. Bennholdt-Thomsen's descriptions of mayordomos/as, festival sponsors, and captains; preparation of food; and the roles of hosts at puestos were elaborated on in several interviews I conducted.

Mr. Mendoza, a retired teacher I interviewed from the nearby town of Espinal, elaborated on the importance of velas in Zapotec culture and went into considerable detail about how the velas are organized, which concurred with what Bennholdt-Thomsen and others have observed (see chapter 5). He impressed on me how great an honor it is to be selected as the mayordomo or sponsor. Like the Olympics, the World Cup, and other major events, selection is made years in advance, and people bid for it, so that if you are not selected as a sponsor for the next year, you can agree to do it in a subsequent year. As the event organizer, the mayordomo gets to select the bands (except the queen's band, which she chooses herself) and invite more people. The mayordomos at the Intrépida Velas have all been muxes.

Each vela also has captains, who assume various functions. Sponsorship is generally not about money but about status or prestige. Biiniza also elaborated on the velas. She mentioned, as Felina did, that Las Intrépidas currently had thirty-six socias, but she added that in order to be accepted as a member, you have to work, be financially stable, and be able to finance a puesto at the vela. She summarized the expense by saying that simply hosting a puesto can cost about ten thousand pesos (approximately eight hundred U.S. dollars).[8] To be eligible for queen, you need to have had a puesto at a prior vela as well as experience as a captain. The queen pays for a band, which is usually about thirty thousand pesos. The mayordomo spends about two hundred thousand pesos (sixteen thousand U.S. dollars), and the entire muxe vela costs more than half a million pesos (more than forty thousand U.S. dollars). In addition to the mayordomo, the primary commercial contributor is the Corona beer company, which sponsors the event. The PRI also contributes, but not much. The group running the vela solicits donations from other organizations and individuals. Biiniza provided a great deal more information and detail on the vela, which is not included here.

Another muxe I interviewed, Mayté, was the Intrépida queen eleven years ago and is a socia (see chapter 4). Like Biiniza, she explained that in order to be a member, you must finance your own puesto. The total cost for being queen is about fifty thousand to sixty thousand pesos, or four to five thousand U.S. dollars. A dress costs about ten thousand pesos, an orchestra, fifteen thousand to twenty thousand pesos, and then you'll still have to pay for your puesto, for the dancers who dance with the queen, and, as noted above, for a band, which will accompany you at the Regada de Frutas. Mayté added that the total cost depends how much you want to pay, but it can be six or seven thousand U.S. dollars.

When I asked how the queen for the vela is selected, Felina told me that the mesa (board) looks at the applicants to make sure they are employed, checks their financial status, and ensures that they are in a position to carry out their function and that they are worthy to be queen. They look at who is applying "y a quién le toca" (and whose turn it is). Each queen tries to outdo the previous one.

## THE GREAT INTRÉPIDA VELA

When I talked with Felina about the vela, she told me that people would be going to set up the night before. This worked out well because I would be able to hang out with Intrépidas and see them relate to one another in an informal setting. The venue where the event was to be held was huge but initially disappointing. A decision had been made to hold the event outdoors this particular year because attendance had just gotten too large. The site was an open field near a local university, and it looked like a large asphalt basketball court surrounded by a dirt floor. Two large stages were set up on opposite ends, connected by an asphalt floor.

I decided to start helping Mandis by opening and arranging the wooden chairs in a large rectangular shape. They were new small wooden chairs that I found hard to unfold and open. They took about three hours to set up, and by the end I was tired and my hands were sore. Each muxe staked out the territory for her guests, and the designated area was set up with chairs around the periphery. More tables were arranged in the middle of the area for food and beer.

I had previously interacted with Mandis, one of the founders of Las Intrépida, and I had walked with him to the vela location from downtown. He was one of the more serious and mature muxes, and I developed some rapport with him. Mandis was in his late sixties at the time and had thinning hair. What was interesting was that he and another muxe, Ángel, were among the muxes I met who did not dress like women or wear traditional Zapotec clothing. They dressed like ordinary men, although Ángel was very flamboyant in his dress at the vela. When I asked Mandis about his attire, he said he could not dress like a muxe because he worked for the government in the Office of Tourism. When we finished setting up, someone brought out and distributed quart-size bottles of beer, and people started to drink and socialize. I had stopped drinking several years ago, so I unfortunately had to pass on the liquor.

On Saturday morning, and before the vela, I observed another surprising example of muxe integration into the Juchitán community, when I attended the Mass that was held for them. Several foreign journalists were also in attendance to cover it. The Intrépidas and another muxe organization were recognized as a society within the Church. It was interesting because the two groups were recognized, and each had sponsors and a banner or standard to represent the group. The main muxe group standard read—"Las Auténticas Intrépidas Buscadoras del Peligro." Many of the muxes were dressed in traditional female Juchiteca dress and had their hair braided with pretty flowers. In his sermon, the priest talked about the muxes and formally welcomed them as a society into the Church, as the priests do for other groups in the community that have velas. He had to be corrected because initially he was recognizing only one group, and there were two. The priest apologized and proceeded to acknowledge and recognize both groups formally as each one and its leaders went up to the altar in a procession, bearing their standard. Padre Francisco (Pancho) noted in his sermon that this culture (muxe) had existed in Juchitán for two thousand years and that respecting these people was a sacred duty (Gage 2009). Padre Francisco made clear in his sermon that he saw muxes as a part of the community; believed that they should be tolerated and respected; and that Juchitán "should serve as an example of tolerance" (Gage 2009).

In addition to the muxes, there was a ceremony for a little girl who was being recognized and incorporated into the Church as a member. She must have been about four years old, and she also wore a Teca dress with flowers braided

FIGURE 1. Intrépida Mass

into her hair. Her mother and father proudly stood at her side. It was interesting to see how Juchitán society integrated these two diverse events into a single ceremony, which included the tribute to the muxes and the introduction of the little girl into the parish community.

As we walked out of the church, we were handed colorful banners. We marched through the downtown area to a hall next to the PRI headquarters, about a mile away, where we had a traditional Oaxacan breakfast with mole and *champurrado*. After breakfast we resumed the march as a group, with banners and balloons, through the middle of town. It was a muxe parade, although we were simply walking down the main street of Juchitán without any decorated cars or floats. While most of the muxes were dressed in traditional Juchiteca attire, with flowers in their hair and a lot of golden jewelry, a few were dressed in ordinary street clothes. Mandis was dressed in civilian attire and had attended the event with another man, who looked like an ordinary heterosexual man but may have been in a relationship with him. I would later learn that he was with Huicho, another muxe whom I would later interview.

In the evening, the venue and celebration were impressive. It was hard to believe that this was the same place we had helped set up the previous day, because it was dramatically transformed and looked beautiful. Tents had been placed around each puesto, and lighting was installed. The two stages were colorfully decorated and well lit. There were three stages now, two for the bands and the other for the muxe celebration and the crowning of the new queen. Interestingly, the fee for the event was a case of beer, which each gentleman bought at the entrance. Ladies could make a cash contribution. The fee and contribution are consistent with the spirit of reciprocity engendered in the community. I bought my case of beer at the entrance, put it on my shoulder, walked in, and went directly to Mandis's puesto and handed it to him. It was early, and he was glad to see me and graciously accepted it. I then walked around and visited with Ángel, who introduced me to another one of the founders of the muxe organization. Ángel struck me as a very nice person. He had a shaved head and, like Mandis, did not dress like a woman. He was, however, dressed in an elaborate white outfit with a large necklace, silver top hat, gray cape, and black cane. He shared proudly that he made his own outfit every year, and that last year, Mandis and some of the other muxes had told him he had to go home and change because his outfit was too outrageous and embarrassing. Ángel looked great during the ceremony honoring the queen. His outfit seemed appropriate for *carnaval* (see chapter 7).

Three bands performed at the vela, but the most famous of them was La Sonora Dinamita, an iconic band that has been around for a long time. They were reputedly paid twelve thousand dollars (U.S.), and the muxe organization clearly had to raise a lot of money to pay for them. The event included two masters of ceremonies. One of them was Amaranta. It was a gala affair with everything, including a red carpet and lots of paparazzi pushing and shoving each other, fighting to get a good view of the contestants.

It was actually difficult to see the contestants and dignitaries as they came down the red carpet. The guest of honor was a young Afro-Latina woman from Guatemala named Karen Davis, who is a supermodel. When they introduced one of the more iconic and popular muxes, Mística, the master of ceremonies humorously said that one (Davis) was a *super-modelo* and the other was a *modelo especial*, which is a play on the name of a popular Mexican beer that means a Special Model. Prior to the coronation, they introduced fifty muxes from throughout the Republic of México. Some were ex-queens while others lived in different cities in Oaxaca or in other regions of the country. Among those introduced were several previous queens, including Felina, who had been the queen around 1998, as I recall.

The culmination of the ceremony and highlight of the evening was the introduction of the queen and her court. The ceremony had all the trappings of a traditional beauty contest. The participants had been practicing for several hours the previous evening, while we were setting up for the event. The new queen, Darina I, was a young muxe, about sixteen or seventeen years old, with a court that consisted of eight male dancers who were about the same age.[9] When they had been practicing the day before, Darina and the boys had been dressed casually. At the time, I had thought the group was entertainment for the evening, consisting of a young woman and her eight male escorts, or, as they call them, *chambelanes*. In any event, the queen and her court danced at the vela and gave a great performance. The lyrics to the song they sang spoke of being queen for the day. Once the queen took the stage, one of the masters of ceremonies asked the other ex-queens to remove their tiaras to properly honor the new reigning monarch.

## LAVADA DE OLLAS

The Lavada de Ollas is an afternoon celebration that takes place the day after the vela, like an after party. On a subsequent visit to Juchitán, I attended another annual Intrépida Vela, and the next day I took a colectivo to the Lavada de Ollas, held at El Campo Che Gómez, near the bus depot.[10] The driver left me about two blocks from the park and pointed me in the right direction. The event started at 4:00 p.m. and was held at an outdoor venue, which was similar to where the Intrépida Vela had been held but much smaller. The setup was interesting. It was like a field with chairs arranged in a rectangle. In the center of the salon was a rectangular asphalt dance floor. A tarp was hung over the floor, with Porta Potties lined up against the wall. The ritual was pretty much the same. You bought your case of beer at the entrance, took it in, and gave it to the host in the puesto where you would be sitting. I didn't know where to sit, so I sat in a random puesto that was centrally located and walked around. Two bands played in succession.

After I had settled in, I spoke to a couple of middle-aged Zapotecas who were sitting near the dance floor and asked them what the Lavada de Ollas meant. They were friendly and responsive, explaining that it meant that the formal vela was over and that you could use this time to unwind and dress informally. As I understood it, this was a more low-key fiesta designed for recovering from the vela, again like an after party. I did notice that people were dressed more casually and not in the *trajes de gala* (formal Zapotec dress) like the night before. The mayordomo, for example, was dressed in plaid madras shorts and a white *playera*, or golf shirt. What was interesting was that although this event started earlier, people danced into the night and drank to excess. In a sense, it also seemed like a continuation of the vela. I heard from another muxe, Felixa (see chapter 3), that Mística, for example, had danced through the night at the Intrépida Vela until 3:00 in the afternoon on Sunday, and then came to the Lavada de Ollas. What is amazing is that since this event started at 4:00 p.m., she had not gotten any sleep in the previous twenty-four hours. I spent some time in Mística's puesto talking to Felixa. I noticed that Mística kept serving her guests and giving them beer. I felt bad about her lack of sleep and asked if I could help her serve, but she answered affectionately, "No, muchas gracias, amor." (No, thanks, dear.)

I didn't stay very late at the lavada. I mostly talked to people and attempted to make more contacts. I spoke to Don Omar (see chapter 3), another founder of the Intrépidas, who appeared to have a lot of money and was known for all the jewelry he wears. I introduced myself, and he gave me his telephone number. I later spoke to Jesús, who was very nice and told me to call him anytime. I also spoke to Enrique and made arrangements to interview him (see chapter 3).

## A MINOR MUXE VELA

On my third trip to Juchitán, I attended a vela organized by a competing muxe group called Vela Muxe. This was a smaller, more modest vela, held at the Salon Acrópolis, an indoor venue across the street from the Che Gómez outdoor venue where the Lavada de Ollas had been held the previous year. I followed the tradition of buying a case of beer at the door. The beer was more expensive this year at 160 pesos, which was about $14 at the time. The case also contained the smaller eight-ounce beer bottles. The bouncer at the door asked for my ticket, I showed him my case of beer, and he stepped aside and let me in.

On the way to the vela, I was chatting with the cab driver, telling him that the muxes were having a vela. He chuckled and said, "Yes, they are crowning Mística." I responded, "She was the queen two years ago." He added, "Es que es muy famosa, todo mundo la concoce." (It's that she is quite famous and every-one knows her.)[11] I had noticed over the past few days that people talked about muxes and Las Intrépidas matter-of-factly, as though they are part of daily life, or at least part of life in Juchitán. Mística appears to be the poster child for the organization, the most popular of the Intrépidas and known by virtually every-one in Juchitán.

I arrived at the vela early, around 10:00 p.m. Many puestos where set up along the perimeter of the dance floor, yet not only was this vela smaller than the Intrépida events I had attended in past years, but they also did not crown a queen. There must have been about fourteen or fifteen puestos, and a few of them had the name of the corresponding muxe in large letters on the wall be-hind them so that guests would know were to go. I looked around and did not recognize anyone, so I arbitrarily approached a puesto for a muxe named Raúl. Someone told me what his artistic or muxe name was, but I don't recall it. Two or three women, clearly family members, were serving food in the back of the stall. The food was modest: a small cheese torta, macaroni salad, sliced sausage, and peanuts. I noticed some puestos had deep-fried tacos and fish. Two stout young men went around offering beer or refrescos to Raúl's guests.

I approached one of these young men as I arrived, introduced myself, told him I did not know anyone, and handed him the case of beer. As I sat watch-ing people rapidly consume the beer, I thought about how some of the people I had interviewed commented that excessive alcohol consumption was a serious problem in the community. I sat for a while and chatted with a man named Julio, in his thirties, from Chiapas. He said they have muxes in Chiapas, but it was not that open. He was visiting, did not know Raúl, and his girlfriend was apparently Raúl's friend and coworker. When I commented that people were very accepting of muxes in Juchitán, he nodded. I also chatted with another young man, named Ismael. He was in his mid-twenties, reeked of alcohol, and was incoherent. It was very difficult to understand him because he was tipsy, and the band was playing loudly, but I heard him say that Raúl was his *primo* (cousin) and had not yet arrived. He pointed out Raúl's mother and *tía* (aunt), who were dressed in traditional Juchiteca clothing and sitting in the front. People at the puestos were clearly family, friends, and invited guests of the cor-responding muxe.

I sat for awhile observing the band and the dancers. Initially there weren't many people, but the crowd began to grow rapidly. Two bands were at the front of the auditorium, on a balcony above the entrance. Huge speakers were located on the dance floor, and the music was extremely loud, especially near the speakers.

I walked around the dance floor, observing people dancing and sitting at various puestos. I recognized Biiniza, who was sitting with two other muxes, went up to her, introduced myself, and told her she had met my daughter at a vela in Oaxaca city several years back and that she had been my first contact in Juchitán. She didn't seem to remember me, although I had interviewed her briefly two years ago at Felina's salon, but she made eye contact and was very gracious with me. She gave me her number and told me to call her. I approached a couple of other muxes. One was a tall, thin muxe named Estrellita (see chapter 4), and there were two other flamboyant muxes who were dressed provocatively in super short, tight-fitting shorts. One was wearing a thong. They were sitting at the edge of the dance floor, and when I asked for permission to take a photograph, they smiled and agreed. I approached one about an interview, and she told me that she was going out of town and would not return until December. The other one, Mayté, agreed to an interview and gave me her phone number (see chapter 4).

I continued to mill around the dance floor and the various puestos. I noticed several muxes entering the men's room, which surprised me because I expected they would use the women's restroom. As the evening wore on, the dance floor kept getting smaller and smaller and more crowded as people arrived and chairs were added in front of the puestos. One puesto in particular, the mayordomo's, located across from the front entrance, was especially large and severely reduced the amount of dance floor space. As I exited the building, people were milling around and trying to enter the event, but it seemed that they were not letting anyone else in. It looked like the place was filled beyond capacity and might constitute a fire hazard.

Several aspects of this vela distinguished it from the previous Intrépida Velas I had attended. The first and most obvious is that a rival group, Vela Muxe, not Las Intrépidas organized it. Second, it was much smaller and was held in an indoor amphitheater. Third, there was no queen or elaborate program as at the Intrépida Velas. Fourth, there were only two bands, and they appeared to be local groups rather than nationally or internationally known groups like La Sonora Dinamita. Finally, and most importantly, the people at the event were dressed mostly in modern dress rather than in the traditional Juchiteca attire. I would later learn that the mode of dress was a main point of contention between Las Intrépidas and some of the splinter groups, who favored more modern clothing. The Intrépidas sought to retain the traditional Zapotec apparel as well as the Zapoteco language, customs, and traditions. Modern dress as opposed to traditional dress, issues with a lack of politically progressive agenda, and vela sponsorship and increasing fees are addressed in subsequent chapters.

Having described my entrance into Juchitán as an outsider and a researcher in the field, the Intrépidas organization, and the important role played by the velas in Isthmus Zapotec culture, I use the metaphor of the mask in chapter 2 to interrogate the relationship between máscara and the macho ideal of manliness—machismo—and how one can reconcile acceptance of muxes in the Isthmus of Tehuantepec with the Mexican cultural conceptions associated with hegemonic Mexican masculinity. A second, related issue I address is the extent to which conceptions of a third gender may have had pre-Columbian origins, and whether acceptance of people of mixed gender can be traced to accounts of cross-dressing Aztec priests and Mayan gods who were at once male and female (Lacey 2008).

# 2

# SEX, SEXUALITY, AND POWER

*The Mexican, whether young or old,* criollo *or* mestizo, *general or laborer, seems to me to be a person who shuts himself away to protect himself: his face is a mask and so is his smile. . . . the ideal of manliness is never to "crack," never to back down. . . . The Mexican* macho—*the male—is a hermetic being, closed up in himself.*

OCTAVIO PAZ (1985, 29-31)

THIS CHAPTER FOCUSES ON TWO THEMES found in Octavio Paz's discussion of "Mexican masks" in his classic treatise on Mexican national character, *The Labyrinth of Solitude.* The first theme is how Mexicans wear various masks to protect themselves from others and from themselves. According to Paz, the Mexican "builds a wall of indifference and remoteness between reality and himself, a wall that is no less impenetrable for being invisible" (1985, 29). The second, related theme is the relationship between *máscaras,* or masking, and the macho ideal of manliness, with a corresponding preoccupation with aggressiveness and violence, as well as an incessant need to prove one's masculinity. In this chapter, I address the relationship between *máscaras* and how one can reconcile acceptance of the muxes in the Isthmus of Tehuantepec with Mexican cultural conceptions of hegemonic Mexican masculinity.

The prototype of the Mexican male is *el gran chingón,* who goes around committing numerous *chingaderas,* creating mayhem, and in the process symbolically ripping open the world. The female *chingada,* in turn, "is metaphorically pure passivity, defenseless against the exterior world" (Paz 1985, 77). The verb *chingar* is "masculine, active, cruel: it stings, wounds, gashes, stains" (77). The word also has innumerable meanings in México, with perhaps as many meanings as emotions, but the verb always denotes violence, or "an emergence from oneself to penetrate another by force" (76).

Paz and others have depicted Mexican society, especially rural areas, as male dominated and driven by the cult of machismo, patriarchy, excessive masculinity, and a corresponding marked intolerance of homosexuality, or what some observers have termed "ranchero masculinity" (Hirsch 2003; Smith 2006).[1] Robert Smith defines ranchero masculinity as "one hegemonic configuration of gender practices that legitimize men's dominant and woman's subordinate position" (2006, 96) so that men exercise authority and women obey. Although relationships of respect resonate with ranchero masculinity and femininity and focus on the man's power and honor with the woman's corresponding deference and modesty, newly emerging forms of companionate marriage emphasize emotional intimacy and friendship between couples, while still maintaining elements of "respect" (97). According to Manuel Peña, machismo and the attendant folkloric theme of the treacherous woman are both intimately tied to Mexican working-class male culture (1991, 31): "Mexican machismo and its vulgar folklore have long been of interest to students of Mexican culture. . . . The folklore of machismo symbolically conflates class and gender by shifting the point of conflict from the public domain of the former to the domestic domain of the latter" (30).

These images of masculinity and femininity are all based on heteronormative conceptions of gender. Smith notes, for example, that among his respondents from Ticuani, a small community in the Mixteca region of Southern Puebla, there was little mention of homosexuality except for two gay men, and he could not recall mention of anyone from Ticuani who was lesbian in either México or New York (2006, 100).

But in Juchitán, a city described as "the most purely indigenous community in Mexico" (Keller 2007), sexual norms are more loosely applied. Male dominance is much less pronounced, and there appears to be greater acceptance not only of homoerotic behavior among men but also of a third gender. As previously noted, *muxe* is a Zapoteco word apparently derived from the Spanish word for woman, which means *afeminado*, or "effeminate," according to Velma Pickett's (2013) *Vocabulario zapoteco del Istmo*. No one knows for certain the origin of the word *muxe*. It is commonly believed that it derives from the Spanish word for woman, *mujer*, but according to Rueda Saynez, it is derived from the Zapoteco word *namuxe'* (Pickett 2013, 82), which means *miedosa*, or cowardly (Bennholdt-Thomsen 1997, 280).

Anthropologists have described muxes as being generally accepted as a third sex or gender category (Bennholdt-Thomsen 1997, 279), analogous to the institutionalized homosexuality found among some Native American groups (Whitehead 1981, 89; Williams 1986). Although lacking the religious significance associated with two-spirit persons among Indian tribes, muxes may have had such significance in the past (Chiñas 2002, 109; Lacey 2008; Williams 1986, 135).

In most Latin American societies, especially in México, residents and outsiders believe that machismo is an important, if not the most important, element of male identity (Sigal 2003, 2). According to Pete Sigal, the *machista* is assumed to be the prototypical male, and the *maricón* "is seen as his opposite, the 'fag' of Spanish-speaking Latin American societies" (2). Yet few scholars have critically examined the concept of machismo, or sought to place this analysis within a broad theoretical or historical context (3). Because of the ideal of machismo, gays and third-gender persons are almost always strongly discriminated against in most parts of México (Bennholdt-Thomsen 1997, 279; Lacey 2008). In Juchitán, however, people are not only aware of this difference,

[p]ero al igual que con muchas otras cosas, la gente en Juchitán está orgullosa de esta diferencia. Y señalar a los muxe's con el dedo sin reparo alguno es parte de un código de aceptación.[2] (Bennholdt-Thomsen 1997, 279)
[but like many other things, the people of Juchitán are proud of this difference. And pointing to muxes with one's finger without reproach is part of a prevailing code of acceptance.]

Despite being born as biological males, muxes wear feminine masks and adopt a distinct persona, which incorporates characteristics of each gender. Acceptance of the muxe lifestyle is not the only feature that distinguishes Juchitán from the larger Mexican society. Another distinguishing feature is that Zapotec culture and language have been maintained since precontact times. Jeffrey Rubin was amazed that Indian peasants taking legal action to protect their lands speak Zapoteco at city hall, and that teenagers from poor neighborhoods write poetry in their native tongue, participate in printmaking workshops, and even read plays by Brecht at the Casa de la Cultura (1997, 1). The appearance and colorful dress of the women of Juchitán is also contrary to Mexican standards of dress and beauty, as well as to Western norms of color and style (1). In addition to challenging Western standards of color and fashion, Juchitecos also defy the gender binary, "with males in varying arrangements of women's dress and body forms dancing with one another at fiestas and playing prominent public roles in work and ritual" (1).

In this chapter, I seek to place the muxe experience in a social and historical context by comparing attitudes toward homosexuality and sodomy held by Spanish colonizers and the precontact indigenous population.

## SEX AND SEXUALITY IN PRE-COLUMBIAN SOCIETY

Before we examine sex and sexuality in pre-Columbian society, several caveats are in order. The first is a word on language and terminology. In keeping with the practice among contemporary Nahua scholars, the term "Nahua" is used to refer to peoples who spoke the Nahuatl language (Sigal 2011, xv). The alternative term "Aztec" suggests a national unity that was not found in the city-state that made up the Aztec Empire (xv). The term "Mexica," in turn, is more focused and reserved for the people who lived in Tenochtitlán. A second caveat is that Nahua conceptions of sex and sexuality do not appear to conform to contemporary views. According to Sigal, "Nahuas did not have a category that a modern scholar can responsibly equate with all of the things that are meant when one uses the category 'sexuality'" (2011, 2). The challenge for contemporary scholars is to determine how one goes about writing a history of sexuality among the Nahuas and other groups who did not have a contemporary conception of sex (2). An additional concern is that discrete modern categories such as "the heterosexual" and "the homosexual" were absent in pre-Conquest and early colonial Nahua society (180). According to Michel Foucault and other social constructionists, these categories did not exist prior to the modern period in Europe, which occurred between the late eighteenth and late nineteenth centuries (Sigal 2011, 180). Because modern conceptions of homosexual identity did not exist, Nahuas instead believed that individuals tended to have certain types of sexual characteristics (181).

Sigal notes that in examining post-Conquest documents, scholars must take into account three additional factors that may have affected these descriptions: (1) medieval and early modern European conceptions that linked sodomy and sin, (2) the tendency among the Spaniards and other conquerors to attribute effeminacy to conquered groups, and (3) indigenous conceptions that associated homosexuality with the passive partner in male homosexuality (178).

Contemporary scholars disagree on how homosexuality was viewed among the Nahuas both before and after Spanish Conquest. Alfredo López Austin contends that the pre-Conquest Nahuas had an extremely negative view of homosexuality, and that the death penalty was imposed on both male and female homosexuals, whether active or passive, and on persons who wore clothing of the opposite sex (1988, 1:305). It was also believed that homosexual relations harmed the participants. One of the ways the cause of "the disease" was tested was to throw kernels of corn on a blanket that was spread on the ground; based on the position in which the kernels fell, one could determine the nature and prognosis of the disease. "When a kernel fell onto and was held by another one, it was proof that the sick person owed his condition to homosexual practices" (1:306).

George C. Vaillant discusses homosexuality only in passing but notes that "sodomy was punished with revolting brutality" (1975, 133). There is, in fact, limited discussion of Nahua homosexuality, with most scholars, like Caso (1958), either not mentioning homosexuality or paying scant attention to the topic (Kimball 1993, 8). Only two texts directly address sexuality in Nahua society, the *Historia de la nación Chichimeca*, by Fernando de Alva Ixtlilxóchitl, written between 1610 and 1640, and *Monarquía Indiana*, published in 1723 by Fray Juan de Torquemada.

Fernando de Alva Ixtlilxóchitl was a historian from Texcoco who identified strongly with his indigenous roots and was proud of his heritage and history (Sigal 2011, 184). Alva Ixtlilxóchitl wrote that the Toltecas and the people of Texcoco punished sodomy with death.

> Y para el buen gobierno . . . [Nezahualcóyotzin] estableció ochenta leyes que vio ser convenientes a la república . . . en donde se castigaban todos los géneros de delitos y pecados, como era el pecado nefando que se castigaba con grandísimo rigor, pues el agente, atado en un palo lo cubrían todos los muchachos de la ciudad con ceniza, de suerte que quedaba en ella sepultado y al paciente, por el se le sacaban las entrañas y asimismo [*sic*] lo sepultaban en la ceniza. (Alva Ixtlilxóchitl 2012, 100)
>
> [And for good governance . . . [Nezahualcóyotzin] established eighty laws that he viewed as beneficial for the republic . . . in which they punished all kinds of infractions and sins, including the abominable sin, which was severely punished with the active partner being bound to a pole while all the city's young men covered him with ashes so that he was buried in them, and as to the passive partner,

his entrails were taken out through the sexual organs and he was buried in the same way in ashes.][3]

Fray Juan de Torquemada similarly notes,

Al que cometía el pecado nefando ahorcaban, y ponían sumo estudio, y diligencia los Jueces, en inquirir, si le cometía esta culpa en las Republicas, para castigarla, por tenerla por bestial, y agena de toda razón . . . pero si eran [los Summo Sacerdotes] notados del pecado nefando, los quemaban en algunas partes, y en otras los ahorcaban o mataban, como les parecía convenir, y satisfice a la gravedad de el caso. ([1723] 1943, 380)

[Those who committed the abominable sin were hanged, and Judges paid careful attention to determine whether this offense was committed in the Republics, since it was considered bestial and alien to all reason . . . and if they [the High Priests] were caught committing the abominable sin, in some parts they were burned and in others hanged or killed in accordance with the gravity of the case.]

If a woman had carnal pleasure (*patlache*) with another woman, they both were killed ([1723] 1943, 380–81).[4] Similarly, men who dressed in women's garments were killed by hanging, as was a woman who wore men's garments ([1723] 1943, 380).[5]

*Historia general de las Indias* by Francisco López de Gómara is generally recognized as one of the principal histories of the Conquest, although this secretary and confidant of Hernán Cortés never came to América. In López de Gómara's *Historia*, he notes that the Natives went around naked, and all slept together in the same room like hens do with one rooster: "They readily couple with women, not unlike crows and snakes, and are in addition great sodomists, indolent, deceitful, untrustworthy, and vile" ([1552] 1954, 1:51). He also wrote that the men of central México were "very much prone to engage in carnal acts with both men and women, without shame or reproach" (López de Gómara [1552] 1954, 2:399) but added that in Tezcuco (Texcoco), "they killed sodomists" as well as "la mujer que anda como hombre y el hombre que anda como mujer" (the woman who acts like a man and the man who acts like a woman; 2:404).[6]

Ironically, while the practice of sodomy was widely condemned by the Catholic Spanish conquistadores, homoerotic behavior among men was widespread throughout the American continent, and nearly all chroniclers of the time commented on its existence (Bennholdt-Thomsen 1997, 295). "At the time of the conquest, same-sex eroticism existed in many, perhaps all, of the indigenous societies of Latin America" (Sigal 2003, 1). This is also true for Native groups of North America. In Yucatán, for example, ritualized transvestism existed among one of the last Mayan societies to be conquered (1). A letter from a priest in seventeenth-century Yucatán reported, "[N]ext to one of their principal temples they had a walled-around large house of very decorous construction solely for the habitation of acquiescents into which entered all of those who wished to have their sodomitic copulations, especially those who are very young, so that they could learn there, these ministers of the Demon wearing women's skirts" (quoted in Sigal 2003, 10). The Spaniards thus demonized what may have been sacred rites for indigenous people.

For the Spanish, sexuality among men, particularly anal sex, or sodomy, was an abominable sin. Hernán Cortés noted in his dispatches to King Charles V that the Natives worshiped false idols, or devils, as he called them, and he was especially appalled by practices such as cannibalism and human sacrifice. He added, "We have learned that they all practice the abominable sin of sodomy" (quoted in Blacker and Rosen 1962, 17). The first indication that the Spaniards had seen transvestism and observed homoeroticism among indigenous groups appears in Cortés's first dispatch to King Charles V of Spain (Bennholdt-Thomsen 1997, 295n55), in which he speaks about the region of Veracruz on July 10, 1519 (Blacker and Rosen 1962, 18). Bernal Díaz del Castillo, one of the soldiers who accompanied Cortés in the Conquest, also makes reference to sodomy among the Mayans, Aztecs, and Huastecs (Bennholdt-Thomsen 1997, 295n55).

Written shortly after the Conquest, *Códice florentino: Historia general de las cosas de Nueva España (Florentine Codex: General History of the Things of New Spain;* 1961), a Nahuatl document, also yields important insights into pre- and post-Conquest Nahua history. Its author, Fray Bernardino de Sahagún, is widely recognized as the father of modern ethnography. Sahagún quickly learned Nahuatl, immersed himself in the Native culture, used Indians as informants, and trained them in ethnographic methods.

## THE *FLORENTINE CODEX*: LOST IN TRANSLATION

The *Florentine Codex* is recognized as one of the most important and complete chronicles of Nahua life in pre-Columbian society. Its principal author, Fray

Bernardino de Sahagún devoted the greater part of the sixty years he spent in New Spain to the production of this text (León-Portilla 1969, 15–16). The impressive research overseen by Sahagún and written in Nahuatl yielded almost one thousand two-sided folios with pictographs. The material provided the basis for his *Historia general de las cosas de Nueva España*, which is not an exact translation but an annotated summary of the main points (16).

Because of Sahagún's advanced age, his aides, the children of the nobility, carried out the bulk of the ethnographic research by interviewing informants and recording their recollections. The methodology used to produce the *Florentine Codex* occurred between 1558 and 1569 (Sigal 2007, 18). Sahagún and his aides went to Tepepolco, a community northeast of Tenochtitlán, and asked the local cabildo (governing body) to support the project and recommend eight to ten older nobles who could remember life before the arrival of the Spanish. The process was then repeated in Tlatelolco and Tenochtitlán (18).

Sigal notes that a filtering process was at work as aides selectively recorded informants' recollections, and that "Sahagún's own filters came into play in organizing and translating the work as well as in preparing the questions" (2007, 20) used by his assistants. Despite Sahagún's obvious affinity for Nahua culture, with regard to its myths, gods, and religious rituals, he "made it clear in the prologues to the various books that his only goal was to destroy these practices" (20).

There are numerous textual references to homosexuality in the *Florentine Codex*, but the meaning of these references often appears to have been literally lost in translation. According to Geoffrey Kimball, though "the *Florentine Codex* has been translated into English, the translators use biased and erroneous translations in the sections of the manuscript which mention homosexuality and the actual meaning is unavailable to anyone who does not know Nahuatl" (1993, 7). Native attitudes toward homosexuals, for example, are found in book 10, chapter 11, which speaks of the vicious and the "perverse" person: "The pervert [is] of feminine speech, of feminine mode of address. [If a woman, she is] of masculine speech, of masculine mode of address" (Sahagún 1961, 37).

Kimball is critical of Dibble and Anderson's translations of the *Florentine Codex*, maintaining that rather than informing, their limited translations of Nahuatl often obscure, mask, or distort the original meaning of the text. For example, he argues that Dibble and Anderson seriously erred in translating *patlache* as "hermaphrodite" rather than as homosexual woman (Kimball 1993, 12). He retranslates their passage, substituting "The one who is homosexual" for

"The pervert": "The one who is a homosexual is: one who has feminine speech, one who has feminine address; one who has masculine speech, one who has masculine address; one who has genital organs . . . one who makes others into homosexuals" (10–11).

Kimball further explains that the word *xochihua* appears to mean homosexual of either sex and is derived from the Nahuatl word for flower, or *xochitl* (11). The fact that homosexuality was often associated with flowers apparently eluded Dibble and Anderson. Sahagún's illustration 61, *The Sodomite*, shows two men seated on the ground with a flower growing between them. Dibble and Anderson incorrectly translate the chewers of chicle as the "effeminates" or "sodomites," and Kimble makes the following corrected translation: "Those sick people that are called homosexual men truly it is their inheritance, the chewing of gum; it is just as if it were their possession, it is just as if it were their fate. And whoever of our men chews gum in public, he arrives to the status of faggotry, he equals the state of male homosexuality" (Kimball 1993, 17).

Native attitudes toward homoerotic behavior thus ranged from acceptance among some groups to dislike among the Nahuas, but not to abhorrence or disdain, as was the case for the Spaniards (Kimball 1993, 15). Instead, the homosexual was viewed as amusing and was often mocked and ridiculed. According to the retranslation of the homosexual in the *Florentine Codex*,

> He is one who is fucked, he is a homosexual man. He is something corrupt; he is obscene (or dirty) he sucks on obscene (or dirty) things, he is an obscene (or dirty), awful thing. He is a corrupt person, he is a lost person. He is amusing, he is humorous . . . he is one who acts the role of a woman. (14)[7]

A single passage contains reference to homosexuals being burned, but as Kimball suggests, "there is linguistic and internal evidence that the attitudes that would lead to this practice were not the previous Aztec ones" (15) but were those of the Spaniards after the Conquest. For example, the passage uses the preterite tense, not the present tense, as was common in descriptions of most professions and personality types, suggesting that the attitudes described in the text were former attitudes. But the subsequent set of verbs, which describe the "burning" of homosexuals, are in the present tense, indicating that they reflect then-current post-Conquest attitudes toward homosexuality (15).

While pre-Columbian societies may have tolerated, ridiculed, or even frowned on homosexuality, under Spanish law, homosexual men were sentenced to death by burning or hanging (Crompton 1978, 70, 72), and the severity of this punishment influenced subsequent views and treatment of homosexuals by Indians in colonial times.[8]

## TRANSLATION AS COLONIZATION

In assessing sexuality in Nahua society, it is important to understand that Sahagún and other Spanish friars were not simply engaged in the translation of indigenous texts and customs; they were also engaged in their creation. Kimball, for example, notes that in the *Florentine Codex*, male and female homosexuality were both known and generally disapproved of, but "there is no evidence for any kind of suppression of homosexuality such as occurred after the Spanish Conquest" (1993, 20). He argues, moreover, that severe punishments for sodomy and homosexuality by hanging or burning were practices not of pre-Conquest Nahuas, but of the conquering Spaniards, who had imposed their views of homosexuality on the Natives (9).

While many laud the *Florentine Codex* for giving us a clear look into Nahua life and culture (Klor de Alva 1988, 35), others assert that the text simply reproduces European views regarding the cultural performance of "savage" cultures (Sigal 2007, 21). Sigal also addresses translations in the *Florentine Codex* and the treatment of a cross-dressing figure called Xochihua. Although translated by Anderson and Dibble as "pervert," as discussed above, the word literally means "flower bearer" (Sigal 2007, 21); the term "xochitl," or the flower, was associated with fertility and sexuality in Nahua ritual and discourse (Sigal 2011, 4–5). Sigal contends, "The text of the flower bearer refers specifically to the cross-dressing figure. . . . And the image accompanying the text shows the flower and signifies it as representing a cross-dressing person who performs various of the functions of women" (2007, 21). But the flower bearer was not viewed positively as, according to the Nahuatl text, the xochihua "has women's speech, women's form of address, . . . corrupts, confuses, and bewitches people" (21). The *cuiloni* was similarly described as "a mockery, annoying, makes people filthy, fills peoples' noses with filth, effeminate; . . . burns, and is scorched; . . . talks like a woman, and passes him or herself as a woman" (21–22).[9]

In the Spanish section of the *Codex*, Sahagún focuses on the acts of the xochihua as a seducer and ignores his image as a cross-dressing figure (Sigal 2007,

22). He also transformed Tezcatlipoca, one of the most important gods in the Nahua pantheon and a paragon of masculinity, into a *puto* (faggot) by transposing him with a lesser god, Titlacauan, who was described as a cuiloni. Sigal argues that we can reconcile the view of Tezcatlipoca as a powerful warrior and as a cuiloni if we recognize that Tezcatlipoca was depicted as a trickster with many identities and forms, a complex figure that in many ways symbolized both masculinity and femininity (2007, 26).

## DISCOURSE ON SEX AND CONQUEST

Although some writers see an important link between sex and conquest, among North American Indian groups, the practice of taking a captive person and making them a berdache who assumed the status of wife appears to have been uncommon (Whitehead 1981, 86). Richard C. Trexler even suggests that all discourse about sexuality and gender is ultimately about hierarchy, dominion, and subordination, and that "sexuality defines gender, a discourse that is about power relations" (1995, 2).

The gendered aspect of war can also be illustrated by descriptions of the sexual practices of Native peoples provided by the Spaniards, since the Iberians were conquerors, and their descriptions of Native practices were unquestionably discourses about power more than they were descriptions of indigenous sexual practices (Trexler 1995, 2). Just as Western anthropologists' descriptions of American Indian practices must be looked at critically (see chapter 6), European accounts of indigenous sexual practices must be interpreted with caution, given that "the Iberians who are our primary informers often stood to gain by accusing them [the Indians] of sodomy" (2). Spanish reports of Native sexual excesses, as noted earlier, were replete with accounts of homosexual behavior, sodomy, and references to "[t]his 'nefarious,' 'unmentionable' and 'abominable sin,'" which was considered to be "against nature" (1). Gendering enemies as female or effeminate also justified the right to conquer the Natives, for if they were seen as "sodomites who engaged in that abominable sin," then they could also be seen as needing salvation, which reinforced conquest as inevitable. In short, once the Iberians demonstrated that the Indians practiced sodomy and other abominable acts, they were justified in conquering them (1). Sigal similarly notes that book 10 of the *Florentine Codex* conformed to the European genre of the encyclopedia, and that the Catholic binary between good and evil "was an attempt to understand Nahua behavior in the Catholic framework" (2011, 194).

In examining the Iberian Conquest of the Américas, Laura A. Lewis has also commented that gender ideals are interlinked with the politics of conquest and the discourse of colonization. The Conquest itself had a gender dimension, so that during the ensuing centuries, "judicial, social, and religious practices in México worked to produce an Indian whose alleged incapacities and vulnerabilities mirrored the qualities dominant gender ideologies assigned to women" (2007, 132). The legitimacy of the Conquest was also upheld by the language of colonial documents, which rendered Indians and women as "weak, sinful, and ignorant" and as lacking "the full capacity to reason" (132–33).

Pete Sigal argues that one cannot understand the cultural, political, or social history of early Latinoamérica without studying how "sexual acts were created, manipulated, and altered" (2003, 3). Society and institutions developed an image of the "successful" man: "The successful man had honor, engaged in sexual activities with at least one woman, and had children. His masculinity was proven through valor in warfare, business, or some similar activity, and through social status. The implied opposite of this position was the man who allowed other men to penetrate him. He was defeated, effeminate, and dishonorable" (3).

Being penetrated was associated with defeat and being "infected," but ironically it was the penetrator who was viewed as the source of contagion and more severely punished (Trexler 1995, 146–47). In fact, archival records indicate that the words *puta*, referring to a woman who was sexually promiscuous, and *puto*, used to refer to a man who was used sexually and acted on by other men, became insults in daily speech, and that these insults were typically leveled at indigenous persons in colonial México (Lewis 2007, 135). Interestingly, some of the men referred to in these texts who were known as male putos assumed the names of well-known Mexico City female putas (Lewis 2007, 135).

Although "puto" was associated with the passive partner in sodomitic male sex, not all putos assumed the passive role. Lewis reports on two cases of mulatto men in colonial México who dressed and acted like women but assumed the active role and mounted other men. In 1658, for example, Juan de la Vega was caught and burned at the stake for committing the *pecado nefando* (nefarious sin) of acting as the penetrating partner (Lewis 2007, 131). De la Vega rented a room from doña Melchora de Estrada and was described by other boarders "as a 'feminized' mulatto *(mulato afeminado)*, whose nickname was

Cotita" (130). Lewis (149n2) states that this would have been a synonym for or nickname derived from *mariquita*, an everyday term used to describe an effeminate man. Witnesses reported that de la Vega cinched his waist, wore a type of handkerchief over his brow that was ordinarily used by women, "adorned the sleeves of his white bodice with ribbons, and he sat like a woman on a small platform placed on the ground as he made tortillas, washed, and cooked" (130).

Another mulatto, Juan Ramírez, was not a transvestite but also reportedly engaged in feminine domestic tasks like cooking, grinding corn, washing clothes, and making chocolate (Lewis 2007, 140). Ramírez also clearly assumed the active sexual role as aggressor. In this study of the muxes of Juchitán, I found that most but not all muxes assumed the *pasivo* role in both oral and anal sex. Yet, there was considerable variation, with a few muxes having engaged in bisexual behavior, and some even having been pressured into marriage.

In the ensuing chapter (3), I turn to an examination of an important and neglected question that has been hotly debated by social scientists in recent years. The question is whether muxes are simply doing gender and reinforcing the Western gender binary by cross-dressing in traditional Zapoteca attire, or redoing gender and representing a third gender category akin to the indigenous berdache of North American groups (see chapter 6). Interviews document internal variations among muxes and reveal several differences between muxes and gay men, as well as the role that mayates (men who have sex with men for money) play in Zapotec society.

# 3

# DOING GENDER IN JUCHITÁN

*[T]he "doing" of gender is undertaken by women and men whose competence as members of society is hostage to its production. Doing gender involves a complex of socially guided perceptual, interactional, and micropolitical activities that cast particular pursuits as expressions of masculine and feminine "natures." . . . Rather than as a property of individuals, we conceive of gender as an emergent feature of social situations: both as an outcome of and a rationale for various social arrangements and as a means of legitimating one of the most fundamental divisions of society.*

CANDACE C. WEST AND DON H. ZIMMERMAN (1987, 126)

I N THIS CHAPTER, I use the muxe experience to interrogate an issue that has been widely debated by sociologists, namely how people go about doing, undoing, and redoing gender. The central question I examine is whether muxes are simply doing gender and reproducing the gender binary or representing a third sex and gender category. A related issue is whether the experiences of muxes are best understood within the context of the Western gender binary or within either Mexican conceptions of masculinity and sexuality or the literature on two-spirit indigenous identity. After presenting an overview of the study sample and discussing the wide range and variety in the muxe experience, I conclude that muxes are a third sex and gender category, which cannot be fully explained or understood through conventional Western conceptions of gender and sexuality or within the emerging field of transgender studies. An alternative explanatory possibility is that the indigenous Zapotec society, dating back to pre-Columbian times, has developed a particular gender system of categories and lifestyles that is similar to two-spirit or other third-gender cultural systems while maintaining its own unique internal codes and logic.

One of the most influential theoretical works on gender over the past thirty years or so has been Candace C. West and Don H. Zimmerman's "Doing Gender" (1987), which attempted to develop a sociological theory that explained how gender is created and reproduced in society. Nearly three decades later, the theory has been so widely accepted that it has nearly attained a canonical or lawlike status (Jurik and Siemsen 2009). In short, doing gender has become not only the hegemonic theoretical framework for understanding gender (C. Connell 2010) but also the "point of reference for Anglophone gender analysis" (R. Connell 2009, 105).

In West and Zimmerman's classic article, they challenge the prevailing "role theory" model of gender differences by drawing on Harold Garfinkle's ethnomethodological case study of "Agnes" (Rogers 1992), a preoperative transsexual who was raised as a boy and who then adopted a female identity as a teenager. West and Zimmerman propose a distinct sociological understanding of gender "as a routine, methodical, and recurring accomplishment" (1987, 126). For these researchers, doing gender was not an internal property but an external social process emergent from social situations and external to the individual.

Seeking to provide greater conceptual clarity than had existed in the past, West and Zimmerman (1987) were careful to distinguish among sex, sex category, and gender. Sex refers to socially constructed biological criteria used in classifying individuals as female or male, such as genital differences at birth or chromosomal differences. Persons are then placed in a sex category through the application of these socially constructed indicators, but in everyday life, such classification is created and maintained "by socially required identification displays that proclaim one's membership in one or the other category" (1987, 127). Although sex category presupposes one's sex and often serves as a proxy for sex, the two can and do vary independently. Agnes, who had to preserve the secret of her penis and present herself to society as a woman, can declare membership in a sex category, even when, as with the muxes, the socially constructed sex criteria are absent (West and Zimmerman 1987, 2009). Gender, on the other hand, entails the process of managing behavior according to normative conceptions of appropriate attitudes and actions that are deemed to correspond to one's sex category (1987). Such membership activities, in turn, develop from and reinforce one's sex category.

Critical theoretical works have started to focus not only on doing gender but also on how one goes about undoing gender, thereby challenging the prevailing gender binary in Western societies and promoting social change (C. Connell 2010; Deutsch 2007; Risman 2009; Lorber 2005, 2006; Davis, Evans, and Lorber 2006; Lucal 1999; and Martin 2003).[1] Judith Lorber (2005, 2006), for example, uses the idea of "breaking the bowls" and calls for a deliberate degendering of society in order to promote equality and social change. The notion of "breaking the bowls" is based on the kabbalah and is a translation of a Hebrew phrase, *lo misbbor et bakelim*, a warning to not go against established customs and traditions. Breaking the bowls is "a metaphor for new ways of thinking about gender" (Lorber 2005, 5) and degendering society.

Although the debate regarding undoing gender has been mostly theoretical (C. Connell 2010), a body of empirical work has begun to interrogate how transgender persons have attempted to undo the heteronormative binary model. Much of this research has examined the workplace experiences of transgender persons (C. Connell 2010).[2] This may not be surprising given that transpeople, by their very existence, disrupt prevailing assumptions that sex, sex category, and gender correspond with one another and are often manifested in the workplace. Transpeople are able not only to transcend conventional notions about how we go about doing gender in our daily interactions (Deutsch 2007; Risman 2009) but also to alter and expand norms associated with gender (C. Connell 2010).

In this chapter I extend the debate on doing and undoing gender by looking beyond Anglophone conceptions and reporting on data from my study of muxes in Juchitán. As noted, muxes upend conventional conceptions of sex, sex category, and gender, as well as the gender binary, by openly dressing in female Zapotec attire and assuming traditional female roles while being widely accepted in the community as a third gender. Rather than focusing exclusively on their workplace experiences, I look at the coming out process and the extent to which muxes are accepted and integrated within the community at large. I conclude by presenting several case studies, based on in-depth personal interviews, that demonstrate the wide range and variation in how muxes go about "breaking the bowls" by actively doing and undoing gender. I place the findings in a global context and suggest that muxes are a hybrid third sex and gender category that cannot be understood by using conventional Western conceptions of gender and sexuality like those articulated by West and Zimmerman (1987), Butler (1990, 2004), Lorber (2005, 2006), and other "doing gender" scholars, as well as within the rapidly emerging field of transgender studies (see Stryker 2008; Stryker and Aizura 2013; Valentine 2007).

The chapter begins with a brief overview of the literature on how transpersons go about doing and undoing gender in the workplace. The study findings reinforce the view of muxes as a third sex and gender category similar to the Native American two-spirit persons and the *hijras* of India and suggest that much can be learned about gender from the muxe experience.[3]

## RESEARCH ON TRANSPERSONS
## IN THE WORKPLACE

Although West and Zimmerman cited various studies to support their theory, they failed to focus on the diverse methods employed by these studies, which included ethnographic observations, case studies, and diaries. "The implication of this omission is that the practices involved in 'doing gender' can be isolated and described by relatively straightforward sociological observation and self-report" (Kitzinger 2009, 94). Celia Kitzinger questions the assumption that the processes in doing gender are self-evident both to observers and to sociological participants, noting that ethnomethodology has always focused on those things that may be seen but often go unnoticed (Garfinkle 1967) and are not the subject of self-report or reflection (Kitzinger 2009).

Raewyn Connell moves the discourse away from identity in earlier studies toward a focus on politics and power, proposing that Agnes's problem was not so much living up to standards of femininity as it was maintaining her categorization as female. Following the work of West and Zimmerman among others, Raewyn Connell calls for the reconceptualization of men and women as "distinct social groups," who are "historically constituted in specific (and changing) social relationships" (2009, 108).

Drawing on an empirical analysis of nineteen in-depth interviews with transpeople, Catherine Connell reports on how they go about negotiating and managing gender interactions in the workplace in her critique of West and Zimmerman. She argues that workplace interactions are important not only because the workplace has been a major site for the reproduction of gender inequality, but also because it is a place where we can observe and document challenges to gender equality (C. Connell 2010).

Five of the nineteen transpersons in Catherine Connell's sample performed stealth in the workplace in that they did not come out or publicly declare that they were transgender, and to the best of their knowledge, they were not identified as transgender by their colleagues. These persons were described as doing gender in the same sense that others do gender daily. Mark, for example, a sixty-four-year-old White transman, had lived and worked as a man for twenty-five years and was able to go stealth at work by changing his name and pertinent background information, such as his driver's license and social security number, and by assimilating appropriate masculinity. Although coworkers initially questioned his gender status because there were things he did not know about or react to as a man, he eventually successfully assimilated appropriate masculinity and was able to transition into his new gender status. Jessica, a twenty-six-year-old Latina transwoman who worked in customer service was also stealth, but unlike Mark, she did not fear discrimination and readily invoked her rights, threatening to take anyone who discriminated against her immediately to Personnel. Jessica's transition had occurred in her previous job, and when asked to describe her transition, she pointed to a more demanding accountability structure, including stringent appearance expectations for women in the workplace (C. Connell 2010, 40).

The majority of participants were said to be "out," and their coworkers, friends, and family knew they were transgender. Rather than simply doing gender, these "out" transpeople describe experiences that fit better into what would be termed "undoing" or "redoing" gender, or "doing transgender." They attempted to blend masculine and feminine gender performances, but at the same time, they "often felt they were gender disciplined and/or reinterpreted according to conventional gender norms" (40). Several "out" transmen related prior experiences as women in which they had been chased out of women's bathrooms for appearing to be too masculine. Other research participants actively worked to "undo" or "redo" gender by deliberately retaining gender characteristics that did not match their gender presentation as a way to chip away at, or challenge, the hegemonic gender order.

Kristen Schilt (2006) similarly examined the reproduction of gender inequality in the workplace through in-depth interviews with female-to-male transsexuals (FTMs). Many FTMs are actively involved in undoing and redoing gender when they enter the workplace as women and then transition to becoming men, an experience that gives them an "outsider-insider" perspective and insight into the patriarchal dividend, giving them advantages and privileges simply for being men. A number of FTMs, for example, found themselves receiving more rewards, authority, and respect in the workplace even if they were doing the same job.

Dana Rosenfeld (2009) looked at how heteronormativity and homonormativity have shaped the identities of lesbian and gay elders, who often opted to "pass" as heterosexual to gain greater societal acceptance. Before the gay liberation movement urged gay people to "come out" and be proud of their gay identity, these elders adopted assimilationist politics that encouraged and justified assuming a heterosexual veneer in order to survive in a heteronormative world. They also strategically employed a homonormative ideology to justify the belief that "heteronormativity provided the tools for personal survival in a hostile society and for the collective production of a respectable homosexual culture" (Rosenfeld 2009, 617). Throughout their lives, these gay elders engaged in impression management, constructing a public heterosexual identity that required assuming a mask and a front as well as the ability to manage separate contradictory claims for different audiences. Several elderly lesbian respondents remarked that they could dress in men's clothing at the homes of their friends, for example, but not in public.

Drawing on a study of sixty-five masculine transgender persons, Patricia Gagné, Richard Tewksbury, and Deanna McGaughey (1997) conclude that while many believe they are radically altering the binary system, the majority of these persons in fact support and reify the very system they are attempting to change.[4] These findings are consistent with West and Zimmerman's (2009) assertion that it is impossible to undo gender, and that efforts to change and subvert the gender binary only work to reinforce heteronormativity.

The fact that much of the research on doing gender has focused on the workplace experiences of transgendered persons who want to change, disrupt, and otherwise reconfigure prevailing assumptions about doing and undoing gender is perhaps not surprising given that in the United States sex, sex category, and gender generally correspond with one another and are openly manifested in the workplace (C. Connell 2010). Despite the obvious theoretical and practical significance of transgender research in the workplace, it is not without limitations. One limitation, noted above and in the literature by Gagné, Tewksbury, and McGaughey (1997) as well as by others, is that in attempting to reconfigure sex and gender roles in the workplace, transpersons may inadvertently reinforce the gender binary and heteronormativity. A second, related limitation is that such research is ultimately based on the Western gender binary.

Many recent studies have focused on doing gender and transgender outside the workplace. In *Global Divas*, Martin F. Manalansan (2003) interrogates gender identity among gay Filipino men in New York City, describing how Filipino gay immigrants, like other queers of color are carving out a new identity and a space that is distinct from that of White gay or transgender men. Manalansan explains his choice to use the Tagalog term *bakla* instead of transgender: "My non-usage of the transgender identity category is due to the dissonance it creates vis-à-vis the bakla, but also as I have mentioned before, cross-dressing and effeminacy, which are the conceptual core of the social construction of the bakla, are not necessarily encompassing realities for all informants" (24).

Although most of his respondents did not cross-dress, they used the bakla as a social category and as a cultural reservoir of meanings for interpreting daily events relative to the intersection of race, gender, and sexuality. In a sense, for many, bakla embodies Filipino queerness, whereas "gay" serves as a symbol for White queerness (24).

According to popular folklore, the bakla possess what is termed the "female heart" (*pusong babae*), an idiom that captures the social construction of the bakla, or the male body within a female heart (25). Their yearnings and desires parallel those of women, which is why some see themselves as looking for a "real man," meaning straight men, who may be married or have girlfriends. Like the muxes, sexual relationships between or among bakla are few because it is generally seen as a form of incest. When a bakla discovers that his lover is also a bakla, he is seen as duped or tricked, which is termed *natnanso* (25).

Another key difference between Western gay men and the bakla is how they envision the transition into homosexuality. While the "coming out" process is central to gay identity and marks an important rite of passage and transition in the United States, many Filipino men have a problem with the notion of coming out and "look at the practice of coming out as a particularly American idea and behavior" (Manalansan 2003, 27). Many bakla see acceptance of their homosexuality not as a coming out nor as an act of revealing or discovering the self, but as the acceptance of an unstated inner self and feminine sensibility (28). Accordingly, "[m]any Filipinos, including scholars, believe that the clothes the bakla wears are external signs of the inner core, or essential qualities of feminine sensibility and emotions," and the "unfurling," rather than revealing a secret self, entails acceptance of an "unfelt or unapprehended presence" (28). A number of respondents reported not only very positive responses from their families when they came out, but also that they didn't actually have to come out because their families already knew they were bakla, without verbalizing it (28). The silence itself is part of the discourse, which makes its verbalization superfluous.

In *Queen for a Day*, Marcia Ochoa (2014) examines the performance of femininity by *transformistas* and beauty queens in Venezuela. Transformistas is a term used in Latinoamérica. In Brazil, it refers to cross-dressers or transvestites, distinct from *travestís*, who have been the focus of a great deal of ethnographic attention (2014, 3). In Argentina and Spain, transformistas are female impersonators. In Venezuela, however, the term refers to people similar to the muxes, those assigned to the male sex at birth who begin to transform their bodies at an early age, seeking to become women through a series of actions over time, such as plucking their eyebrows, using makeup, wearing women's clothing, taking hormones, getting breast implants, and doing women's work (3). The term is associated with sex workers and is considered an insult by some, although it is sometimes used for self-definition. Because these changes are made gradually and silently, unlike the norm in the United States, there is no "coming out" moment as in lesbian and gay identity formation (4).

While muxes are broadly accepted in Juchitán, transformistas in Venezuela are subjected to gender policing nearly everywhere, including in the home as well as in public spaces, such as on the street, in shopping malls, at schools, and in other institutional settings. In fact, "the life of many *transformistas* in Venezuela is defined by social exclusion and violence" (Ochoa 2014, 4). During the course of the research, Ochoa found that a large number of transformistas were subjected to extreme violence at the hands of police, private security, family members, and other individuals. A report compiled with Edgar Carrasco concluded that "the overwhelming majority of transgender and transsexual people we surveyed (including transformistas) had experienced some form of physical or structural violence" (4). Their exclusion from mainstream education and occupational opportunities forces many to turn to sex work, although some work in beauty, food preparation, nursing, or spiritual work.

Unlike Manalansan, Ochoa sees transformistas as fitting within the concept of transgender, although the latter term is new to Venezuela, and some transgender folks are careful to use the term to differentiate themselves from transformistas. She defines transgender as "a general category that refers to people who take identitarian, physical, and social measures to express a gender that society says does not belong to the sex assigned to them at birth" (2014, 4). While transformistas, and muxes, fit within the broad rubric of transgender, obviously not all transgender persons are transformistas.

Rather than seeing transgender femininities as deviant or exceptional, Ochoa uses a parallel conceptual structure to better understand the production of both cisgender and transgender femininities. Employing Harold Garfinkel's concept of the "accomplishment of femininity" and Simone de Beauvoir's observation that "one is not born, but rather becomes, a woman," Ochoa draws parallels between the accomplishment of femininity by transformistas and by participants in the Miss Venezuela beauty pageant (2014, 5). In fact, she sees the country of Venezuela as transformista in that both the transformistas and the nation "use beauty and glamour to negotiate power and marginality" (6).

## WORK AND GENDER IN JUCHITÁN

Although a rigid gender-based division of labor characterizes Isthmus Zapotec society, some occupations are not assigned to one gender or the other and are instead recognized as the domain of muxes. Counter to the gender binary, lighter work in music, poetry, and art, for example, is typically defined as men's work, whereas women's domain, including working in the market and planning fiestas and velas, is linked to subsistence and heavy work. Making decorations for the velas or ornaments for parade floats does not readily fit into either one of these categories and is considered appropriate for muxes. The patterns for embroidery and for traditional Zapotec clothing are also usually designed and made by muxes.

Ironically, the sharp division of sex and gender roles facilitates acceptance of the muxes as a third sex and gender category, as does the prevalence of gender equity in Isthmus Zapotec society. Multiple researchers have noted that Juchitán is not a matriarchal society (see introduction), yet in the face of patriarchy, a matrifocal family system persists, in which both men and women have important cultural and ritual roles, and women exercise a great deal of power and autonomy economically and socially, as well as in the kinship system (Chiñas 2002; Bennholdt-Thomsen 1997). Because women assume the role of merchants and traders in the market, they also typically control familial resources and are recognized as the economic heads of households. Muxes often become heads of households in traditionally caring for their elderly parents.

The prevailing view in the community is that being muxe is not a voluntary choice. Zapotec parents, especially mothers and women in general, are said to readily defend muxes, believing that they have a right to "be themselves" and that "God made them that way" (Chiñas 2002, 108–9). Since being muxe is seen as an immutable characteristic, perhaps it is not surprising that people, including muxes themselves, easily distinguish between genuine muxes and those who simply cross-dress or mimic the muxe lifestyle. Biiniza, for example, noted that only a handful of muxes were among the hundreds of transvestite men attending the vela in Oaxaca city.

Julie, the gay hair stylist in the city of Oaxaca whom I met before embarking on my research, was acquainted with a number of muxes and provided an "insider/outsider" view that distinguished sexuality, sex, and gender. She observed that although muxes have sex with men, they distinguish themselves from gays because they identify as a third sex and gender category, and like the bakla, they do not have sex with one another. Most also live the muxe lifestyle 24/7 and are always out of the closet.

Another outsider perspective came from Marcos, the young gay waiter who worked at a local restaurant near my hotel. Marcos was not originally from Juchitán, and he agreed that muxes were different from gays in that they generally dressed in Zapoteca attire, considered themselves a third sex and gender category, and continuously lived the muxe lifestyle.

The idea of going stealth in the workplace is thus antithetical to muxe identity, since they are out and readily identifiable in public by the Zapoteca outfits they don in daily life. Their workplace, or better yet, their work ethic, reinforces their identity. On the other hand, the two young men Bennholdt-Thomsen observed in the marketplace, and one of the muxes I interviewed, Tifani, were going stealth in that they were men trying to dress like women in order to be accepted in the marketplace, the domain of women.

While my interviewees adopted modes of dress that ranged from traditional male to traditional Juchiteca, most were not trying to pass as women. They openly take on some of the characteristics of each gender and have historically been recognized as a third gender by the Juchitán community and by the Church. Like two-spirit indigenous persons, when asked whether they identify as men or as women, muxes invariably respond that they are neither; they are muxe. Muxes are therefore continuously not only doing but also undoing and redoing gender.[5]

## SUMMARY OF DATA AND MUXE RESPONDENTS

The following is a summary of data I collected during several visits to Juchitán and neighboring communities. The list of muxes interviewed appears in appendix A, including their names, ages, and occupations, as well as whether they are *internacionales* (inters), meaning both active and passive, in their sexual relations (see below and chapter 7).[6] The data capture how muxes generally opt to go public in the workplace, going stealth and reverting to more traditional male dress only when dictated by public occupations, such as politics or teaching.

There was a total of fifty-two muxe respondents, ranging in age from nineteen to seventy years, with three being sixty-five years or older.[7] Almost 40 percent (twenty) were in their twenties or teens, 25 percent (thirteen) were between thirty and thirty-nine, 15 percent (eight) were between forty and forty-nine, and 21 percent (eleven) were fifty years of age or older. A wide range of occupations was also represented in appendix A. Although many of the respondents worked in traditional muxe trades, as dressmakers, huipil designers, clothing designers, decoration makers, hair stylists, merchants, and so forth, a number of professions were also represented (teachers, accountants, nurses, government workers, and politicians). In fact, respondents were fairly evenly distributed between professions and muxe-related occupations. Three hair stylists (Felina, Kike, and Francis) were also independent entrepreneurs who owned their own businesses (hair salons). Mitzary similarly was an independent entrepreneur and businessperson, in addition to a huipil vendor. Notably, they are all professionals in traditionally muxe trades. Since a number of muxes held more that one job, appendix B gives a more detailed accounting of the various occupations represented.

The respondents are also grouped in appendix A according to whether they were classified as *vestidas*, those who regularly dressed in women's clothing, or

FIGURE 2. Muxes in traditional male attire.

FIGURE 3. Vestidas tradicionales.

*pintadas*, those who wore men's attire but used makeup and/or jewelry. Forty-three of the fifty-two respondents are in one of these two groups. There was further distinction made between vestidas *tradicionales*, like Biiniza and Felina, who dress in traditional Zapoteca clothing every day, and vestidas *modernas*, those who, except for fiestas, dress in jeans and a blouse. The sample is fairly evenly divided between vestidas and pintadas, with twenty-four (56 percent of the forty-three; 46 percent of all respondents) classified as vestidas, who dress like women daily, and nineteen (44 percent, or 37 percent of all respondents) as pintadas, who dress like men but wear makeup and/or jewelry such as neck-laces, bracelets, or earrings. Variations occurred among the pintadas. Anilú, Johnny, Camelia, and Ángel Rolán did dress as women for special occasions like the velas, while others, like Enrique, Mandis, and Omar, never dressed up but wore light makeup, jewelry, or embroidered shirts to distinguish themselves as muxe.

Ten of the remaining muxe respondents, Armando, Gabriel, Felix(a), Ferni, César, Romi, Jade, Sofia, Kike, and Huicho, could not be classified as either vestidas or pintadas because they dressed like ordinary men in guayaberas and pants, never donned women's attire, and did not use makeup or jewelry. Others, like Franki, Sofia, and Kike, only dressed for the velas. Kike alternated between ordinarily dressing as a man and transforming into the female Kika, La Performancera, on special occasions. The term *vestida* was thus reserved for those who dressed as women 24/7.

Respondents were also classified according to whether they assumed an *activo* (active) or *pasivo* (passive) role in sexual relations. Those who were the insertees in anal and/or oral sex with other men were termed pasivos. The vast majority (88 percent) of muxes interviewed assumed the pasivo, anal receptor position in sex with men, and only six (12 percent) were internacionales (inter), alternating between the pasivo and activo roles. Those classified as inter included Ángel Rolán, Armando, Becky, Franki, Huicho, and Marian. Finally, only three of the muxes (6 percent), Armando, Enrique, and Huicho, identified as bisexual, and both Enrique and Huicho have been married and have children.[8]

FIGURE 4. Vestidas modernas.

# VARIETIES OF MUXES: CASE STUDIES

In the following section, I present several in-depth case studies gathered in my research to demonstrate the variety in muxe experience, lifestyle, and sexuality. These case studies also represent the range of how muxes go about doing and redoing gender. The interviews were taped and conducted in Spanish. When I translated them into English, I carefully preserved the "voice" of the respondent, including individual variations in usage, syntax, and grammar.

## BIINIZA, THE IMPETUOUS BREEZE

When I was finally able to interview Biiniza, after several attempts, she came dressed in traditional Juchiteca apparel. I met her in front of the Restaurante Internacional, but the restaurants in the immediate area were crowded, so we took a moto-taxi to another restaurant, in la séptima sección. Biiniza knew the driver of the mini moto-taxi. She said that he was Mayté's brother, and he acknowledged that he was.

Biiniza explained that her name reflected what she was like. In Zapoteco it means *viento y agua* (wind and water), or somewhat like an impetuous breeze or mist. Biiniza is vestida, one of the muxes who dresses and acts like a woman 24/7. At the restaurant, the proprietor, who also obviously knew her, referred to her as "Señora." She has lighter skin than most people in Juchitán, yet she referred to me as being güero, or light complected.

Biiniza was born in Niltepec, a town in the municipal district of Juchitán, and feels that she was raised between the two communities. Her father was from the North and an engineer, and her mother, a teacher and politician who became the presidente municipal of her community. When her parents divorced, her father moved back to the North, so he wasn't around for much of her childhood and adolescence. She gets along well with him, and her mother is now deceased.

Biiniza grew up with her grandmother and great-grandmother. They would play games, listen to music, dress up, and dance. She feels that grandmothers always have a sixth sense about gender identity. They would bathe her, play with her, and spend so much time around her that they sensed her inclination toward the feminine. Interestingly, her great-grandmother was more open to her sexual orientation and accepting of it. Biiniza also suggested that in an all-male family, they may have wanted a girl, which might have affected her upbringing. She has identified as a girl for as long as she can remember.

Her first year in school, *kinder*, was very traumatic because it shattered the world she had constructed with her grandmother and great-grandmother. For the first time, she began to experience contact with boys, who were somewhat homophobic. She also discovered a boy she was attracted to, whom she described as gorgeous. Biiniza still knows his family and tells his mother that her son has always been "beautiful."

She attended a Catholic elementary school and found it difficult because the teachers had the children line up according to gender, with boys in one line and girls in another. She had no place to go and was forced to line up in the boys' line, learn to be physical, play sports, and play rough with other boys. But Biiniza was always bored and not interested in boys' games. One thing that saved her was that she had always been intelligent and strong willed, so she was not readily intimidated by the boys. In fact, there was a sense in which boys had to conform to her expectations.

Biiniza came into her own in junior high school, when she started wearing makeup and fixing her hair. She got some flack from the school, but she told them that she was paying her tuition, was not violating any school rules, and had a right to dress the way she pleased. At about age thirteen, she fell in love for the first time, at the *preparatoria* (high school), with a boy who was fifteen. For her, this boy was *lo máximo* (the greatest), and their courtship "Era muy bonito" (was lovely); she really fell in love. At that time, there was a lot of talk about AIDS, so she went to the pharmacy to purchase a condom. Her aunt worked there and asked why she needed one, and she told her that they were talking about them at school, and she wanted a sample. Other girls also talked about boys as well as about maintaining their virginity, but she had sex for the first time with this boy. The relationship lasted eight months, and she facetiously termed it a "horrible pregnancy." Predictably, the boy had a girlfriend, and he ended up being with her.

Biiniza has not been involved in a long-term relationship since then. Her first sexual encounter was beautiful, but she learned never to let anyone take advantage of her or exploit her. On the contrary, this experience taught her to use and control others, particularly men, instead of letting anyone use or control her. Since then, she has used men to satisfy her own needs and interests. I asked where muxes have sex, and she said in places just like other people. "You have sex in hotels, someone's apartment, or wherever you can." She and the boy she first had sex with got together in a house that was under construction; only he and she had access to it. I asked whether they kissed and did other things, and she said, "A, sí, como cualquier persona." (Oh, yes, just like anyone else.)

She said muxes have a good relationship with the local priest, although they are not bound to religion the way people are in Oaxaca city, which is the center of the Catholic Church. The Church is just one of many institutions in society. Father Pancho was good. He met with them and explained that they could not have a Mass for the muxes per se. They could have Masses for a person who died, for a saint, or for other occasions acknowledged by the Church. Biiniza also mentioned that the bishop had issued a declaration saying that muxes were God's children and could not be denied the services of the Church, which helped a great deal in gaining acceptance.

Biiniza went to Oaxaca city to study. She took courses and studied for a short career in *turismo*, which was popular at the time. She also trained as a health expert and now works in a hospital outside Juchitán as well as running her own consulting agency, providing services to various governmental agencies. She explained, as Felina had, that there were currently three muxe organizations: Las Intrépidas, El Santa Cruz Baila Conmigo, and Vela Muxe. One of the issues that had arisen, and the reason some had broken away from the Intrépidas, was that some muxes want to be more modern and dress in contemporary outfits. These muxes dressed in modern clothes at the vela and more traditionally at the lavada. The Intrépidas want to protect Zapotec traditions.

One of the most interesting things Biiniza said was that many Intrépidas were not pursuing advanced degrees or going into professional careers even though they are very capable. Although things are changing, many professions still require dressing in conservative, modern, gendered clothing. You cannot dress like a Teca. There were exceptions. Biiniza mentioned a college professor, an anthropologist in another state, and a politician who openly cross-dressed, for example. This reinforced the finding that half the muxes worked in muxe-related occupations.

## ENRIQUE: A CONFLICTED BISEXUAL POLITICIAN

One of the reasons some muxes, like Mandis, do not dress as women or in traditional Zapoteca attire is that they are employed in mainstream occupations, for example, as accountants, medics, teachers, school administrators, and computer instructors. Enrique, a twenty-four-year-old muxe, was an elected public official in a nearby municipality who did not dress in traditional Zapotec women's clothing.

Enrique is a heavy-set person of average height but with the build of an American football player. He has short hair and uses a little bit of makeup on his eyes but is not effeminate. If you didn't look very carefully and didn't notice the makeup, he could easily be mistaken for an ordinary man. In my interview with him, he said that life was difficult, and his eyes got glassy as he told me his story. Enrique is not like other muxes because he is bisexual, which he has known since he was about ten years old. At an early age, he knew that he had a thing for boys and liked to play and dress up with his sisters. He was the same way through high school, although he was also attracted to girls. Enrique's mother knows about his sexuality. His father, who is very traditional and drives a taxi, suspects but doesn't ask because he is afraid to find out and doesn't want to know. Enrique lives at home, and his family is aware that he takes time in the bathroom primping, putting on a bit of makeup and doing his eyes, but they don't say anything. Enrique was wearing black pants and a white guayabera, which is traditional male dress. The only distinguishing muxe trait, other than the light makeup, was that he wore a large gold medallion necklace, gold rings, and a gold bracelet. He admitted that dressing up as a woman was *una fantasía* (a fantasy), but he couldn't do it because of his work. Elections were coming up shortly, and he had to be very careful because any kind of negative publicity could be used against him politically. He paused briefly and speculated on what might happen if a picture of him dressed like a woman was made public and concluded that it would be political suicide.

The day after a vela, Enrique invited me to a local fair in his hometown, about eighteen kilometers outside Juchitán. It was a traditional Mexican event, with charros, a rodeo, games, and a lot of food and drinking. As we walked across the town square and entered the fairgrounds, I was impressed with the number of people he knew as we were warmly greeted, and I was introduced to various persons. Town residents clearly knew and respected him, but again, his outward demeanor was that of an ordinary man.

Enrique had a two-year-old son from his previous marriage, which had ended in divorce. He had been candid with his wife about his bisexuality, but the marriage hadn't worked out. He seemed very sad and kept saying how difficult life was for someone who is bisexual, noting, "Es muy, muy difícil." (It's very, very difficult.)

Enrique also told me about several reported, though rare, incidents of violence against transgender persons, particularly at the large truck stop on the outskirts of Juchitán, where some people go looking for sex. He believes that there are people *que no respetan* (who are not respectful) or who do not honor the muxe identity, and they have problems, but overall this is not a major issue. In fact, there was pretty much total acceptance of muxes in Juchitán. As an example of muxes who were not respectful, he related an incident that took place at the tail end of an Intrépida Vela I had happened to attend. It was about 6:00 a.m., and security had gone home. He needed to use the bathroom, but outside the Porta Potties was a group of six or seven men performing oral sex on men. He told me in disgust that several of them had yelled out, "Come and have a taste," inviting him to join in the orgy, but he thought having sex in public like that was inappropriate, disrespectful, and gave muxes a bad name.

## FELIX(A): A DEDICATED TEACHER

Felix(a) is a forty-something muxe who teaches third grade in a nearby town and also dresses in regular male attire.[9] When we met for the interview, he was clean-cut and impeccably dressed in a light green guayabera and dark green slacks, looking neat and well groomed, with his hair spiked with mousse. Felixa has been involved with Las Intrépidas for about twenty years but is not a socia. He knows Enrique and explained that, like Enrique, he cannot dress like a muxe because of his profession. But his students know Felixa is muxe, and they still accept and respect him.

I met Felixa at Estética Felina as a large crowd was gathering outside, waiting for the Regada de Frutas parade, which was held the night before the vela. Traditionally, women threw fruit from the floats, but on this occasion, muxes on the floats threw candy and toys to the children. It was interesting to sit outside Felina's salon and see families and children lining the street along the parade route, much as people in the United States would line up for a Fourth of July parade. This was another indication of the acceptance of muxes in the community, which I observed on this and several other occasions. Felixa and I made arrangements to meet at the bus station the next day between 3:00 and 3:30 p.m. He was going to a birthday party for an aunt and would pick me up at the bus depot so we would have an opportunity to talk.

We traveled to a nice Oaxacan party in Unión Hidalgo, a historic town near Juchitán, for the celebration of Felixa's aunt's seventy-fifth birthday. The trip

FIGURE 5. Regada de Frutas.

was an adventure because we took a second-class bus, which was open and very crowded, to the center of town, and then took a moto-taxi to the aunt's house. The party reminded me of the Intrépida Vela because people were sitting on plastic lawn chairs with the men on one side and the women on the other. The women were dressed in traditional Isthmus apparel but not in the fancy trajes de gala. The men were dressed casually. There was a live band and some danc-ing, but other than one heterosexual couple, women were dancing with other women. As at the Intrépida Vela and the Lavada de Ollas, the practice here was to buy a case of beer at the entrance to the event and take it in to the host. Fe-lixa had a bad back and asked if I would carry in the beer, which I did, handing it to the host, Felixa's uncle, when he stood up to accept the case.

Growing up, Felixa liked to play with his sisters and was always attracted to boys, an attraction he has been aware of since the age of ten. He believes that he was born that way. Felixa has always been accepted by family and, like many muxes, lived with his parents until they died, then continued to live in the house where he had grown up.

FIGURE 6. Intrépidas with banner at Regada de Frutas.

Felixa's first sexual experience, at the age of eighteen, was with a neighbor boy who was straight, an encounter initiated by the boy. Felixa had *novios* (boyfriends) in high school and in college, and though they had always been straight, they aren't called that. They are simply hombres, or men. Felixa likes being in a stable relationship and was in one until about a year ago. They were together for about five years, and the boy had been only fifteen when they'd met. I asked whether one person or another was dominant, and Felixa said, "No." Some muxes have problems because they want to control their men, but Felixa lets his partner go out with women. This is consistent with the flexibility of sex roles in Juchitán and suggests that even though muxes are involved in sexual liaisons with men, most do not insist on monogamy and do allow their partners to go out with women.

As mentioned earlier, Felixa doesn't dress like a muxe because of his job. At the vela, he had shared that he didn't like it when muxes dressed in provocative or outlandish ways. There had been a muxe, for example, wearing a white mesh see-through dress with a black thong underneath it. Another had worn a

Brazilian carnaval-style outfit with wings and short-shorts. When a couple of other muxes wearing very short skirts came by Mística's puesto, where Felixa and I were sitting, he explained that he didn't like the way they dressed because it was outlandish and vulgar.

When I asked about violence against muxes, Felixa, like Enrique, blamed people who did not know how to behave, who would disrespect other people and themselves. He gave as an example the sex workers who go to the *cruzero* or truck stop looking for sex.[10] Truckers sometimes think they are with a woman and respond violently when they find out they are actually with a man.

## CAMELIA, LA TEJANA

Before discussing my interview with Camelia, I should mention that the song "Camelia, la Tejana" is a well-known *narco-corrido*. According to legend, Camelia was a Mexican drug-smuggling queen who allegedly shot and killed her lover Emilio in a jealous rage. There is some question as to whether she really existed or not, but in one version, Camelia is transgender. The legend inspired an opera, which played in Long Beach among other locations (Johnson 2013). Camelia, la Tejana, was also made famous by the popular norteño singing group Los Tigres del Norte. In their song "Contrabando y Traición," Camelia is reportedly from San Antonio, Texas, and is smuggling marijuana into the United States.

Like the woman in the famous narco-corrido, Camelia is from the North and lived for a long time in el DF. She appears to be in her early fifties, was previously a secondary school teacher, and now spends her time going back and forth between El Norte and Juchitán. Camelia seems to be very well educated, intelligent, and articulate. Interestingly, she uses the terms "gay" and "muxe" interchangeably, clarifying that she used the term gay because she was from Mexico City, and muxe was more appropriate for people from Juchitán and the Isthmus region. During our interview, she talked about the early days when the muxes started meeting in the little town of Comitancillo.[11] She also talked about how things had changed for the better and how in the past, the police in la Zona Rosa in Mexico City raided gay dances, grabbed gays by their wigs, beat them up, and arrested them. The police in Mexico City are now much more tolerant of gays, especially in Zona Rosa, which is viewed as a gay-friendly section of the city.

Camelia is clearly an activist and an advocate. She said that even in Juchitán, the police used to chase them and harass them. She wears some makeup but normally does not dress like a woman, although she had dressed up for the vela.

She told me that for her, dressing up is fulfilling "totalmente una fantasía" (a total fantasy) and added, "Y no todos lo pueden hacer. Es muy difícil vestirse y actuar como mujer." In other words, she feels that dressing up and acting like a woman is extremely difficult and that not everyone can pull it off.

Camelia had been involved with Las Intrépidas since the beginning, when the first few velas were very small. Omar, one of the original founders, had opened a dance hall where the muxes started having meetings. At first only muxes attended the meetings and danced there, but eventually they started inviting women and other people in the community.

## DON OMAR: EL PADRINO MUXE (THE MUXE GODFATHER)

I met Don Omar at the Lavada de Ollas. He agreed to an interview and invited me to his home, which was a large house near downtown. It took several attempts before I was able to interview him, and on one of those attempts I spoke briefly to an elderly woman who identified herself as his aunt. Several other houseguests also called her Tía. She had come from out of town for the Intrépida Vela. When I asked her what she thought of the muxe lifestyle, she said that it was fine and added, "No, es que es natural. Así nacieron." (No, it's natural. That's how they were born.) She seemed totally accepting of Omar, his friends, and their way of life.

I returned later the same day to see if I could interview Omar. Luckily, he was home, but he was very busy, as usual, and we were interrupted several times during the interview. Omar is a short, stout man around sixty-five who looks somewhat Middle Eastern, with curly graying hair and small eyes. His face, hair, way of dressing, and demeanor were very flamboyant. He wore a large gold necklace with a ruby stone and lots of gold bracelets and rings. We sat in an anteroom, a reception area at the entrance to his house. Omar was barefoot and wearing shorts. He looked comfortable and acted very much like a powerful don, like Don Vito Andolini Corleone in *The Godfather*. He sat in a glossy wooden chair with armrests and was constantly interrupted. In addition to his large house and a hotel, Omar owns several businesses where he sells clothing. He used to sell gold jewelry, but it was too expensive now, and he had been robbed a couple of times. Now he only sells la fantasía—fake, gold-plated metal jewelry rather than real gold.

Omar is not shy about taking credit for establishing Las Intrépidas in Comitancillo, but apparently another man, named Néstor, claims that he founded the group and that Omar stole the name.[12] According to Néstor, the muxes from Comitancillo, rather than those from Juchitán, were the original Auténticas Intrépidas Buscadoras del Peligro. They were a group of about six muxes known as Las Panteras Negras, or Black Panthers, that the others, including Omar, started gathering with in Comitancillo, before they eventually came to Juchitán. Omar opened the dance hall where the first muxe gatherings were held. As Camelia had remembered, Omar said that at first just men came to the hall to dance, but then they started inviting women, and eventually it evolved into a vela for the entire community. The vela got too large for the hall, so they shifted the event to el Campo Che Gómez, which is larger and where the Lavada de Ollas had recently been held.

Omar grew up in Juchitán. His family has always been in commerce, and he started early on as an entrepreneur, quickly outselling others. Gregarious and charismatic, he has always had an eye for business. He has known he was muxe for as long as he can remember, and he doesn't believe that you can make a person muxe through abuse or anything like that. He said that muxes are born, not made. "El muxe nace, no se hace." He has two sisters. His mother was accepting of his sexual orientation, but his father was a bit disappointed since Omar was the only male in the family and, presumably, would not have any children.

During the interview two Intrépidas came to visit and take care of some business. One was Mandis, the secretary of the organization and the person I had helped with setup for the first vela I had attended. The other was Alex, who apparently was president at the time. They were doing an accounting of beer sold at the vela and wanted to know how many cases Omar had taken. Omar complained that when he had arrived, there had been no beer or ice, so he had taken ten cases. He still had five cases and told them they could return them and get a refund. They were trying to *hacer cuentas*, or "square up," with the beer distributor because several cases were unaccounted for. Omar stood his ground and implied that the distributor was trying to take advantage of them. He told them to have the distributor call him if he had any questions about the discrepancies.

## "COMING OUT" OR UNFURLING?

Whereas the respondents discussed in the previous section identified as muxes and assumed a clearly established and distinct gender identity, this section turns to a discussion of how some go about becoming muxe and adopting a muxe identity and lifestyle. The first person discussed, Francisco (Franki), is a young man in the midst of making the transition from a closeted gay person to adopting a full-fledged identity as a third-gender person. The second, Tifani, recently accepted herself as muxe and has been dressing up as a woman for about a year, yet she has remained a virgin, having never had sex with either a man or a woman.

## FRANCISCO (FRANKI), A WOULD-BE MUXE

Since Felina's salon was a communication center for my research, Roque, a muxe who works there, whom I had previously interviewed, told me that Francisco (Franki), a young man I had met at the estética, had come in looking for me. I was disappointed because Francisco had not shown up for a scheduled interview, so I asked Roque if he knew where Francisco lived, and he told me that he did. Roque was sitting at Felina's desk with Mandis, making adornments for an event on Sunday at the plaza, where the Intrépidas would be passing out condoms. Roque said he could go with me to find Francisco. He worked for a few more minutes, and then we took a moto-taxi to la octava sección, an indigenous barrio, where Roque and Anilú also live. When we got to Francisco's house, his older sister came out and wanted to know why I wanted to speak to her younger brother. I explained, without mentioning the muxes, that I was doing interviews and collecting biographies about people from Juchitán. She seemed very leery, but Roque intervened by speaking to her in Zapoteco, and she eventually, and somewhat reluctantly, showed us to the patio to talk to Francisco. He had just gotten home from work and came out to greet us, wearing jeans and a scarf around his neck. We made another appointment, agreeing to meet the next day at Felina's at 4:30 p.m., after he got off work.

Francisco is twenty-three but looks younger. He is average in height (5′10″) and weight, and he's güero, with light skin and hair. His tight-fitting skinny jeans made him look more effeminate, although he was dressed as a man. Francisco seemed fairly nervous when I met him the next day for the interview. He didn't want to go have coffee or a soda and suggested that we go to my hotel to do the interview. He confided that he was in the process of coming out.

Francisco was born and raised in Juchitán, but at age eighteen, when he finished prepa (high school, short for preparatoria), he went to live in the state of México for three years. During this period his sexual identity began to take form. Now that he was back and living in Juchitán, he said, "Ahora estoy vivi-endo una doble vida, como hombre en el día [Francisco] y mujer en la noche [Franki] cuando salgo." (I'm leading a double life now, as a man during the day [Francisco], and as a woman at night [Franki] when I go out.) He added, "Qui-ero ser una persona." (I want to be one person.) His sexual preference is inter, or internacional, and therefore he plays both passive and active roles in sex. He has never had a stable relationship or had sex with a girl. He almost had sex with a girl once, who was bisexual.

Like Enrique, Francisco's family doesn't know about his sexual and gender identity, but they suspect that he is muxe. His mother tells him that he can share anything he wants with her and that "she would love him anyway," sort of inviting him to come out. He believes that his sisters also suspect. He said, "As you can see, my sisters are really protective of me," making reference to his older sister, the one who had been reluctant to have me speak to him. She is married and doesn't live at the house but was visiting because their mother is sick with diabetes and is on dialysis.

Francisco comes from a large family of three boys and four girls and is the youngest of the seven. He has known he's had muxe tendencies since he was very little. His sisters would dress him as a girl and dance with him, and he loved it. He has identified with being a girl since he was about five. I asked if he thought this identification was a factor in his being muxe, and he said, "Yes, definitely."

Francisco's mother accepted that her youngest son was effeminate, but his father had a hard time with it and complained because Francisco wanted to play with girls and not with boys. When Francisco was about eight, his father passed away. He had been an *albañil* (bricklayer) and was working in Salina Cruz, a nearby community, when he fell off a ladder and died instantly. Had his father lived, he would have had difficulty accepting Francisco as muxe. His father was also the one who worked and controlled the money in the house-hold. Francisco's mother didn't work and is now supported by her children. Five people currently live in Francisco's household, including his mother, an uncle, and two brothers. All of his sisters are married.

Francisco got along well in school and has never really been teased, harassed, rejected, or sexually assaulted. One thing that saved him was being the smartest boy in his class. He'd do homework for the boys in his group, and they would simply put their names on the papers. He also played *fútbol* (soccer) in school. They had a boy's team and a girl's team, and he played for both at different times. Francisco believes he was accepted because he played sports and did well in school, so his friends respected and looked up to him.

His first sexual experiences were with some of his classmates, but his sexual orientation didn't solidify until he moved to the state of México. There, he started going out with friends and dressing up like a woman, and he liked it. Two years ago in November, *una amiga* (a friend) told him that she wanted to go to the Intrépida Vela in Juchitán. They went to the vela, stayed at a hotel, and had a great time. His friend introduced him to some of the muxes and told them he was from Juchitán. Several Intrépidas invited Franki to come by so they could introduce him to the group. Now that he is back in Juchitán, he has started going to various events, hanging out at Felina's, and socializing with Las Intrépidas. They have been very supportive of having him come out. Roque, for example, asked, "Why do you want to pretend that you are something you are not?"

As an adult, Francisco has never been harassed or assaulted for being feminine. One of the most interesting things he said was that mayates are very brazen and open today. In fact, most of them charge for having sex with muxes. A lot of muxes, especially the older ones, have a mayate who lives with them. The most shocking thing he shared is that the mothers of some mayates will shop their sons around and say, "Yo te vendo a mi hijo." (I'll sell you my son.) At the end of the interview, he showed me some photographs of himself dressed as Franki. He was wearing a blonde wig and looked just like a woman.

## LORENZO ANTONIO (TIFANI), A MUXE VIRGIN

Tifani is a twenty-one-year-old "woman" who works at a shoe and sandal store, a zapatería around the corner from Hotel Central, where I stayed. I had seen her daily as I walked in the neighborhood, both in the shop and at a mobile hot dog/hamburger cart on the corner. Her good friend works at the stand, and Tifani often visits her during breaks and on her day off. I worked up the nerve to go into the sandal shop, approach Tifani, and ask discreetly if she was muxe. She smiled and appeared to be glad that I had noticed. I asked her about an interview, and she agreed to meet me on her day off.

Tifani goes by her male name, Lorenzo Antonio, during the day and by Tifani Alexander when she attends velas or goes out to bars at night. She seemed very reticent about being interviewed on tape, so I took notes instead and recorded them immediately after the interview. We sat on two white plastic chairs next to the hot dog/hamburger cart. Tifani had completed four semesters of prepa and seemed bright. Since the age of fifteen, she has worked for the same man, who treats her well. At some point she stopped working to try to complete prepa but returned to work because he asked her to come back. She has been at this location for about a year.

Tifani's mother is a housewife and her father an albañil and a *maestro de obras* (foreman) for bricklayers. "Ostensibly my father was the dominant partner in the household," Tifani told me, "but they both respected each other's decisions." Tifani was born in Chiapas and has been in Juchitán for ten years, about half of her life. She came here when she started *secundaria* (middle school). Her father is from Chiapas, and her mother is from here. Tifani has one older brother and a younger sister. Her parents and siblings had accepted her as muxe when they had lived in Chiapas. She had not had any problems, and they had not tried to change her. Once she moved to Juchitán, however, her tíos and tías criticized her and gossiped about her. Although she was accepted by her immediate family, Tifani had problems in school, "because the boys used to make fun of me and ridicule me." They made fun of her because she did not like the games boys play, so she always tried to keep to herself.

Tifani has become more and more accepted here, but she has had problems, not only with her extended family, but also with strangers. Once, when she was coming out of a bar dressed as a woman, she was followed by three young men, ages twenty to twenty-two, who beat her, cut her lip, and kicked her. On another occasion, some men got out of a taxi and tried to grab her and pull her into the taxi. She resisted and ran away. When I asked if they were going to rape her, she said, "I don't know what they were going to do."

She has always been a bit of a loner, hanging out with neither boys nor girls. As far as her sexual experiences are concerned, she has not had any and is very leery of people and of getting involved with someone. She is attracted to men. Some day she would like to be with a man, but she has not been with one nor, presumably, with a woman.

Muxes are more accepted here than in any other places. She has only been dressing in a feminine style for about a year. She was wearing jeans with a sweater, some makeup, and her hair swept up like a woman's, but it would be more accurate to say that she was sexually indeterminate. She likes to dress like a woman at the velas of Las Intrépidas, both in the traditional Teca attire and in more modern wear, but she is not an Intrépida.

Tifani shared that she has friends and "enemies" who are muxe. Muxes are more accepted because they help more around the house, more than men or women. And they are also accepted because they are more creative, sociable, and intelligent. In other words, they are accepted because of what they do and how they work.

## TWO GAY JUCHITECOS

While much of the general population conflates the words "gay" and "muxe," the two terms are not synonymous. I asked one of the young men who worked at the hotel if he knew any muxes, and he put me in touch with a young man who sold piñatas at the market. But he turned out to be gay and did not identify as muxe. Davíd, my trainer, arranged a meeting with another young man, named Mario, whom Davíd described as muxe, but Mario was also gay. Interviewing these two young men proved to be instructive, however, because it pointed to important differences between gay and muxe identity from their perspectives as gays, reinforcing Julie's observation that muxes distinguished themselves from gays, although both were attracted to men.

### MARIO, A GAY PHOTOGRAPHER

Mario is a pleasant, somewhat shy and reserved but intelligent and articulate twenty-four-year-old man. He has a younger brother whom I believe is nineteen. Davíd and Mario are very good friends, and I appreciated that Davíd went to considerable effort to set up the meeting. Mario was born in the city of Oaxaca and lived there until age twelve, when he and his family moved to Juchitán. His parents divorced when he was sixteen, and his father now lives in another state. His mother has remarried. He doesn't know who is more controlling between his parents because they are both independent. He has a good relationship with his mother but hardly any contact with his father. Both of his parents are teachers; his mother is a preschool teacher, and his father teaches elementary school. Mario has a *licenciatura* (bachelor's degree) in marketing, and at the time we met, he worked for a magazine that focuses on *sociales* (social events, like weddings and *quinceañeras*).

I began the interview by asking Mario how long he had known that he was muxe, and he responded, "For me a muxe is a man who identifies as a woman and likes to dress like a woman. I am not muxe. I am gay because I have never wanted to dress like a woman or to be one. And they do women's work. I know that I am a man." Mario has known that he was attracted to boys since he was five or six years old. I asked whether his parents accepted him and the fact that he is gay. He responded, "Bueno, la familia Mexicana es muy machista, y no, no me aceptaban." (Well, the Mexican family is very sexist, and no, they did not accept me.) His father abused him physically and verbally and did not accept that he had an effeminate son. His mother was more tolerant but also did not accept that he was gay. She sat him down and talked to him and even sent him to psychological therapy. This was when he was about ten years old. "She wanted to change me," he said.

He went on to talk about his father, saying that he was extremely macho and came from a part of Oaxaca, Putla Villa de Guerrero, where men are machos and some practice polygamy, having more than one wife living in the same household. Mario also said that his father was a *mujeriego* (a womanizer). I asked whether this was a factor in his parents' divorce, and he said, "Yes, definitely." His father had taken up with another woman and had wanted to bring her to live with them, but Mario's mother would have no part of that. "Las Tecas son muy fuertes." (Women from Juchitán are very strong.) So neither parent accepted him, although his father was more overt, rejecting, and violent.

I asked Mario about his first sexual relationship, and he said that he had been twenty. It had happened with a good friend. The boy was eighteen and not from the same school. Mario said that neither one initiated it; they just fell into it and had sex without planning it. When asked how he was treated in school, Mario said, "I had a very normal childhood. I played soccer. I played with the boys." He was not harassed at all in elementary school, but "junior high school was the most difficult period." He added that in adolescence, you begin to question your identity and who you are. All his friends were hombres, not gay, and he got along well with them, but he questioned his identity and sexual orientation. "That's when I decided to experiment." His first sexual relationship, as noted, occurred at age twenty with a very good friend. His friend considers himself to be a man in every sense of the word and goes out with women. They are no longer friends.

Mario is in a stable relationship with a young man who is nineteen, whom he considers a novio, but they don't live together. They are both gay, but Mario considers himself to be totally inter and practices oral, anal, and every other kind of sex. When asked if he has experienced harassment or discrimination because he is gay, he said, "Not really" because he works in a setting with people who are educated and tolerant and where people are treated with a lot of respect. Most of his amigos are *heterosexuales*, and he gets along well with them.

No one kids him about being gay. He noted that Davíd (my trainer), a heterosexual, is a very good friend. Mario goes out to bars and to "antros," but he doesn't have gay friends and doesn't hang out at gay bars or anything like that.[13]

Mario believes that most muxes spend their lives prostituting themselves by paying mayates for sex. I asked whether he thought that was really the case, and he responded emphatically. "¡Yo sé que es así!" (I know that that's how it is!) Many of the mayates are very open. "You can go into any bar or antro and see them come and ask if you will buy them a drink, and after a few drinks, one thing leads to another, and they end up having sex." Mario was not very positively inclined toward mayates and felt that, in the end, they were also gay. "Ser gay es que te gustan los hombres, y el que busca tener sexo con un hombre es gay." (To be gay is to like or to be attracted to men, so anyone who seeks out men for sex is gay.) He said that mayates have sex for economic profit. People know who they are, and they are accepted. Some are more reserved in their approach, but most are pretty open. They don't accept the fact that they are gay. Most of them have girlfriends. He added that here in Juchitán, you are going to find a little bit of everything. It's very diverse here. You are going to find gays, muxes, and mayates at the antros.

Mario is fairly open in his relationship with his novio. They go out together to the movies, to dinner, or whatever. If people disapprove, he said, "the problem is not with me; it is with those who don't understand." He repeated that his friends are heterosexual and that he doesn't participate in a gay community as such. When asked why muxes are accepted, he responded that it was because many of the muxes come from lower social classes and are the main source of income for the family. They are also not bad people. They earn their living decently.

Near the end of the interview, Mario shared that he had been molested when he was four both anally and orally by a cousin who was twenty. The boy penetrated him and made him perform oral sex on him. This may have contributed to his being gay. He didn't know.

## DALHIT, THE GAY PIÑATERO

Dalhit is twenty-eight years old, probably about five foot six, and a bit overweight, but he gives the appearance of being larger because of his girth and the way he carries himself. He sells piñatas he makes out of clay, as they were made in the past, or from paper, as they are made in the United States. He has bright, shining eyes and a very expressive personality, the kind of personality that, like Omar's, lends itself to sales. I guess you could say that he is extremely person- able and attentive, immediately asking how he could be of service. We talked about piñatas and how I could take one home with me. He said, "We can pack it, and it will go as luggage."

Dalhit's puesto in the mercado was easy to spot because of all his wonder- ful piñatas of Dora, Mickey Mouse, Spider-Man, and various other television characters, like SpongeBob, that my granddaughter, Pilar, watches on Nick- elodeon. Dalhit worked the back of the puesto, and his mother, the front, al- though there were piñatas all over the shop. He is the proprietor.

His mother sells fruit and is very charming. She has missing teeth and looks as though she is in her sixties or seventies but is probably younger. She really pushes sales by offering samples and insisting that you purchase some of her fruit. Every time I went back to buy more of the delicious little bananas she sold, she would put extra fruit in my bag.

I introduced myself to Dalhit and asked whether he had time to talk. He responded that it was a busy time for fiestas and piñatas and would be very difficult. He works from 10:00 in the morning until 8:00 at night every day. I stopped by a couple of days later, and we set up an appointment for a Sunday at about 8:30 p.m., after he got off work.

The piñatero's father had also been in sales and had *un puesto ambulante* (a mobile shop) from which he sold clothing and other items by going from town to town. He passed away about ten years ago, but Dalhit still lives with his mother and family. His mother has always been a fruit vendor. Dalhit has three siblings and is next to last in the birth order. His two older sisters are thirty- three and thirty-four, and his younger brother is twenty-six.

Dalhit seemed both nervous and excited about being interviewed, perhaps because he is somewhat closeted, although his being gay doesn't seem to be a very well-kept secret, since René, a hotel worker, had identified him as muxe when he'd referred him to me. Dalhit came to the Hotel Central, where I was staying, and was sitting on a bench when I came down. I told him we could talk in my room if he wanted privacy. Instead, we sat on a second-floor bench in the hallway, which was very comfortable and quiet. Only two guests came by during the course of the interview, and I was very discreet and stopped talking as they passed. I reassured Dalhit that this was an academic exercise and that he would not be identified by his true name in any book or article that would be published. I said, "I can call you Juan, or you can pick a name." He seemed to like the idea of picking a name, smiled, reflected for a while, and proudly came up with Dalhit. I asked if it was Zapoteco, and he said proudly, "No, but I like it."[14]

He first became aware that he was different, attracted to men and identifying more with women, when he was fifteen. It was at this age that he became more confident and secure in his identity, although he would not have his first sexual experience until he was older. Like Mario, he emphasized that he considered himself gay and not muxe because muxes dress like women and "want to supplant women." Dalhit doesn't dress like a woman and apparently has no desire to do so, although the reason he would not dress like a woman is out of respect for the family. He hasn't come out as gay, and he has both male friends and female friends he goes out with. It was clear that, like Mario's friends, Dalhit's were not gay.

"I had a boyfriend who identified as a man and who trusted me more as a man," Dalhit said. He clarified that his novio was not a mayate because he didn't do it for money. The boyfriend did not identify as gay and also went out with women. I asked if he, Dalhit, had a stable relationship or lived with a man, and he said again, "No, out of respect for my family. I have been respectful, and I demand respect from others."

He said that his family might suspect and would not be surprised that he is gay, but he is not openly gay out of consideration for them. He seemed to be very family oriented and concerned that his actions always reflect well on them. But he added that if they found out he was gay, "no es algo del otro mundo" (it wouldn't be anything out of the ordinary). They would continue to accept and love him anyway. There is a muxe in Dalhit's family, a paternal uncle on his father's side who is respected "because his sexual preference was evident prior to adolescence."

There are people who disrespect gays. He sees this at work, where someone will say, "Oye puto, tráeme esto o aquello." (Hey faggot, bring me this or that.) Gay-targeted joking or ridicule is always expected. This hasn't happened to him, but he has observed it at work. He added, "Muxes are very hardworking. That is their defense or saving grace." And many of them pay mayates for sex. Mayates are not viewed negatively. Some are more conservative and don't want be seen publicly with muxes, but others are brazen and open. He added, "El mayate nunca paga." (Mayates never pay.) Then I asked, "Cómo se ve el mayate aquí?"[15] And he laughed and responded, "Se ven bien. Los muxes los visten bien y se ven muy guapos algunos." (They look good. Muxes dress them well, and some of them look very handsome.) Although he took my question literally, it was evident that he thought mayates were accepted and not frowned on.

He expanded on the reasons that muxes are accepted. They are very hard workers. They work for the welfare of their family and to support it. They make floats, huipiles, decorations. As to who had *la manda*, or control, en la familia, he responded, "Here on the Isthmus, women dominate. They do everything; cook, take care of the children, control the money."

## EL MAYATE

A number of respondents in the study brought up the topic of mayates, but they had divergent views of them. Mario had a fairly negative take and noted that many of the mayates were very open; they would come to you in the antros, buy you a drink, and solicit you for sex. He believed that they were technically gay because they had sex with other men. Dalhit, on the other hand, felt that mayates were not viewed negatively, noting that some are more conservative and don't want to be seen publicly with muxes, although others are brazen and open. He added that the muxes dressed them well, and that "they looked good." Francisco saw some mayates as being very bold and said that sometimes mothers will even shop their sons around to the highest bidder.

These polar images of the mayate were reflected in interviews with muxes and community members as well. A common thread, however, is that mayates are extremely secretive and reluctant to admit that they have sex with other men. I found it very difficult to locate mayates who were willing to be interviewed, and once they agreed to be interviewed, they were careful to conceal their identity. When I interviewed Pedro, for example, we met at the central park at the plaza and then proceeded to what I thought was a safe locale—ironically, as it turned out—the rear patio at San Vincente Ferrer Catholic Church. Pedro was apprehensive and nervous during the entire interview and, at the end, confided that initially, he had been afraid that he might be sequestered by the contact person or by me.[16]

I made many attempts through my contacts and social notables to get interviews and was finally able to meet and interview five mayates and construct a composite profile of them. They represented a range of occupations and backgrounds, but they were largely young, under thirty, married, and working class, men from poor neighborhoods who have sex with gays or muxes for money (see appendix C). Edgar was currently a moto-taxi driver and had previously driven a cab, while Juan had worked at a pizza place and now drove a semitruck for a large retail store. Wilmer was a low-level restaurant worker, Pedro worked as a carpenter, and Javier was a student. All of the men were difficult to find and reluctant to grant an interview for fear they might be identified.

Javier is only nineteen and became financially needy after his girlfriend got pregnant. He now has to support his common law wife and infant daughter, so he had to drop out of school to work in a low-paying job. Javier related how he got into being a mayate inadvertently. He was horsing around with a gay friend when the friend suggested that they have sex. Javier asked jokingly, "How much would you be willing to pay?" When the friend said 2,000 pesos, Javier reluctantly agreed because it was so much, and he needed the money. The friend performed oral sex on Javier, and to date, Javier has only engaged in sex work about three times. He was not brazen, is not proud of his behavior, and was reluctant to share his story.

## PEDRO, EL CARPINTERO

Pedro arrived on a bicycle at the kiosk for our interview, looking like he was loaded, as his eyes were red and watery. He wore a baseball cap and was unkempt. At twenty-four years old, he is the eldest brother of three: one of his brothers is twenty, and the other is only two. He seems close to his middle brother. His father is a bricklayer, and his mother, a housewife. Pedro and his middle brother do carpentry. Pedro's education did not go beyond *primaria* (elementary school).

Although other men maintained that they had become mayates out of economic necessity, Pedro admitted that he enjoyed the sex. He started doing it when he was sixteen or seventeen. As to why he does it, he said that he was "hot blooded," very sexual, masturbating two or three times daily, and that it feels "bien rico" (really good); "it gets your blood boiling." Then he added, "You pretend and fantasize that it's someone else. It feels great, especially if you do it after you've had two or three beers."

He said that men pay him 100 or 200 pesos, or they might buy him a beer. "Sometimes I feel like it, and it satisfies me. They do almost everything that a woman will do." As to what happens in sex, Pedro stressed,

Yo soy el hombre. Dejo que me toquen pero no me gusta que me agarren por las nalgas. Es todo, pero por las nalgas, no. Nomas por adelante.

[I am the man. I don't like for them to touch me from the rear. We do everything but not from the rear. Only from the front.]

Most of his buddies (*camaradas*) also do it, either for money or for pleasure. There are times when he does not charge, implying that he gets some pleasure from it. He has had a novia but is not married. One relationship lasted about six months, another not very long at all, and one lasted for four years. It doesn't make any difference whether he has sex with a man or a woman. "Ando con uno por un rato, nomás en la calle." (I will go out with one [a man] for a while, only in public.) They have sex at the man's house or sometimes pay for a room. When asked if he allowed men to kiss him, he said, "Yes, sometimes when I've had too much to drink." From time to time, he goes out with men or with his twenty-year-old brother. They are very close and will do it together with two men. He talks and jokes about it with his friends.

Pedro considers himself mayate because he has sex with other men for money and acknowledges that some mayates are closeted gays, and others are bisexual. What they have in common is "Siempre lo hacen a escondidas." (They always do it on the sly.) His family knows about it, and they "me hacen una regañadita" (bawl me out a bit).

## EDGAR, THE MOTO-TAXI DRIVER

Edgar, a moto-taxi driver, remarked that everyone has a *don*, or gift, and his is driving. He can drive anything, including a fourteen-meter truck. We met at the patio of San Vicente Parish, which provided privacy and some protection from the strong winds, gusting at about forty to fifty miles per hour. Edgar currently lives in la segunda sección. He is separated from his wife and has a four-year-old daughter. Born near Ixtepec, Edgar is the youngest of his parents' seven children. His father died before his birth, and when Edgar was about five, his mother remarried and moved to Veracruz, leaving Edgar with his grandparents for the next three years. He has ten siblings, ranging in age from seventeen to thirty-eight, and there are more girls than boys. His younger siblings are from his mother's second relationship.

When asked if he is a mayate, he said, "Prácticamente así nos dicen." (That's essentially what they call us.) He lived in Veracruz for several years and started being a mayate when he was about seventeen. He said that things are more *libre* (open) in Juchitán. Referring to his work as a mayate, he noted, "Aquí lo ven como cosa normal." (It's seen as something normal here.) As to why he does it, he said, "La neta lo hago por dinero. Me pagan o me emborrachan." (The truth is that I do it for money. They either pay me or get me drunk.) He generally gets paid between 300 and 400 pesos (25 to 35 U.S. dollars) but doesn't do it very often. He mentioned that he'd met Gabriel on the moto-taxi. They had talked and learned that they had a lot in common, including both having family in Veracruz. Gabriel had invited him to have some beers, and the two became friends.

Edgar engages in all types of sexual activity, including oral and anal sex, but he is activo and doesn't like to be kissed. In talking about his gay partners, he said, "La mayoría de ellos son muy alegres. A veces lo hago por amistad. Tengo amigos que son así, pero la neta es que lo hago por lana." (Most of them are very cheerful. Sometimes I'll do it out of friendship. I have friends that are like that [gay], but the bottom line is that I do it for the dough.) He added that most of the time it isn't talked about. "I am very discreet." He felt that nowadays, "there is nothing wrong with it," that it's more accepted now that many places have legalized gay marriage. He drew a parallel to lesbian relationships in which there is a feminine partner and a *machorra* (masculine woman), indicating that similarly, passive gay men have sex with dominant hombres.[17]

Edgar's estranged wife does not know he is a mayate and would not approve. He doesn't talk about it with his brothers. "Es algo personal. Entre amigos, sí, a veces se platica." (It's something personal. Among friends, yes, sometimes we do talk about it.) He thought back to when he used to be a cab driver and "saw a lot of things." People would offer him money "to do certain things." He concluded that most mayates have sex for the money.

I asked about the difference between muxes and gays. He answered that muxes are different from gays in the way they speak. Muxes can be identified right away because they speak like women. Gays are more masculine, and they socialize more with men, rather than with women. He gets contacted more by muxes than gays. Like other respondents, he felt that one of the reasons men have sex with muxes is that muxes will engage in sexual activities that some women will not. Some women don't want to have anal sex, or even oral sex. He again said that a lot of men do it but don't talk about it.

## JUAN, THE PIZZA DELIVERY MAN

Juan was very nervous and reluctant to be interviewed. I met him in a bar, which had blaring music, and while we talked, he put the recorder a couple of inches from his mouth and spoke directly into it because the music was so loud. Juan is twenty-eight, originally from Juchitán, and has two sisters and a brother who passed away. Juan is the middle child. His father worked for Pemex as a laborer and is now retired; his mother is a housewife. When I asked if he identified as a mayate, he said, "Soy hombre."

Juan started having sex with other men at age twenty, when he and a friend worked at a pizzeria. On Saturday nights, gay men would pay them to go have a drink with them. "One time my friend and I didn't have any money, and we had to call *un gay* to make some money." He did it "por dinero." Between the ages of twenty and twenty-five, he had sex as a mayate regularly, about twice per week. Juan indicated that a lot of gays were voyeurs and would take photos of his penis, elaborating that if you were well endowed and were willing, you could make quite a bit of money. He added, "I work out. I am in good shape."

I asked whether people knew that he was a mayate, and he responded, "Buenos conocidos lo sabían." (People who knew me well knew.) His sisters know. "They hear rumors. Somebody will say this or that. People tell them stuff." Juan was married, and after he split up with his wife, he hooked up with a twenty-two-year-old woman. When asked if his partner knew he was a mayate, he again said that she had "oído rumores" (heard rumors).

I was surprised when he said that he didn't receive monetary payment for sex. Instead, in addition to getting free drinks, Juan received gifts, like pants or a watch, and had been involved in relations with as many as three men at a time. He stressed that what was important, in addition to having the physical attributes and being fit, was a willingness to go out with his gay partners, "como novios" (like a couple in public). He is currently doing just fine but doesn't make much money. He drives a trailer truck for a large superstore and makes 2,100 pesos every two weeks (approximately $260 per month). He repeated several times that being a mayate was all about money. He does it because of the money he receives (directly and indirectly). "It's all about the money. If I had more money, I wouldn't do it. But I would do it with women for the money." Juan added that when he was drunk, he had no remorse about the sex, but when he was sober, he was embarrassed.

When asked if he distinguished between gays and muxes, he expressed a surprisingly negative view of muxes.[18]

Un gay es un hombre con dinero, que tiene carrera, tiene coche, trabaja, y luce lo que trabaja. Un muxe es un puto barato que dejo de trabajar. El muxe habla con todos, no es discreto y no es profesional. Hay muchos muxes por el nivel económico, que es bajo.

[A gay is a man with money, with a career. He has a car, he works, and he shows off what he's earned. A muxe is a cheap queer who has stopped working. The muxe will gossip with everyone and is not discreet. There are many muxes at a low economic level.]

It was clear that he typically has sex with gays, not with muxes, and he seemed to be saying that muxes did not protect the identities of mayates. He talked about certain secciones of the city with high rates of poverty, crime, and delinquency, and said that 70 percent of the muxes come from la séptima sección. He doesn't think about stopping what he does because "es buen empleo" (it's good work). Juan believes he has two paths he can take in his life, being a criminal or being a gigolo, and he has chosen the latter.

## LESBIANAS OR MACHORRAS

Although the focus of this book is on muxes and their acceptance in the community, the acceptance of lesbian women also arose several times during the course of the study. Some people noted that while lesbianas may be less visible, they are even more accepted than muxes or gay men. After my interview with Mayté, as we were exiting the restaurant, I noticed two women passionately making out at a table near the exit. When I inquired about this, she said that lesbianas were more accepted. Roque observed that the community is so female centered that people don't think twice when they see two women on the street holding hands, or even kissing, but when they see two men together, they always assume that one is muxe and the other one mayate. Edgar drew a parallel between the relationships of mayates and their partners and those of lesbians in which there is a feminine partner and a machorra, just as passive gay men have sex with dominant hombres.

During the study, I had the opportunity to interview three lesbianas, and to construct a brief composite of them. All the women were masculine, identified with men, had played with boys as children, had been attracted to women at an early age, dressed in shorts or jeans, and were involved with feminine women, or mujeres normales, who had been previously married to men. Chano was typical of the lesbianas interviewed in the study.

### CHANO, A LESBIANA INTRÉPIDA

One of the Intrépidas, Chuchín, had mentioned during my interview with him that his sister-in-law, Chano (his sister's partner), was lesbiana. Chano, who identifies as male, had been involved with the Intrépidas and was even part of the mesa directiva of the organization. Chuchín put me in touch with him, and I interviewed Chano at Chuchín's bar.

Chano is thirty-seven years old and originally from la cuarto sección, although he now lives in la octava with his partner. He has four siblings: an older sister, thirty-nine; a younger sister, thirty-four; and two younger brothers, thirty-three and twenty-five. Chano's father was a physics and chemistry teacher in secundaria, and his mother was a homemaker.

Chano is short and stocky, with a classic Zapoteco build—that is, close to the ground. He wore jean shorts, a tank top, and a baseball cap tilted down so that you could hardly see his eyes. He had a three-stripe tattoo on each of his bare arms, and he acted like a man. He had become aware of his tendencies in elementary school, where he always played with the boys. "Desde el kínder, no me gustaba vestirme de vestido. Yo convivía con los chavos." (I didn't like wearing a dress, since kindergarten. I hung out with the boys.) Chano is a physical education teacher and never had any problems with discrimination until he attended Normal University, where he had a problem with a machista teacher because they were both attracted to the same woman in the class and competed for her affection. All of Chano's partners have been heterosexual women, and his current partner was previously married and has a fourteen-year-old son. When we talked about sex, he confided that he was activo and that only a woman knew how to satisfy another woman. He's had conversations with grown men that left him amazed at how little they knew about a woman's anatomy or how to satisfy her.

Chano noted that he always dresses like a man, and that his mother always knew and was just waiting for Chano to tell her. "My father was more difficult. He saw it as a machista and took about a year before he accepted it." Chano added that he and his partner go out together to fiestas and are accepted. "They accept us, and friends and family defend us. I am the godfather and she is the godmother of many children." It's clear that they are a common law couple and accepted by family, friends, and neighbors. They have no problems on the streets with people bothering them or harassing them.

They also participate with Las Intrépidas and have a joint puesto in la vela. Chano's partner is an administrator for the government. Interestingly, he made reference to an unwritten code of conduct, just as some of the muxes had. "Ahora salen más lesbianas, pero hay unas que no se saben comportar." (There are more lesbians who are out now but some don't know how to behave.) Some get drunk or act out, which makes it worse for the rest. They might engage in

inappropriate public displays of affection or public drunkenness. According to
Chano, the lesbians are not as organized or as accepted as the muxes.

As to why muxes are accepted in Zapotec society, he noted that mothers accept them because they know that muxes will take care of them. The muxe is
going to work to make sure that the family "se adelante" (advances). "Saben que
el muxe es el que se va a quedar en la casa, y el que va a cuidar a sus papas cuando
sean ancianos." (They know that the muxe is the one who is going to make sure
the family prospers, stay home, and the one who will take care of the parents when
they are elderly.) Chano believes that acceptance of the muxe is linked to Zapotec
culture. He noted that on his mom's side there are many muxes, and on his dad's
side, there are also lesbians. His mother was the oldest and the first to have a child,
and when he turned out to be masculine and not feminine, his mother's family
had initially felt betrayed. They had expected Chano's mother to have a machito.

Chano's first sexual experience was at age thirteen. He had some boyfriends,
and he had a novia. "She was mujer, not lesbiana. We were neighbors." He
would see her at her grandparents' home. His mom's family was totally accepting. His grandfather and uncle would take him to work, where they sold this
material that was like bamboo and that was used to construct patios and other
structures in patios. Chano has had several novias, all heterosexual, and has
been involved with them after they have been in failed heterosexual relationships. She didn't go into detail about the sex but noted that she was activa and
that they engaged in mutual oral sex. "Hay que satisfacer a la mujer." (One has
to satisfy the woman.)

Chano pointed out that the muxe is accepted more than the lesbian in Juchitán. The muxe seeks to retain traditional Zapotec culture, but there is nothing traditional about this generation. One bar in town caters to lesbianas, and
the lesbian couples who have been publicly accepted have had money. Chano's
partner's husband (deceased) was machista, and he used to provoke Chano, but
nothing ever happened. "Es lo que más le duele a un hombre es saber que su
mujer se vaya con otra mujer." (What's most painful to a man is knowing that
his wife has left him for another woman.)

## GAY, TRANSGENDER, OR MUXE?

The section above presented narratives of muxes, two gay Juchitecos who distinguished themselves from muxes, several mayates, and one lesbiana. Before

elaborating on how muxes differentiate themselves from gay and transgender persons, I discuss how various scholars have interpreted terms applied to gay and transgender people.

In an excellent ethnography of "transgender," David Valentine takes a genealogical approach, examining transgender and homosexuality as distinct *categories* throughout history. Following Foucault, he posits that these categories are not simply descriptions of history but *products of* the very phenomena they seek to describe (2007, 30). Working under the basic anthropological assumption that language shapes the way we make sense of and organize our worlds, Valentine contends that transgender is a relatively recent term that only emerged as a collective and institutionalized category in the early 1990s. Since homosexuality itself is also a relatively recent concept used to describe transgender forebears, he asks, how is it possible to conflate these categories and "to extract certain actors from the categorical embrace of 'homosexuality' and into 'transgender'?" (31). In other words, what have been the social and political consequences of this process of labeling and reorganization?

According to Valentine, "transgender" in this political, collective, and institutionalized sense arose in the United States in uneven and often contested ways, mostly in New York and California and in largely White, middle-class activist contexts, although it had antecedents in 1980s California and England (31). Within these activist and social service settings, transgender

> was seen as a way of wresting control over the meanings and definitions of gender variance from medical and mental health professionals to replace an assumption of individual pathology with a series of claims about citizenship, self-determination, and freedom from violence and discrimination. Just as importantly, it was seen as a way of organizing a politics of gender variance that differentiated it from homosexuality.[19] (31)

In the introduction to *The Transgender Studies Reader 2*, Susan Stryker and Aren Aizura also document the rapid growth of the transgender category in the 1990s, noting that a Google Books search revealed that "since about 1992, *transgender* has experienced a meteoric rise in popularity compared to other familiar terms for describing gender nonconforming practices" (2013, 2). During that time about 2,500 books were published with the words "transgender" or "transsexual" in the title, exclusive of those with some variation of phrase, such as "gay, lesbian, bisexual, and transgender." Some 40,000 academic articles and about two million newspaper and magazine stories also referenced transgender topics (2). Finally, a recent poll showed that 91 percent of the people interviewed had heard the term "transgender," and most knew what it meant (2).

One of the most extensive studies of transgender identity and acceptance was carried out by Genny Beemyn and Sue Rankin (2011), who interviewed nearly 3,500 participants and then conducted more than 400 follow-up interviews. The researchers cast a wide net, as the sample included transsexual men and women, cross-dressers, and gender queer individuals. Their research differed from most previous studies in that it did not attempt to determine a priori who qualified as transgender. All people living in the United States who currently identified as transgender or gender nonconforming in some way or had done so in the past were encouraged to participate (2011, 6). Beemyn and Rankin used "transgender" as a generic term that included "all individuals whose gender histories cannot be described as simply female or male, even if they now identify and express themselves as strictly female or male" (6).

With regard to gender identity, they found more specifically that among persons designated as female at birth, 45 percent refer to themselves as male, 36 percent as transgender, and only 13 percent as other, whereas for those designated as male at birth, almost half now identified as female, 35 percent as transgender, and only 6 percent as other (2011, 22).

Valentine spent eighteen months during the late 1990s doing fieldwork in New York, working as a safer-sex activist in Manhattan, where he was part of a support group of transgender-identified people with HIV at a New York hospital. While he and the group facilitator were White, middle-class professionals who self-identified as gay men, the other five members of the transgender support group were either African Americans or Latinas who, though born male, lived their lives as feminine people. One member of the support group, Fiona, said that, "I've been gay all my life, been a woman all my life" (2007, 3). Valentine found that while the people in his research among mostly male-to-female transgender-identified persons were labeled by activists and service providers as transgender, many of the participants were unfamiliar with the term or resisted its use and instead self-identified as gay. He concluded that the term transgender has been adopted by researchers because it is consistent with an emergent model that sees gender and sexuality as distinct areas of human experience, but that unfortunately erases the experiences of gender-variant people, especially poor people of color who have a different view of their gender and sexuality.

Beemyn and Rankin similarly point to the power of language, particularly when it is used in naming groups of people (2011, 16). They note not only the absence of neutral terms to describe transgender people (Valentine 2007, 31) but also the lack of neutral strategies for classifying, treating, or empowering them. The words we use to refer to ourselves and to others in terms of characteristics like race, class, gender, and sexuality thus reflect our own cultural values and those of the dominant society (Beemyn and Rankin 2011, 16). As a result, the terms we use to describe individuals and their communities have real consequences, as is evident from the discourse surrounding transgender people (16).

The same is true for the muxes in the present study. Muxe and other respondents in Juchitán do not use the term "transgender" (*transgénero*) to describe themselves or others. Although some respondents, like Camelia, occasionally refer to themselves as "gay," most muxes readily distinguish themselves from gay persons, largely in terms of gender rather than sexuality.[20] Coni, one of the Intrépidas, commented on the distinction between gays and muxes, noting that gays are more masculine and less visible (more closeted). Muxes, by comparison, are out and very visible, typically dressed like women in Zapoteca clothing. It was interesting that Coni linked being muxe to maintaining Zapotec culture and traditions as well as to retaining the language. She added that most Intrépidas speak Zapoteco. This reminded me of Mayté's statement that all muxes were Intrépidas in the sense that they had the courage to come out and be open about their sexuality. Kike, a flamboyant and charismatic hair stylist and performance artist discussed further in chapter 4, believes that gays are more reserved in their dress, and that muxes are more open in public and out of the closet: "We can dress in a manly way or as women." Julie also noted that muxes are more open and that gays are masculine, not vestidas. Biiniza was perhaps the most eloquent, noting that being muxe is not something you put on and then take off. It is a way of being that includes not only dressing like a Teca, but also maintaining, incorporating, and respecting Zapotec customs and traditions. She felt that one of the *retos*, or challenges, faced by the Intrépidas is being able to recruit people who will continue to represent the organization's values and maintain their local traditions.

Many other respondents indicated that the acceptance of the muxe is rooted in Zapotec culture and noted that muxes are more accepted in certain sections of the city, like la séptima, that are historically more Zapotec and poor. Darina, the 2009 Intrépida queen, who has an older muxe sister, pointed out that some nuclear families in la séptima have up to three muxes. Gabriel noted that muxes have lots of support in la séptima because it is 100 percent Zapotec. Johnny also said that muxes have Zapotec roots and are fully accepted in secciones like la séptima, octava, and novena, which are heavily Zapotec, as did Valera and Ángel Rolán, a young personal trainer from la séptima. Finally, Estrellita and Coni both reiterated that muxe Zapotec roots ran in certain families across generations, particularly in the more indigenous sections of Juchitán.

Unlike Dalhit, the piñatero, and the older gays studied by Rosenfeld (2009), who were pressured to engage in a lifetime of impression management, constructing and maintaining public heterosexual personas, muxes are openly recognized among themselves and by others in Juchitán as a third gender. That muxes are not simply doing gender but are actively undoing and redoing gender is one reason that they must be understood through social rather than sexual categories.

In chapter 4, I turn to a critical examination of the popular belief that having a muxe child is always viewed as a blessing from God by relating the life histories of several more muxe respondents, based on in-depth personal interviews.

# 4

## A BLESSING FROM GOD?

### Muxe Narratives

---

*Muxes are a blessing from God because they look after you when you are sick more than a woman would. . . . They are a very important part of life.*
VICENTA TOLEDO, QUOTED IN CBS NEWS (2013, 13)

VICENTA TOLEDO MADE THE STATEMENT QUOTED ABOVE while attending a muxe vela in Mexico City with her muxe son. The CBS News story that quoted her focused on how the vela brought together indigenous muxes from Juchitán and members of the Mexico City gay community. The broadcast added that according to anthropologists, some Juchitecas actually "encourage their sons' muxe leanings because they tend to stay home and care for their parents rather than get married" (CBS News 2013, 2).

In chapter 3, I looked at how third-gender muxes in Juchitán have redefined the research on doing and undoing gender, focusing first on workplace studies, including the concept of going stealth, and ending with a new look at transgender studies, all informed by case studies revealing the voices, characteristics, and lived realities of the Juchitán muxes and their surrounding community. This chapter presents additional case studies in which muxes themselves address the commonly held idea that they are gifts from God. The biographies of several muxes I interviewed give intimate descriptions of a wide range of lifestyles and views—from how they perceive themselves to how they perceive their treatment in their families, among peers, and in society at large.

## MUXE NARRATIVES

Like CBS News, multiple journalists and social scientists have reported that parents and grandparents in Juchitán generally accept muxe children, and some have even suggested that having a muxe child is "a blessing from God."[1] Carmelo López Bernál, a young muxe featured in a *New York Times* article, was accepted by his family. When Carmelo's grandmother was asked how she felt about her muxe grandson, she said that she felt normal about it because that was "how God sent him" (Lacey 2008). Certainly, many Zapotec families like Carmelo's do readily accept muxe children, yet some of the findings in this study call into question the idyllic view of universal family acceptance.

The narratives in this section generally support this idea of Juchitán families accepting their muxe sons, but several muxes reported having difficult and traumatic childhood experiences and not being readily accepted by their parents. Fathers seemed especially punitive and resistant to having a muxe son. As in chapter 3, my interview translations into English preserve the "voice" of each respondent, including each person's colloquial language, syntax, and grammar.

### ROQUE, THE HAIR STYLIST

I had made arrangements to interview Roque at Felina's salon, where he worked at the time, at 2:00 p.m. because his daily dinner break is 2:00–4:00 p.m. When I arrived he was sitting on a sofa waiting for me and chatting with Anilú, who is also muxe. They were speaking with Felina, who greeted me and asked how I was. She remembered me and wondered why I had not attended the vela the previous weekend. I told her that I had attended Intrépida Velas in prior years and found that people were very busy during that time, so I felt it would be better to come after the vela. She nodded knowingly in agreement.

Roque, Anilú, and I left the salon, crossed the bridge that goes over the Río de Los Perros behind Felina's estética, and then took a moto-taxi to Roque's home. He lives in la octava sección, known by its Zapoteco name Cheguigo (*después del río*, or "past the river"). Roque said that he has lived in the same house since he was born and that his parents always accepted him. His brother lives in a house across the way.

Homes in the neighborhood are simple, made of stucco with tin roofs, but seem comfortable. An uncle who lives around the corner is also muxe. Roque opened the lock on the door, and we went in. The interior was modest, with several sofas in the center of the room and a hammock to the side. It was one large room that was not divided into different rooms. He asked whether I wanted to sit inside or outside. It was very hot and the logical choice was to sit outside, so we sat on the porch on white plastic chairs around a small square plastic table.

Roque just turned fifty-three but looks younger and is average in height and weight. He has shoulder-length dark brown wavy hair and is somewhat effeminate but clearly identifies as a man. Although Roque likes hombres, he has never dressed or tried to act like a woman. His parents are now deceased, but he stayed with them, not exactly to take care of them, but simply because he never left home. It was strange and difficult for him to think about leaving home because he had never lived by himself. He has eight siblings, is the second oldest, and all the others are married and on their own.

Roque showed feminine tendencies for as long as he can remember and was always completely accepted by his family. While growing up, he never felt that he was discriminated against or mistreated by classmates because of his sexual orientation. He had straight friends who never bothered him or harassed him in any way.

His first sexual experience occurred when he was in prepa. It was consensual and the other boy, "era un hombre." Roque has had a number of novios but has never lived with them. He always assumes the pasivo role during sex and acts as if that is the only natural role for him; otherwise he would be straight. He has been in long-term relationships, one lasting eight years, and sometimes goes out in public with his partner. Others want to keep it on the "down low," he said, but he is open about his relationships. He had just ended a relationship and started to say that they had *unos problemas*, then corrected himself and said, "Well, it wasn't problems. It was that I learned that he was married, and I don't want anything to do with that." It was evident that he didn't want to incur any problems or retributions from his partner's family. He mentioned that there were some men who only had sex with muxes and yet identified as hombres. Others had sex with both men and women and were bisexual. And some muxes were married and had children, so he clearly saw being muxe as separate from one's sexuality.

When I told him that I was interested in interviewing men who have sex with muxes but identified as men (mayates), he said that this would be difficult because they don't want society to find out that they have sex with muxes. They want it kept secret. I commented that it was ironic because it seemed that these hombres were the ones who were truly in the closet or hiding behind a cultural mask, and he nodded knowingly. Some men pay and ask for particular sexual favors, but Roque didn't seem comfortable with the idea of getting paid for having sex because it's like prostitution.

He has been involved with the Intrépidas since early in their history, back in the days when they organized a basketball team. Roque played on the team in the early years. It was very popular and had great success, winning one tournament and coming in second in another. He never felt like they were discriminated against or mistreated. On the contrary, people loved to see them play, and when they played at the park in Juchitán, they drew large crowds of people who came out to watch them.[2]

Roque is not a formal member, or socia, of the Intrépidas, although he hangs out with them and participates in their various activities. He confided that they really don't do much, other than hosting the annual vela. I asked about the name of the organization, and he said it meant that they were supposed to take risks and take on unpopular causes, but he doesn't see them doing much of anything. He believes that they should form something like a self-help or *mutualista* group (mutual aid association) that would help fellow muxes in need. He added, "Sometimes people [other muxes] are in need, because of an illness or some other emergency, but they don't seem to be moving in this direction."

I asked how I would go about meeting other muxes, and he suggested Anilú. He is an accountant who looks like an ordinary man. When I said this, Roque laughed and said that he was like that until he had a few drinks and then got all *loca* (crazy). Roque also said he would contact his uncle who is also a muxe to see if he would agree to an interview.

I thanked him for the interview, and he walked me out to the street, where I waited for another moto-taxi. As we were walking, he advised me that some muxes now charged for interviews, but he didn't believe in doing this. He just wanted to put me on notice that this might occur. I thanked him again, shook his hand, and left.

## ANILÚ (ANIBAL), THE BATTERED CHILD

Anilú is fifty-two and fairly bald, with graying, thinning hair. He doesn't look or act particularly effeminate until you start talking to him. He wears glasses and is average in height and weight. He has diabetes, and his feet were wrapped in bandages. I had met him at Felina's and noticed that as we drove through the neighborhood (Section Eight), many people waved and acknowledged him. Similarly, when we sat outside his house to do the interview, people walking or driving by waved to or greeted him.

Anilú lives in a well-maintained two-story yellow house with shiny tile floors and a hammock in the middle of the patio. We sat on two white lawn chairs at the entrance to the house to take advantage of the breeze, because it was a very hot day. He lives with two of his sisters in the same place where his parents had lived, but he noted proudly that he had built this house with his earnings on the same site where his parents' house had previously stood.

Anilú seemed to take great pride in the fact that he has always contributed financially to the support of his family and his sisters and that he currently lives with two of them, who love and accept him as he is. Anilú has not been able to work for the past two years because of the diabetes, so his sisters help and support him, just as he helped and supported them in the past.

Anilú's story was a sad, tragic tale. He began, teary eyed, by confiding that he had a very violent, machista father, who could not accept the fact that he had a muxe son. Anilú is the middle child and the only male, with two older and two younger sisters. I asked whether the fact that he was the only male influenced his father, and he said, "Yes. . . . He would ask, 'how is it that my only son is going to end up being a homosexual?' He tried to beat it out of me, but it was to no avail."

Anilú noticed that he was different at an early age, perhaps around ten, when he started acting in an effeminate way. His father worked in the fields and would take him out, trying to get him to like working in the field, "like a man." His mother did not work outside the home. Anilú's father also worked in the *pilas* (vats) where they cured hides to prepare them for making huaraches. The process is long and arduous and requires soaking the skins in lime baths and in other pilas. Despite his father's efforts, Anilú was not attracted to working in the fields or acting like a man and continued to act in an effeminate manner, all to his father's dismay.

His father did not beat his mother, but he beat Anilú, and his mother would try to protect him from the beatings. Anilú's saving grace was that he was always an excellent student, left to study in Mexico City around 1981, and he graduated first in his class with a degree in accounting. When he revealed his intention of going away to study in Mexico City, his father was strongly opposed. Getting through school was difficult because he had no economic support from his family and always had to work and study. It fact, it wasn't until he graduated first in his class that his father began to recognize him. They managed to reconcile later, when his father was older and before he died, but he was never really very close to him. Anilú was visibly shaken and in tears as he shared these childhood recollections of his father.

Like Roque, Anilú had always lived with his parents. It is a Zapotec custom for children to live with the parents until they get married, and sometimes even after they are married, with the husband's parents. Anilú's parents, for example, first lived with his paternal grandparents until they got enough money together to build their own house, on the same lot where the current house stands. His uncle lives next door and, like Roque's uncle, is also muxe. While growing up, he had two other uncles who were muxe and lived openly as such their entire lives. They are now deceased.

Anilú's first sexual encounter occurred when he was in prepa between the ages of fifteen and sixteen. A classmate took him to a cemetery near the school. They went inside one of the large tombs and had sex. Using his arms and hands to graphically demonstrate a thrusting sexual motion, he said the boy penetrated him from the rear. Anilú then put his hand toward his back to illustrate, saying that he noticed he was bleeding from the rectum. The boy took him back to the cemetery a few weeks later, and he bled once again. After a while, though, Anilú started to like it. He said that he was the one who had to receive anally and to *chupar* (suck) the penis, saying this while simulating a sucking motion with his hand and mouth. He always assumed the pasivo role in sex, whether it was anal or oral.

He has had long-term relationships, which have lasted for several years. One with a particular novio lasted three years. At first they had lived with Anilú's mother, as his father was deceased, but the boy was violent and fought a lot, and Anilú's mother disliked him. The novio also beat Anilú. Eventually, the novio talked to his own mother, and they lived with the boy's parents for some time. Normally muxes do not live with their partners. This was unusual and suggests that the boy's parents accepted the fact that their son was in a relationship with a muxe.

Anilú normally dresses like a man, and when I asked whether he ever fantasized about dressing like a woman, he smiled and said, "Solamente una vez, hace como veinte años" (just once, about twenty years ago), when he bought a green dress and a wig. He kept it at a friend's house and dressed up there, instead of at his house. He referred to straight men who have sex with muxes as mayates and noted that many of them are attracted to the muxes for financial reasons, because muxes will work and take care of them. I asked how these men could see themselves as hombres or heterosexuals when they have sex with other men. He agreed that they were technically gay because they were having sex with another man but that the mayates would vehemently deny it, saying they were hombres because they assumed an activo role in sex. Anilú suggested I call him tomorrow. He would talk to some of the men who hang out at the bar on the corner near his house to see if they might be willing to talk to me. They might talk to me, he said, but they will deny being gay.

When asked about living with their male partners, he said most muxes do not, although some do. He has known some who live openly with hombres and go out in public with them. In fact, he mentioned someone he knew who was married and had three children but was still muxe. He was bisexual, and the wife and children knew that he was muxe. The man eventually left his wife and lived openly with men in several relationships until he died. When the man's partner died, he was in *luto* (mourning) and dressed in black for a long time.

Anilú has lived away from Juchitán for more time than he has lived there. After he graduated, he worked in Mexico City for a while as an accountant and then took another job as an accountant in Ciudad Juárez. He also worked for about fifteen years for a private company that subcontracts with Pemex, the Mexican national oil company, as a head chef on a petroleum tanker in Campeche. He periodically returned to Juchitán and finally came back to live there after being away for some twenty years. He has cooperated with the Intrépidas but is not an active member and is a good friend of theirs and hangs out at Felina's salon.

## INO: A WOMAN TRAPPED IN A MAN'S BODY

Ino was recommended to me by Anilú, who told me that Ino's house was in his neighborhood, indicating that it was next to an Apostolic Church. I asked the moto-taxi driver to take me to the Apostolic Church in Cheguigo, but he drove me to the wrong church. I finally found the correct church, and people showed me an alleyway where Ino's place was located.

A neighbor told me to knock on a window that faced the alley. Ino opened the window and asked me how he could help. He was wearing a hot pink tank top and shorts. Ino is about average height and fairly muscular. He has curly dark hair with some gray in it, brown skin, and broad shoulders. I got the sense that he engaged in physically demanding work. It also looked like he was wearing some eye makeup. Ino turned toward the back of the room and told me that he would like to talk to me but that he couldn't because he had company (*visitas*). His houseguest was his nineteen-year-old lover, who was visible when I glanced in the window. Ino's young lover was güero and a normal-looking young man.

I told Ino that Anilú had strongly recommended that I speak with him, and I suggested that we do the interview under a tree in an open area beside the alley. He somewhat reluctantly agreed and came outside. I placed the tape recorder on a motorcycle that was parked in the alley so that I could take notes. It was awkward and very hot, and it was difficult to take notes standing up, but it would prove to be a compelling narrative.

Anilú and Ino were about the same age and had been friends since childhood. His father was a friend of Anilú's father, and they often worked together. Like Anilú's father, Ino's father worked in the fields, was very machista, and also took him to the fields and tried to make him into a man. Ino's father cut firewood and *guamúchiles*, trees with sharp thorns.[3] This was difficult and demanding work, which required that they hollow out the inside of the tree. He said, "Mi papá era muy machista y me pegaba." (My father was very machista and he would beat me.) His father even tried to choke him once with a *soga* (rope) because of Ino's sexual orientation. Ino would refer to beatings several times during the interview. His younger brother also used to hit him, but Ino's mother accepted him.

Ino said that he wanted to be a tailor. He did *puntos o vestidos* (needlepoint or made dresses), but his father wanted him to undertake more manly work. By the age of fourteen, Ino had gotten together with another boy. He had about three relationships around this time. "My first relationship was at age fourteen. My father saw me talking to the boy. He hit me, he dragged me, and he punctured a hole in my earlobe. I had sex out of spite for my father. It hurt both oral and anal. It hurt but I enjoyed it. I identify as homosexual. It's all the same. Muxes dress like women and are more *vulgares* [vulgar]."

Ino's father forced him to marry a woman at age eighteen. He was with her for only about three months. "My father would beat me. He would try to strangle me. I had sex with her *por venganza* [out of spite]. We had three children, ages twelve, nine, and six. I discussed it with her, but she still saw me as a man. We had an amicable separation. Little by little, I entered the homosexual life." He added that his children accepted him because he dresses like a man. The girls tell him that they want to be with him. His children come over to visit even when his partner is there. In describing himself, he said, "I am a woman trapped in a man's body."

Ino has been involved in three long-term relationships with men. They sometimes go to fiestas, and many of his novios like to go out with him. He declared, "I am a beast [ *fiera*] in bed. Being activo does not interest me [*No me llama la atención*]. I would rather masturbate." He doesn't have sex with women. Referring back to his father, he said, "Mi papá no me aceptó hasta al último. Yo le velé y lo cuidé." (My father did not accept me until the very end. I watched over him until he passed away.) Ino had an older brother who was gay and came out when he was twenty. His father reportedly also had a gay brother, and family members would hit the brother, and they also forced him to marry, so it seems to run in his family.

Ino returned to discussing how he would go out with his father to cut guamúchiles. They would take off the bark, cut out the inside, and make pulp out of it. It was very hard, demanding work, and you had to be strong to work with the guamúchil. Today he makes piñatas and owns a small establishment where he makes lencia, a drink made with beer, lemon juice, and chile. He took pride in saying, "It's delicious and is good for hangovers," adding, "This is my job as a man."

## ESTRELLITA, THE DWINDLING LITTLE STAR

Estrellita is from the novena sección, known as Cheguigo Guete (Cheguigo South). She is thirty-one and has been dressing like a woman for the past twelve years. We decided to meet at Felina's estética, then have lunch at the Casa Grande, a very nice restaurant she suggested, located across from the zócalo.

She arrived about fifteen minutes late, wearing jeans, a midriff blouse, heels, long earrings, and some makeup. She usually dresses this way, except around the house, where she wears shorts or jeans. Estrellita is tall, about six feet in heels, and very thin. As we walked the three or four blocks to the restaurant, I didn't sense that anyone was looking at us or staring in any way. Estrellita greeted a number of people and seemed to be well recognized and regarded. The waiter was courteous and also acted normally. In fact, he brought a small coat rack and suggested that Estrellita put her purse on it.

Like Anilú and Ino, Estrellita has a tragic story to tell. She is the middle child of five children, with two older brothers and a younger sister and brother.

Her father was good to the other children, loved them, and brought them presents, but he always rejected her because she was muxe. She has known she was different since about the age of five and believes that being muxe runs in families. She has an uncle who is muxe. Like Anilú's family, his insisted that he marry, and he did, but he is still muxe and maintains the muxe lifestyle on the side. Estrellita's mother makes tortillas and sells them from home. Her father worked as an *obrero* (laborer) and now works as a gardener or landscaper. Estrellita creates designs for huipiles and works out of her home, where she lives with her parents. She feels that both parents had equal say in the family and that neither one was dominant.

Estrellita said that when she was young, her father would yell and beat her repeatedly because of the way she was. He did not accept her as muxe. He wanted her to change. From an early age of, say, around eight, he would take her out to do hard manual labor in the field, like carrying wood, bricks, or other heavy material. Anilú and Ino had presented similar stories. Her mother tried to protect her against him. Sometimes Estrellita went to her grandparents' house nearby, just to get away from her father. She had a good relationship with them and with her mother. She has had an operation, partly as a result of the beatings her father gave her, and pointed to a deep scar, an indention on the left side of her face.

Estrellita has stayed in her parents' home because of her mother. Even now she has a bad relationship with her father. She gets along fine with her siblings, although it took the oldest one a long time to get used to the fact that she was different. Estrellita went as far as sixth grade. From an early age, she saw things that she wanted but didn't know how to get them, so she started growing plants when she was about ten and selling them at the plaza to earn money.

Her first sexual encounter was when she was ten. There was a party in the neighborhood near her house. When she left the party, a boy followed her. She thinks he was also at the party. He took her to a *barda* (wall or fence) and raped her. Her second sexual experience was also when she was ten. There was a man about thirty who lived in the neighborhood and was almost like an uncle. He started talking to her about various subjects, including sex, and asked whether she wanted to try different things. He finally had sex with Estrellita, and because of her age, she now sees it as a form of sexual molestation and doesn't have good associations with it. She looked like she was going to cry as she related these incidents to me.

Estrellita's first serious relationship was with a young man, un hombre. They were novios for about four years, but it is the only long-term relationship she's had. She does have a relationship with someone now, but he just comes to have sex with her and leaves. They are not really novios and don't go out and do things together as a couple. She has had the nickname Estrellita since she was a child, so it's not a muxe, or an artistic, name but a childhood nickname.

Like Roque and Anilú, Estrellita always assumes the pasivo role in sex and is the insertee in both anal and oral sex, rather than the inserter. She said that some muxes assume both roles. She has never been in a threesome but has been in situations where several couples were having sex in the same room at the same time. I asked if it was true that muxes are very promiscuous, that, as Biiniza said, "Somos más putas que las galiinas." (We are more promiscuous than hens.) She conceded that muxes do have a way of seeking out and getting men to notice them. They will see someone and say, "A ése me lo quiero coger." (I want to screw that one.) They look at the man or go by and rub against him to get his attention until he responds. Men like to go to muxes because they can satisfy them and will do things most women won't do. Estrellita added that a lot of men are muxe but won't come out publicly or dress as women. One example is a prominent lawyer who wears a suit all the time. This person finally got the nerve to dress up like a woman and go to the vela. When Estrellita saw him there, he was in "seventh heaven." Estrellita has been involved with the Intrépidas group for several years but is not a socia, or formal member, although they invite her to their functions.

We talked candidly about parents who don't accept their muxe children. I mentioned a few people I met who seem to accept them, like César's father (see chapter 5). She said that people here don't have the sense to do this, but she wishes that they would just sit their children down and talk to them, and ask them whether they want to change or not. She is sure they could change, if they wanted to.

## RICARDO (TÁMARA), THE MEDIC

Ricardo's story contrasts sharply with the experiences of others, like Anilú, Ino, and Estrellita, who were rejected and severely beaten by their fathers because they were muxe. Ricardo's father, Héctor, was very accepting of his son. Ricardo is thirty and the oldest of five boys. At about age nine, he realized he was attracted to men. Asked whether he liked to play with dolls and do feminine things, he responded, "At first I had a great deal of responsibility as the oldest. I did not like working in the fields, but I had to help my father. I was fascinated with sewing, and I also helped my mother with her household chores." I couldn't help but notice during my visit that in his interaction with his younger siblings, Ricardo was treated with a great deal of respect and authority as the oldest.

Regarding how his parents responded to his being muxe, he said that his dad noticed he was different but thought that Ricardo would assume responsibility for talking to them about it.

A los diez y siete yo tomé la decisión de hablar con mis papás. Entonces llamé a mi tía, la hermana de mi mama, que me apoyaba más, y me junté con mis papás. Yo les dije que si no me aceptaban, yo tendría que irme con mi tía. Mi papá si me aceptó, pero mi mamá no. Ella se tardó un rato.

[At age seventeen, I decided to speak to my parents. So I called my aunt, my mother's sister, who was the most supportive of me, and met with my parents. I told them that if they did not accept me, I would have to go live with my aunt. My father did accept me, but my mother did not. It took her a while to accept me.]

In the long run, his mother accepted him because he helped her with sewing and with other responsibilities at home. "She accepted me after about eighteen months," he said.

As to whether he was a vestida, he said, "I dress. I put makeup on here at home. I will wear a blouse or a man's shirt, sort of unisex, but I don't dress like a woman, except at the velas." He said that at work he has to wear a uniform and dress like a man. At school he always showed his feminine tendencies and dressed as he dresses at home, and his friends "me cotorreaban" (would tease me). One of them gave him the artistic name Támara. He didn't like it at first and would say that his name was not Támara, but his friend insisted on calling him by that name. He later came to accept it, and it stuck. He assumed the name in prepa and later at the university. He was called Támara. Even the teachers called him Támara, except when they took roll. Teachers treated him like a woman, and sometimes they would say, "Bueno ustedes las mujeres, hagan ésto o aquello y me incluían." (Okay, you girls do this or that and they included me.) For the most part, he was not teased at school. He got along really well with his friends and classmates.

Ricardo's first sexual experience was at about ten years old. His partner was a classmate he had been in love with from the age of nine. He had known him since grade school and sat behind him, but he was older, about eighteen. The classmate started to show him about sex, and that's how they got started. They went to the river. The boy was a mayate. Ricardo bought him gifts or gave him money to please him. He fell in love with him and would tell the girls that the boy was his husband. The boy got wind of this, and he didn't like it because of his pride as a man. He bawled him out, and they broke up. He sees Ricardo on the street but doesn't acknowledge or greet him. Ricardo had only one stable relationship, but his novio was gay and more inter. Ricardo considers himself pasivo in both anal and oral sex.

In response to what a mayate is, Ricardo explained, "A mayate is a man who becomes a muxe's lover. He does not consider himself to be muxe. He has a wife and sleeps with muxes." He added that the difference between muxe and gay is that the word "muxe" is Zapoteco and the Spanish word "gay" is actually English. A muxe is one who has a partner and doesn't have the resources to support him. He shared a joke.

> Si le preguntas a alguien, bueno, "¿Tú qué eres?" Si dice "Soy gay" y le preguntas, "¿Tienes coche?" "No." Entonces tu eres un pinche muxe; no eres gay.
> [If you ask someone, "What are you?" [and] if he answers, "I am gay," and you ask him, "Do you have a car?" [and he answers] "No." Then you are a lousy muxe. You are not gay.]

Like Juan, Ricardo said that gays are the ones who have cars, the ones who pay mayates. When I asked him whether he was muxe or gay, he laughed and said, "If you don't have a car or money, you are muxe," meaning he was muxe. He continued by saying that two gays can go about as a couple because they are masculine and they look like a couple of friends, but a gay and a vestida can't go out together because everyone will assume that one of them is a mayate. A gay and a vestida won't last because people will talk and point fingers at them. He added, "Es muy aceptado el muxe aquí como una bendición de Dios. Son los que cuidan a los padres y luego se quedan con ellos." (Muxes are well accepted here as a blessing from God. They are the ones who take care of their parents and will stay with them.)

He talked about having had a friend whose father would take him to work. His friend can whistle like a man and is very masculine because he learned to work like a man in the fields. The friend still works in the field, although he's muxe. When his friend's sister got married, he had to help his mother with knitting and feminine tasks, and the mother finally accepted him. But his father continued to reject him.

Ricardo mentioned an organization named Gasela there in San Blas. He said he has been their muxe queen and will be the queen for this group again next year. The chosen queen is one who will do things right. She has to pay about 5,000 pesos (400 U.S. dollars) for a band and overall will spend about 15,000 to 20,000 pesos (1,500 to 1,800 U.S. dollars) in expenses. He invited me to the next San Blas Vela, where Támara would be the reigning queen.

## CONI, COMFORTABLE IN HER OWN SKIN

Coni is thirty-nine and the oldest of five children, two girls and three boys, and lives with her father, two sisters, and their husbands in a fairly large but modest two-story house about three blocks from the center of Juchitán. She is about five foot three and plain, with blond shoulder-length hair and a bad complexion. Dressed casually in shorts and a shirt, with no makeup, Coni indicated that when she goes out, she generally wears a dress. She did not look as feminine as other muxes, as the stubbles of her beard and moustache were visible. Her father sold fruits and vegetables, and her mother was a housewife. She answered that her father was in charge when asked; he was the one who controlled everything.

Her parents divorced when she was about twenty years old. Divorce used to be rare but is quite common today. Her mother lives in a nearby town, and she sees her and gets along well with her. Coni described her father as very machista, set in his ways and hard to get along with, especially now that he was older.

I met her father when I came to ask for her. He was sitting in a chair in the open doorway and very gruffly said, "¿Quién? No, no la conozco." (Who? No, no I don't know her.) He had an amputated leg and diabetes, which seems to be very common in Juchitán. Coni grew up in one of the neighborhoods of Juchitán. She was accepted by all her family except her father, who had a hard time dealing with the fact that she was muxe, but he is a difficult person to get along with and has always been like that. With time, he grew to accept her and has accepted her since she was eighteen.

When she goes out, people generally also accept her, although there are always exceptions. When asked if she has ever been physically or verbally assaulted, she responded, "No," but that "most of the girls [muxes] have experienced problems of some sort. Some have been beaten, and one was even assassinated, but this is the exception rather than the rule." She added, "Some people treat you well and others might bad mouth you or stab you in the back."

Coni became aware that she had feminine tendencies at the age of five because she loved to play with dolls and she played with girls. Like Biiniza, she was raised primarily by her maternal grandmother, who only spoke to her in Zapoteco and was very accepting of her being muxe. Coni's sisters understand Zapoteco but don't speak it.

She said that in school she never got along well with the boys. "We were discriminated against in elementary and junior high school." Her first really negative experiences with being teased were in fifth grade. I asked how she dressed when she was little, and she responded that students always wore uniforms, with boys wearing jeans and a white shirt, and girls wearing skirts, so she dressed like the boys. She attended public school.[4] "I also had problems in junior high school, and boys ridiculed me." She finished school and went on to prepa but did not finish, dropping out at age sixteen.

Her first sexual experience was in prepa when she was eighteen. She reflected and then admitted that it was hard to remember because it was a long time ago. Since she had dropped out of prepa at sixteen, perhaps she had been younger than eighteen. Her partner had been a *compañero* (classmate), and they had been in the same group. It had happened only once. Coni added that she "never had boyfriends in school; none at all."

Coni's first novio and the only long-term relationship she has had was when she was twenty-two. She's had a lot of partners, but their relationships haven't lasted long. Some have been hombres, others bisexual. On two occasions, she had sex with someone who was gay, but he was dressed like a man. She wouldn't be attracted to anyone in a dress because she is attracted to men. Coni shared that some of the girls take female hormones, especially the younger ones, when they are trying to transform their bodies into women. In some cities you can be "hormonized" and take all the female hormones. She used to take hormones, "Pero ahora, ¿para qué?" (But now, what's the point?)

Like a number of other respondents, Coni added that there is a long tradition of muxes in Juchitán families. "In my family we are accepted because there is a long tradition of muxes *entre mis antepasados*" (among my ancestors). She has uncles who are muxe, and even her maternal great-grandfather was muxe. "There are muxes in our ancient origins as Zapotecs." She estimated that about 60 percent of families in Juchitán have one or more family members who are muxe—an uncle, brother, or someone.

As to who has the power in relationships, it varies. In her case, when she was in a long-term relationship, she was the one *que mandaba*. She lived with a male partner and was the dominant one.

## KIKE/KIKA, THE PERFORMANCE ARTIST

Kike's Estética is filled with artwork, mementos, and pictures of various muxes, dressed in traditional Zapotec attire. Kike is forty-eight years old but is youthful, animated, masculine, and charismatic. He lives in a loft above his studio. Another muxe, Mayté, described him as un travestí (a transvestite). I took this to mean that he normally dresses like a man and dresses as a woman as part of a performance. He was wearing male clothing and looked very stylish. Kike's hair is so short that it looks shaved, and he uses a wig when he transforms into a woman. He pointed to pictures of himself in the salon dressed in the traditional feminine Juchiteca clothing, and they showed a dramatic transformation. He wore extreme multicolored eye makeup with penciled wings arched toward the sides of his head. His feminine Intrépida name is Kika, so he transforms from Kike to Kika.

Kike was born and raised in Juchitán, but like several other muxes, he went to Mexico City to study hair styling after secundaria, at age fifteen, and spent several years there. He comes from a family of seven children, five girls and two boys, and he was next to last in the birth order. Kike's father worked for the railroad as a watchman, and his mother was a housewife.

When he was little, Kike liked to take breakfast or dinner to his father at work. His father's coworkers made comments about him because of his effeminacy, and would say that he was spying on them. He smiled and admitted that he did like to look at the men when they weren't looking. His effeminate behavior embarrassed and bothered his father because of his coworkers' comments. Like Coni's father, Kike's was machista and didn't like to see his son in the kitchen, but Kike loved to be in the kitchen with his mother. I mentioned that I was also raised with the same tradition, that men were not allowed in the kitchen.

Although Kike's father was machista, his mother ruled and had power in the family. Kike was rebellious and fought constantly in school when other children teased him because of his feminine mannerisms. He reflected on his mother, noting that she was his *protectora* and spent a lot of time at school defending him. Although he fought a lot, he eventually made friends and has two close friends who are not muxe.

Kike also had girlfriends in school and having them as friends helped to shield him from criticism and *choteos* (kidding or ridiculing). "They were my armor," he said. Kike is attractive and charming, and he said proudly that he was always with the prettiest girl. I asked if he had ever been attracted to women, and he said he fell in love with the prettiest girl in his school, Marít. But he has never had sex with a woman. "No me llamaban la atención." (I wasn't attracted to them.)

Kike's first sexual experience was at age eleven and quite negative and traumatic because several older boys raped him. This reminded me of Anilú, because it was very painful and they also made him bleed. The experience traumatized him forever, and for this reason, to this day, he does not like to assume the passive role in sex. He prefers to be el activo in *sexo anal* rather than pasivo or to engage in mutual oral sex and other sexual acts.

Kike's next sexual relationship was in Mexico City when he was about eighteen. A man who was about thirty picked him up on el metro (the subway).[5] The man took him with him, and they had sex, but he has never liked being the receptor in anal sex. He reiterated that anal sex was painful, and he had negative associations because of being raped. The relationship with the man in Mexico City lasted three years, but Kike has not had a lot of other long-term relationships.

Kike has a novio with whom he has reciprocal oral and manual sex, and he again repeated that he does not like to assume the passive role in anal sex. He believes that men who have sex with muxes are in fact bisexual because they seek out muxes at velas and other places and keep having sex with them. He commented on a bisexual female, a South American researcher and professor that he spent time with. They were never intimate, but she wanted to marry him and have his children. He added that she wanted them to be the first couple to have a muxe child, perhaps through artificial insemination. She really pursued and harassed him, to the point that he had to cut off the relationship.

Kike said, "Soy activista, y me cuido." (I am an activist and I protect myself).[6] He described his transformations as a performance artist into a man, a woman, and several other variations. When making reference to his feminine self, La Kika Performancera, he described her in the third person. We talked about the prior week's vela, and he said he had been there. He'd worn a short black knit skirt with a thong underneath it. Kike said that he is open about his relationship with his novio and that his boyfriend accompanied him to the event.

Kike is active in Las Intrépidas. Felina was currently the directora de la diversidad sexual (director of sexual diversity) for the Municipal District of Juchitán on behalf of the dominant political party (PRI). At the time, Kike was negotiating to assume the equivalent post representing the PRD (Leftist party) or COCEI, which are linked, and he assumed the position in December of the same year. One of the interesting proposals he's made is to provide a "third" bathroom for transpersons. Another is to have a communal kitchen for persons who don't have resources or anything to eat, including those who pass through the area from Guatemala and other places. This would be a proposal at the municipio level.

Kike reinforced information provided by other respondents, explaining that the term Intrépida meant they are *luchadoras* (fighters). They are very hard workers and like to be "envueltas con todo" (involved in everything). He said that muxes were accepted in the past but were not as open or out in public as they are today. He recalls that in the 1970s, when he was a *chavalito* (little kid), muxes dressed in brightly colored guayaberas, perhaps with a flower embroidered on them, golden buttons, and cufflinks, but they didn't dress like women. Those with more money dressed this way. "We are like a third sex," he concluded.[7] Kike also believes that the muxe tradition has Zapotec roots but did not elaborate and ended by noting that Las Intrépidas also has several lesbian members.

## HUICHO, EL JAROCHO

Luis, who goes by Huicho, is a muxe respondent who looks, dresses, and behaves like an ordinary man. Huicho is fifty years old, about five foot ten, with a medium complexion and dark curly hair. He seems to be in good shape, athletic. I spoke with him at the basketball courts, where he coaches the Intrépida basketball team. In the past, he played center on the team. I had seen him with Mandis at the Mass for the Intrépidas and at the velas. I initially thought that he was a mayate, because he is not a vestida or pintada in any sense of the word. In fact, he and Kike strike me as being hypermasculine and unquestionably macho.

Huicho is also very personable and gregarious. When I explained my research and asked for an interview, he readily complied but told me that I had made "a serious mistake" by speaking to a lot of other people before talking to him, because he had founded Las Intrépidas and had all the answers I needed. We agreed to meet the next day at 2:00 in the afternoon during his dinner break at the restaurant where he works as executive chef. The restaurant is new and one of the better ones in Juchitán. Everyone calls him El Jarocho because his father is originally from Veracruz. I arrived promptly at 2:00 and Huicho led me to a private dining area. He smoked and drank coffee while we did the interview. This was one of the most interesting interviews I conducted, but he spoke very fast, and I found him somewhat difficult to follow.

Huicho comes from a family of three girls and two boys. His father was a merchant in *las ferias* (the fairs), and his parents sold a variety of foods, like tortas and tacos, there. His father is from Veracruz, and his mother from Tiltepec (Santa María Magdalena, Tiltepec, Oaxaca). His father is machista and is now seventy-four years old. His mother is in charge of the household. As a child he was interested in assuming household chores, and since the age of seven or eight, he could iron clothes. He was raped when he was seven by the sixteen-year-old son of the owner of the house. His parents had a concession stand for a restaurant at Juchitán's Parque Central, but when there was a change in political parties, and a new government came into power, they lost the concession. Huicho used to help out at the restaurant.

He told me that he has been independent since he was three. He left Juchitán for about twenty-five years. "Bailé mucho," he said. (I danced a lot.) His father was also an excellent dancer and once beat Resortes, an old-time comic who was a great dancer, in a dance contest. His father performed at all the carnivals and fairs. The family traveled from town to town with *carpa* (the carnival), and his father entered and won many dance contests. Huicho has also won many dance contests. He can do any sort of dance, and he stressed that he dances the role of a man, not that of a woman. He added that he has a very extensive social network and knows a lot of people in high places—politicians, entertainers, and celebrities—and that they all respect him.

He has always been *priísta*, or a member of the dominant political party. El Jarocho proceeded to name drop. He said that he knew the ex-presidente of Juchitán Hector Sánchez López, who had visited Tuxtepec, where Huicho met him. When he lived in Cancún, he worked at the Fiesta Americana hotel, where he also met a lot of people.

Jumping back to his childhood, he said, "Hasta ahorita mi papá no me acepta. Soy bisexual. Mi papá me hizo así. Nunca me he vestido." (To this day, my father does not accept me. I am bisexual. My father made me this way. I have never dressed like a woman.) On the same theme, he said that he used to be upright and responsible.

He went into more detail about his childhood and noted that his father used to beat him. His mother was very strong and has three children from a second marriage, ages thirty-three, twenty-nine, and twenty, who live in Cancún.

When Huicho was eleven or twelve years old, the muxe group that Omar had mentioned to me, Panteras Negras, already existed. Néstor hadn't liked the name Las Intrépidas. They put on an event in these early years in Comitancillo, and he later became the first mayordomo of the vela.

Huicho elaborated on his romantic and active sexual life. He has been involved with famous male songwriters and composers who have written and dedicated songs to him. When he was thirteen or fourteen, the song "Perfume de Gardenia" was dedicated to him. The song "Amor de mi Vida" (Love of My Life) was written for him. He declared, "Lo puto lo tengo por atrás. De frente soy muy macho." (The gay in me is in my rear. Up front I'm very macho.) He continued to elaborate on his sex life:

> En un día me eché a diez y siete personas. Tengo un muchachito que fue el lunes. El me paga. El es activo. Con el soy muy pasivo.
>
> [One day I had sex with seventeen people. I have a young boy who comes over on Mondays. He pays me. He is active. I am very passive with him.][8]

He looks at mayates as being normal but has gotten into fights with some *locas* who ridicule women who are very beautiful.

## MAYTÉ, THE EX–SEX WORKER

I met Mayté at a vela and asked her for an interview. When we met, she was wearing short shorts. For our interview, she showed up in pedal pusher pants, a midriff white blouse, long hooped earrings, and high heels. Mayté is twenty-eight, tall, and dark. She has stylish short straight hair with a part on the side, like a bob, and wears a lot of makeup. She looks like she tries hard to appear feminine. She had stood me up a couple of times, but I persisted and was ecstatic when she showed up at the kiosk in Plaza Principal. Mayté is a busy dress designer (*modelista*) who also designs traditional Zapotec dresses. She explained that she couldn't make the other appointments because she had been very busy completing an order.

She selected a nice restaurant for our conversation, about four blocks from the plaza. As we walked toward the restaurant, I felt like people were staring at us. She even got some whistles from passing cars when she bent down to fix her socks outside the restaurant. This reminded me of a comment another muxe, Roque, had made, that every time someone sees you with a muxe, they think you are hooking up. They think the same thing when a man is with a woman.

Mayté is from la séptima sección and has three older brothers. Her father was a fisherman, and her mother worked at home. Mayté currently lives with her mother and her mother's partner, who appears to be her common law husband. Her mother sells seasonal items. For example, she was currently selling Christmas merchandise, which would change in January. Her mother generally cooks, but Mayté cooks for herself when her mother is working.

Mayté doesn't have many recollections of her father, except that he was an alcoholic and would come home, drink, and sleep. Her mother separated from him and was divorced by the time Mayté was five. She thinks that her father accepted her the way she was, although he wasn't around much, and would have accepted her as muxe, even though she had very little contact with him. He never hit her or anything, but he was machista and sometimes beat her mother. Mayté's father is now deceased. He not only was a fisherman, but also made boats while her mother sold the fish he caught in the market. Her mother has always been a *comerciante* (merchant). She was also a *panadera* (baker) and made and sold bread on the street. Mayté said, "In effect, it was my mother who ran and controlled the household because my father was an alcoholic."

Mayté had a good childhood and was completely accepted by her mother and siblings. Her brothers started to notice that she was different when she was young, but they accepted her nonetheless. Two of her brothers were considerably older, but one was still in primaria when she was in school and protected her if someone messed with her. I shared that it was the same way with my older brothers because I was the youngest of three boys.

She had a sense of being different and attracted to boys "desde que era consciente de razón" (for as long I can remember). Early on, she was not aware of gender differences, but by preschool, she was always attracted to boys. There was some teasing in school, but she was able to handle it. Mayté normally hung around with girls and had some very good girlfriends. In fact, one of her best girlfriends fell in love with her, and she had to stop talking to her because she couldn't handle having a woman attracted to her.

In grade school she hung out with girls, but when she got to high school, she feared that she would be detected as being muxe. Yet she was accepted and very popular in school and got along well with everyone. "They accepted me." There were other muxe classmates she hung out with, "but I got along with everyone and was the most popular."

I asked if some of the muchachas took female hormones, and she said that some did so that their hips would get wider and their breasts would grow. Her first sexual experience was when she was in secundaria, at about age fourteen. She was in a chemistry class and students were working in teams of three. One team was made up of girls, the other of boys, and she was with the boys. They had to go to the bathroom to get water for an experiment. She went into the bathroom with a boy, and he "showed his intentions." They started kissing and fooling around. Later she made a date with him, and they had both anal and oral sex. The boy is now grown, married, and has several children. Mayté finished secundaria but could not go on to prepa for financial reasons.

Mayté has lived all her life in Juchitán, except when she went to Mexico City (México, DF) at about seventeen and was employed as a sex worker for several years. She went to México because she had friends who were sex workers, and she never looked for a regular job. She did well and was able to make a living. She will sometimes spend three years in México, DF, at a time and return to Juchitán, or she might spend a few months in Juchitán until she gets bored, and then go back to DF. She has been going back and forth for the past eleven years.

Mayté has not had any long-term relationships. Her novios are open and accompany her to the velas and to certain bars. She lived with one for a while but then learned that he was involved with another muxe. She also later discovered that he was gay or bisexual. Mayté could accept a man being with another woman but not with another muxe. She termed him an internacional. Mayté has always assumed the pasivo role, like a woman, and has never had sex with a woman.

Regarding mayates, she explained that although mayates vary in that some are more reserved than others, some will meet you at a bar but won't kiss you in public or anything like that. Things are changing now, and some young men are more open about going out in public with muxes. She has had men who will go with her to bars and be out with her openly on the street. She went to the Lavada de Ollas with a few of her male friends and bought cartons of beer for them. It's not like the old days. Here, sometimes the muxes will pay the man; not pay him, but buy presents and things like that. The muxe gets paid here, but "in Mexico City they pay us for sex." A man who is kept by a muxe is called *un mayate mantenido* (a kept mayate). Normally, a woman (muxe) does not support a mayate.

Mayté has gotten into fights just as anyone else would, but not because people disrespect her as a muxe. Mayté was the queen of the muxe vela eleven years ago and is a member of Las Intrépidas. As others confirmed in interviews, she said that there are three muxe groups but that the Intrépidas are the main one. One group is Vela Santa Cruz Baila Conmigo, who had their vela in December, and the other group, Vela Muxe, had their vela recently, but it has only been held for five years, whereas the Intrépidas will soon be celebrating forty years.

## FELINA, THE HAIR STYLIST AND DIRECTOR
## OF SEXUAL DIVERSITY

I spoke with Felina several times but finally conducted a more formal and extensive interview. Felina was born and raised in Juchitán, although she was gone for five years, studying to be a hair stylist in Mexico City, like many other muxes. She attended school through preparatoria. Felina comes from a family of four brothers and three sisters and was in the middle of the birth order. Her father was a campesino, or farmworker, and her mother a housewife. Although women in El Istmo tend to control the money in the family, her parents each had power and authority in their respective domains. Felina could not remember when she first realized that she was muxe, but it was very early on. "Los papás siempre resisten más" (Fathers always resist [accepting muxes] more), but her father eventually accepted her the way she was. Boys in school made fun of muxes, but she didn't have a lot of problems. Surprisingly, there were six muxes in her grade, three in one classroom, and three in another, so she hung around with them as well as with girls. Her mother is deceased, and she has a good relationship with her father and lives with him.

When asked about the acceptance of muxes, she suggested, "Viene de las mujeres porque ellas controlan el dinero en la familia." (It comes from the women because they control the money in the household.) Consequently, when they have a muxe son, they see him as "one more pair of hands" because "muxes are very good workers."

Felina's first sexual relationship was when she was thirteen or fourteen "cuando se presentó el momento" (when the opportunity arose). She has been involved in a number of long-term relationships, one lasting eight years. Muxes do not typically live with the men they are seeing, and many of these men also have novias, but this doesn't bother Felina because she is not jealous of them. She and the man agree on a place to meet or to go out. Where they have sex varies. It might be in a motel or in someone's house when available. The previous place where she worked was a large house, and she was able to have sex there. Like most muxes, she always assumes the pasivo role in sex.

Felina linked the popularity and acceptance of muxes to the importance of virginity in Juchitán, meaning that men don't generally have a sexual outlet. Things are changing, but muxes continue to play an important role in providing a sexual outlet for young men. Men simply see sex with muxes as a way to satisfy their sexual needs and nothing more. Los hombres don't see themselves as gay because they separate the sex act from their sexual orientation, and because they assume the active role in sex. Many men are therefore able to have sex with muxes and also be in relationships with women, but they generally don't want people to find out about it.

Felina works as an AIDS information consultant. Her formal title is director of sexual diversity for the Municipio of Juchitán, which is part of her political involvement as an Intrépida, but she makes her living as a hair stylist and hair salon owner. There are about forty active members in the Intrépidas organization, with many others who are on the periphery and help out with various activities. There are only about forty members of the mesa directiva because they don't have space for any more.

Like other respondents, Felina pointed out the good relationship the organization has with the Church as well as with a number of political entities. The Church accepts them because they participate in the Church, celebrating various saints' days, observing *cuaresma* (Lent), and taking part in other activities. She also believes that the Intrépidas have to demonstrate to the community that they are responsible citizens and involved in civic affairs. Members get invited by schools and other agencies to make presentations on safe sex and AIDS prevention. The group has been supported financially by the PRI, the dominant political party.

Despite the general acceptance of muxes, Felina said there are always exceptions. There are muxes who are drunks, who are obnoxious, who are aggressive, and even violent, and they get a corresponding response. Sex work is not generally appealing to people from El Istmo. People who do this kind of work in Juchitán are from other areas.[9]

Interestingly, Felina said that muxes participate in Juchitán's principal velas for San Vicente de Ferrer in May, but they are not allowed to dress as women. This change occurred about six years ago. Prior to that, they could dress as women. According to Felina, the primary challenge currently facing the muxes is recruiting more young members who will be able to maintain the strong values and traditions of the Zapotec community.

Although this interview with Felina went well, I had a very embarrassing moment. The "hundred-dollar misunderstanding" began when I went to Felina's estética to see if Biiniza would show up for an interview. I suspect that the confusion occurred because Biiniza and Felina share a telephone number. When I thought I was speaking with Biiniza on the phone, I was actually speaking with Felina. I was glad to see Biiniza when I arrived and proceeded to conduct my interview with her. But I had a strange feeling because "Biiniza" looked different, more tired, and much less animated than when I had seen her in the past. In any event, I had screwed up and interviewed Felina mistakenly, thinking that she was Biiniza. I wrote the following account of this incident in my field journal.

I am quickly learning that in Juchitán it's much easier to make appointments than to keep them. I was stood up by Señor Héctor in Tehuantepec on Sunday and, this morning, by Mayté. I also had an appointment at 2:30 with Biiniza. I waited until 3:05 and was about to leave when a large van of at least twelve passengers stopped in front of Felina's Estética and a muxe emerged from it. I was glad to see her but she proceeded to tell me that she had to go take care of her father. Because she was working with the people in the van who were visiting from Japan, she was pretty much at their disposal whenever they called. She is a community worker and provides AIDS information. She told me to come by around 6:00 tonight and she would be there, if she didn't get called. I came at six and completed the interview.

Of course, the person I saw getting out of the van was actually Felina, *not* Biiniza. When the interview was completed, Felina graciously said, "By the way, Yo soy Felina, no Biiniza." (I am Felina, not Biiniza.) Needless to say, I was very embarrassed yet she seemed unfazed by the confusion. I subsequently also interviewed Biiniza.

# 5

# COMMUNITY ACCEPTANCE

FLORENCIO MENDOZA, a retired teacher from Espinal, a town near Juchi-tán, reiterated the community view that muxes were very much accepted in El Istmo. "Es una cultura"; it is a distinct culture, he explained. As to why they were accepted, he said that "sometimes mothers want to have some-one to help them with household chores and other things, so they will select one of the male children and teach him to cook, knit, and take care of chores and household tasks."

The previous chapter presented the personal narratives of muxes with per-spectives on childhood experiences, family acceptance, and relationships with peers and partners. Since community acceptance is grounded in a muxe *cultura* and Zapotec traditions, this chapter presents an analysis of the societal views of muxes garnered from interviews with community respondents, including teach-ers like Florencio Mendoza, public officials, local priests, students, and ordinary citizens. In addition to formal in-depth interviews, others are more informal, and shorter, impromptu interviews that I characterize as encuentros (encounters).

The interviews revealed the many muxe characteristics that the community values—muxes are hardworking, help with household duties, take care of their parents into old age, contribute to the economic well-being of their family, and excel in both feminine and muxe arts and skills. Chiñas also found, "Muxes are considered to be highly intelligent and artistic and their work is believed to be done even more artistically and carefully than when it is done by women"

(Chiñas 2002, 109). In addition to being hardworking, muxes are believed to be the brightest and most gifted children (109). Parents generally consider them as the most likely to get educated but will only support them beyond sixth grade if they demonstrate superior intellectual ability because of the cost of pursuing higher education. Some muxes also engage in traditional male jobs, such as crafting silver and gold jewelry.

Given Juchitán's matrifocal emphasis, it is perhaps not surprising that the birth of a girl is celebrated. Marina Meneses Velázquez describes how, after the birth of a daughter, a seventy-eight-year-old family friend, Rosita, an expert in raising children and assisting in the delivery of babies, told the mother, "It's great that it's a girl, now you have someone who will take you by the hand when you are not able to walk" (Velázquez 1997, 99). The birth of a boy is more problematic and can lead older women to feel sorry for the mother: "A bachelor was born, you are going to have to get him married" (99), referring to how difficult and costly a boy's wedding is for a mother.

Most parents, however, are not embarrassed or burdened by having a muxe son. On the contrary, to have a muxe son in Zapotec culture is often said to be a blessing because muxes generally do not abandon the home but stay to help their elderly parents. Community acceptance of muxes is such that it would be misleading and condescending to say that they are "tolerated," which implies token and reluctant acceptance. When I interviewed Father Luis, the priest at the Parish of San Vicente Ferrer, he made an important point, that because Zapotec culture is very familistic, muxe children are accepted not because they are muxe per se but because they are part of the family.

Maria Fernanda, the thirty-five-year-old queen of the muxe vela in la novena sección (Cheguigo Guete) related that she was identified as muxe even while she was still in the womb. She said that the *partera* (midwife) told her mother that because of the way the baby was positioned, she was going to have a girl: "Esperó niña y cuando nací la partera le dijo que este niño va a ser muxe, porque llegó en la parte de la mujer." (She was expecting a girl, and when I was born, the midwife told her that this child is going to be muxe because he came from the female side of the womb.)

While it is generally accepted that muxe children are warmly accepted in Zapotec families, especially by women, a few reported being rejected by mothers. Valera, for example, a fifty-year-old designer of traditional huipiles from la octava sección, knew that he was muxe from an early age but kept it to himself because he was beaten.

Me pegaba más mi mamá. Mi mamá hasta me obligó a casarme a los diez y siete años. Nomás dos meses aguanté. Al final si me aceptaron. Mí mamá falleció hace veinte años. . . . Mi mamá no lo aceptó hasta una semana antes de que falleciera.

[My mother spanked me more. My mother even forced me to get married. I only tolerated the marriage for two months. In the end, they accepted me. My mother died twenty years ago. She didn't accept it until a week before her death.]

Gabriel, a forty-year-old computer salesman, lives with his sister in a house next to his mother, who rejected him. We became friends, and he once shared after he had a few beers how his father discovered he was muxe when he caught him at home with a boy, but he was not machista and readily accepted him. His father is now deceased, and Gabriel was teary eyed when he confided that to this day, his mother refuses to accept him or his friends.

Muxes generally appear to take great pride in the fact that they are socially accepted and integrated into the society. The acceptance and respect most were accorded was evident when I walked with them in Juchitán or rode in moto-taxis on our way to interview locations. Some, like Felina, Biiniza, and Mística, were publicly acknowledged, appeared to be well known, and were treated like public figures and granted considerable deference and respect.

## COMMUNITY SAMPLE

The following is a brief summary of background information on the forty-nine community respondents included in the study. The complete list of interviewees is found in appendix D, which includes their pseudonyms, occupation, age, the location where the interview or encuentro took place, and where they reside. Occupations ranged from housewives and students to farmers, food vendors, cab drivers, retail clerks, personal trainers, security guards, nurses and teachers to priests, the associate director at CONALEP (a technical and vocational school), the director of Casa de la Cultura, and the assistant to the mayor of Juchitán. There were also three muxe parents and a few relatives and visitors who came to Juchitán on business or for the velas.

Twenty-eight of the forty-nine community interviewees were male (57 percent) and twenty-one (43 percent) female. Their ages ranged from fifteen to seventy-three. More specifically, eighteen of the sample respondents (37 percent) were fifty years of age or older, six between forty and forty-nine (12 percent), ten thirty to thirty-nine (20 percent), six twenty to twenty-nine (12 percent), and nine under twenty years of age (18 percent). Overall, half of the sample (49 percent) was forty or older and another half under forty (51 percent). Forty-one of the forty-nine respondents lived in Juchitán or surrounding communities like Espinal, Unión Hidalgo, and San Blas Atempa (84 percent).

## THE ROAD TO JUCHITÁN: TWO TEACHERS' VIEWS OF MUXES

### FLORENCIO MENDOZA, A RETIRED TEACHER

I met Florencio Mendoza and his family at the Veracruz restaurant next to the Oaxaca city bus station on one of my trips to Juchitán. While waiting to be seated for breakfast, a woman in her early sixties and a younger woman in her thirties, the woman's daughter, were standing in front of me. I asked whether they were waiting to be seated, and they indicated that they were. It turned out that they were also going to Juchitán. We chatted for a while, and I finally got up the nerve to ask them about the muxes. What do they think of them? Were they really accepted in El Istmo? If so, why were they so accepted?

The mother said that muxes are much more accepted now than they were in the past. I noticed that although a mature woman, she was wearing purple and Vans-type sneakers, which looked comfortable. The daughter, like her father, is a teacher who lives and works in the city of Oaxaca. Her parents had been visiting her for several days. This was to be a great experience as I had the opportunity to gather a lot of information on the muxes and velas from this family. It seemed rude to record the conversation during breakfast, so I decided to pay close attention and write down what they said shortly after I arrived in Juchitán.

As we waited to be seated, the father showed up and kind of took control of the conversation. El señor Mendoza is a small Zapoteco, about five feet five inches tall. He was suffering from the flu and had his face covered with a checkered black-and-white scarf. He has been retired for thirteen years. I subsequently learned that you can't retire from teaching in México before the age of fifty-two, so he would be about sixty-five.

The Mendozas sat at a large table, and he kindly motioned me to join them. The restaurant was very crowded, and, parenthetically, I should note that restaurants in México often have tables that seat eight to twelve people family style, and unrelated individuals might sit together. A nun who was already at the table joined our conversation. She is also a teacher, at a Catholic school in Oaxaca, and was going to a conference, so we had four teachers at the table. When the conversation turned to the muxes, she quoted a recent statement by the Pope that described gays as being God's children and said that muxes should be accepted just like everyone else. Florencio agreed that muxes were very much accepted in El Istmo.

"It's a distinct lifestyle," he said. Mothers will sometimes select one of the male children to help with chores and other household tasks, including knitting and embroidery. Florencio was very demonstrative as he spoke and touched my shirtsleeve for emphasis, rubbing it gently between his fingers to illustrate the texture of fabric when he was talking about various fabrics muxes work with.

Espinal, the town he is from, is a small agricultural community just outside Juchitán. He talked about the velas, explaining that three velas are held there. One is the muxe vela on the penultimate weekend in April. The other velas are for San Juan and Vela Primavera (spring) in May. The principal vela in Juchitán is for San Vicente Ferrer, goes on for about a month, and starts on May 20.

Florencio Mendoza said that the economy of Espinal had taken a downward turn, and that the town was in the midst of entering into an agreement with some Spanish investors to install electric wind energy turbines to generate extra revenue for the community. Espinal is unique in being the first pueblo that sought community input about the project. He invited me to this important event at the municipal auditorium, which would focus on the project. He said that most people went along with it, but leftist people like the ones in COCEI are opposed. He looked at me and winked as he said this, implying that I might be one of those leftist persons who felt that this was another example of Spaniards wanting to reconquer and exploit indigenous people. He had agreed to support the project because it made sense, and it has really helped boost the town's economy. Florencio gave me his telephone number and his daughter's e-mail address. He wanted me to meet a friend and fellow farmer, Héctor Contreras, who has a muxe son and has accepted him completely.

After the bus arrived in Juchitán, I said good-bye, told him it was a pleasure to meet them, and thanked him for his warmth and hospitality. Florencio was self-effacing and said that people from Oaxaca are known for being *amigable* (friendly).

## PROYECTO EÓLICA DEL SUR:
## THE SOUTHERN RENEWABLE ENERGY PROJECT

I did attend the community meeting in Espinal that Florencio had recommended. Although much of what transpired is not directly relevant to this study, I met some interesting folks and learned about issues surrounding wind turbines and the local economy. I also had the opportunity to gather opinions about muxes from the locals.

The meeting was held at the municipal auditorium, and a total of 210 people signed in. After a wait of more than an hour, while they tested the microphones, set up the tables for the dignitaries, and played dance music, the program began with a lot of fanfare, welcomes, and introductions by at least twenty dignitaries. The distinguished guests ranged from representatives of the federal department of energy, to state and local community leaders, including the assistant to the municipal president.

I had met several people before the meeting. One man in particular was señor Virgilio who is about sixty-five years old and bilingual. He is a friend of Florencio Mendoza's and was quite responsive. People about his age all speak Zapoteco because it is their first language. Virgilio first learned Spanish in school. He believes that the Zapoteco language is being lost, although some schools now have bilingual education. Virgilio agreed that muxes are accepted because they are hard workers and help out in the family. For example, in Juchitán today, schoolteachers will ask boys to form a line and girls to form another but allow muxe boys to line up with the girls.

He is participating in this program because Espinal is an economically blighted community, and the project gives everyone a steady income from the wind turbines. For example, if you own ten thousand hectares, you will earn one hundred thousand pesos per year, which at the time was about eight thousand U.S. dollars in two installments of four thousand dollars every six months. He commented that the city went for a period of forty-five days without rain, and then for another forty-five, it never stopped raining, but that's how it is in this region. Most people grow corn or sorgo (sorghum), which are used to feed cattle, but these crops provide little income. The project gives people a more stable income from their land.

I spoke to the people who were sitting next to me, telling them I was a visitor and a sociologist who was interested in the muxes. A woman named Socorro said that parents saw having a muxe child as a blessing from God because they now had a child who would take care of them when they were older. Although I had the opportunity to meet a number of other interesting people, I had to leave before the end of the meeting because I knew the muxes were having a Regada de Frutas parade in Juchitán that evening.

When I returned to Juchitán, the cab driver said that traffic was congested because Las Intrépidas had already started the Regada de Frutas. I learned that the regada was organized not by Las Intrépidas, but by a rival group. I spoke to two young women who were waiting for the parade. One, Sandra, was about twenty and from Salina Cruz. She said that they have muxes in her town, but they are not as open in their lifestyle as here, so she came because she wanted to see them. I asked if they were accepted, and she said, "Sí." The other was a thirty-something mother, Brenda, who had a girl, two, and a boy, seven, and was also waiting patiently for the regada. She defined "muxe" as a Zapoteco word that means someone who is biologically male but has the social characteristics of a woman. She said muxes were accepted because "they are now part of our culture; not something separate and apart."

## JOSÉ ABÉL ACEVEDO, TEACHER

On another bus trip from Oaxaca to Juchitán, I sat next to another teacher, José Abél Acevedo, who is also from a town near Juchitán. He had just turned fifty-two and was returning from Oaxaca city, where he had gone to arrange paperwork for his retirement in January. He was slim, of average height, with a dark ruddy complexion, and he was wearing a light blue Filipina-style guayabera.[1] Teachers' pensions don't pay much, he said, so he wants to coordinate his retirement with his oldest daughter, who is about to graduate from college, so she can help out until he gets another job. He also has a seven-year-old son. José Abél's wife is also a teacher.

José Abél agreed that muxes are accepted by everyone in society and believes it has ancient origins in Zapotec culture. Like Brenda, he defined "muxe" as a Zapoteco word that means someone who is biologically male but has the social characteristics of a woman. He also linked them to the economy, noting that although they don't have a matriarchy in El Istmo, women are not just housewives. They are very industrious, and many work outside the home, either in the market or somewhere else. Like Florencio, José Abél also said that women sometimes take a son who has feminine tendencies and teach him to do feminine work like embroidery, making flowers, or working in the market.

Like other respondents, he added that muxes earn money by making decorations for fiestas and velas or flowers and decorations for parade floats. A lot of them are also hired for organizing weddings or quinceañeras. For quinceañeras, for example, they do the hair and apply makeup on the girls, make the dresses, and even coordinate dancing for the event. He was familiar with Las Intrépidas and said they were in more demand and made more money because they have a higher status in society than other muxes, so people take their business to them. He has friends who are muxe, including a young neighbor boy who does not hide his sexual orientation and comes around to help with household chores.

After I settled into the hotel, I went to Felina's hair salon, but it was closed. I noticed in the window of the estética that I had missed a conference on muxes held earlier in the month at la Casa de la Cultura. I also noticed a flyer on the door announcing that they did makeup and hair for weddings, quinceañeras, anniversaries, and other events.

## HÉCTOR CONTRERAS, A PROUD MUXE FATHER

Héctor Contreras and his muxe son, Ricardo (see chapter 4), live in the historic town of San Blas Atempa, on the outskirts of Tehuantepec, and finding them proved to be an odyssey.[2] I had gotten Héctor Contreras's contact information from Florencio Mendoza. Héctor told me to call him on his cell on Sunday morning. I called numerous times from various locations over a period of several hours after I arrived, but the telephone repeatedly went to message. Because people generally know one another in the community, I asked around to see if anyone knew a man by that name who had a muxe son and went to several homes in search of Héctor, but they all proved to be dead ends. As I was about to give up and return to Juchitán, I went to an Internet café near a small plaza. Miraculously, as I was calling again, a clean-cut young man who was on a nearby computer interrupted me and asked politely, "Are you looking for señor Héctor Contreras? I am his son." It was unbelievable that I had simply run into him at the Internet café just as I was about to abandon the project. Ricardo gave me directions to the house, which was about eight blocks away. I took a moto-taxi and finally found Héctor.[3] Ricardo joined us after a few minutes, and his interview is in the previous chapter.

Héctor Contreras is a large man, about fifty, and very gracious. He invited me into the family kitchen, where we sat on small wooden folding chairs. He has five sons ages thirty, twenty-eight, twenty-four, twenty, and seventeen. The oldest, Ricardo, is muxe. Héctor said that he is a farmer and grows basic food staples like corn, sorghum, and tomatoes. His wife has a small puesto where she sells tomatoes, fruit, and tortillas. When asked who had la manda, or controlled the household, he answered, "Los dos mandamos." (We both do.)

Héctor Contreras had noticed that his son was different when Ricardo was about ten. Héctor worked in the fields and would take Ricardo out with him, but he noticed that the boy didn't like working in the fields. Instead, he liked to work and help out with his mother's tasks around the house. Since Héctor recognized this early on and knew that Ricardo did not want to work in the fields, he attempted to come to an understanding with his son that he would have to have a profession to fall back on. Unlike other fathers, like Anilú's and Ino's, he was not violent with his son.

Ricardo has a BA in *enfermería* (nursing).[4] Román, the twenty-eight-year-old, works for Coca-Cola and is head of a worker's union. Claudio (twenty-four) has a degree in business administration and is a schoolteacher. Eduardo (twenty) is pursuing an engineering degree in *agricultura*. The youngest, Roberto (seventeen), is in prepa.

When Ricardo was little, he liked to play with dolls and with girls. He was interested in sewing and designing dresses, or *la vestidura*. Héctor explained that it wasn't difficult to accept a muxe son.

No fue difícil. No, al contrario. Era una bendición de Dios tener un hijo tan inteligente. No hay otros que sean muxes en la familia. Le fue muy bien en la escuela. Fue muy inteligente. Yo lo apoyé económicamente y psicológicamente.

[No, it wasn't difficult [for me]. On the contrary. It was a blessing from God to have such an intelligent son. There aren't any other muxes in the family. He did very well in school. He was very intelligent. I supported him financially and psychologically.]

Only one of the boys, the youngest, likes soccer. They all like dancing and folklórico, and they are members of a dance group. His brothers are very cheerful. Ricardo is responsible, but Héctor told him not to act out because people would judge him. There is communication and respect among them here. People accept Ricardo because of his chosen profession. Héctor added,

Aquí sí se acepta al muxe más, aunque hay familias que no lo aceptan, especial-
mente cuando están chicos. Y después cuando están más grandes y ven el dinero
que ganan, entonces sí los aceptan. Pero él no.
[Muxes are more accepted here, although there are families who don't accept
them, especially when they are young. But later, when the money starts flowing
in, then they accept them. But that was not the case with him.]

I asked whether he would accept having his son bringing his partner home, and
he said,

That's a decision that is totally up to him. I only ask that he would do it with
discretion. I spoke with him and told him that he shouldn't think that I would
reject him. I accepted him like he is. I only wanted him to have a profession for
his future.

He concluded by saying that God listened to him and that he was very proud
to have a son who graduated from college and is a nurse. As I was interviewing his dad, Ricardo came in. His father suggested that I speak directly with
Ricardo, but I wanted to finish the interview with the father first.

After closing the interview, the father smiled and invited me to the San Blas
Vela next year, where Ricardo would be the queen, and said that I could bring
copies of the book for the participants. I was very impressed because, unlike
some of my respondents, this was a father who had not only come to accept but
was extremely proud of his muxe son.

## LA LAVADA DE OLLAS AND A MUXE'S FATHER

I attended another vela and Lavada de Ollas organized by a rival muxe group,
Vela Muxe. I didn't realize that the lavada was being held until I called Biiniza
and she asked if I was going. It started at 5:00 p.m. I was feeling a bit nauseous
at the time because of something I ate, so I wasn't excited about going. I was
looking forward to staying in and relaxing, but I decided to go, and I am very
glad that I did.

It was early in the evening, and the atmosphere at the lavada was much more
laid back than it had been the night before at the vela. Rather than sitting in
one puesto, I opted to make the rounds to try to establish some contacts. I was

proud of myself because, with time, I'd become much more focused and strategic in my approach to getting interviews. It was like "working the room" at a cocktail party.

I spent a little bit of time watching the dancers, but people were not dancing much. I saw a couple of older ladies in Juchiteca outfits dancing to "Zandunga," a traditional Isthmus song played on a marimba.[5] They grabbed the edges of their skirts and turned slowly and rhythmically from side to side in time with the music. They were very graceful and clearly had presencia.

My first contact was with a man at the back of Raúl's puesto. He had had a few drinks. The music was so loud that it was hard for me to hear his discussion of the symbolism and importance of the velas, but I asked if I could talk to him in the next couple of days. He readily agreed and gave me his telephone number. He also suggested that I talk to the mayordomo and pointed to César's puesto.

I approached a man at the back of the puesto who was wearing a white guayabera and black pants, the traditional male attire at velas. He was thin, short, and looked like an important person, although he spoke Spanish simply, in an unpretentious manner, with a distinct Zapoteco accent, and he was clearly an obrero, or working-class man.

The man told me in a self-effacing way that he was not the mayordomo but that his son, César, was. I found out that he is also named César. Talking with César Senior proved to be the highlight of the evening. In fact, it made me rethink the wisdom of conducting only formal interviews, since sometimes the richest information and insights occur in encuentros—informal, spontaneous moments like this one, with very little fanfare or forethought.

The elder César is fifty-two years old and was born in Juchitán. He works at a beer refinery in a nearby community as a night watchman. His wife is a homemaker. While I was talking to him, his son arrived and proceeded to actively host his puesto, greeting people and making sure they had plenty of food and drink. Young César is a tall, somewhat hefty man, who weighs about 220 pounds. He appeared to be a gentle, very amiable, and pleasant young man. His mother was busy preparing the dishes that were distributed, and his father kept running around also passing out food and drinks and putting out chairs for people as they arrived. The family seemed united and proud in hosting the event. A couple of other young men also helped serve food and drinks.

The younger César is twenty-five years old and makes decorations for fiestas and velas. He has two sisters. As the mayordomo, he had planned and organized the vela, had paid for the bands, and was also allowed to invite more guests. He clearly had the largest puesto with the most guests.

I asked César Sr. how he felt about having a muxe son, and he responded with a distinct Zapoteco accent in his Spanish, "Así nació!" (That's how he was born!) "Of course, I accept him, what else could I do?" The words were spoken without reproach and in a matter-of-fact way. He told me that he had noticed that César was different when he was about "that age," pointing to a four- or five-year-old boy, who was playing between an adjoining puesto and the dance floor. From an early age, his son identified with girls, even though he does not dress as a woman.

I asked if he ever tried to beat him or to dissuade him from being muxe, and he emphatically answered, "No, por qué? Así es él" (No, why? That's how he is). When asked if César was harassed or bullied by classmates, his dad said, "No, he didn't associate with boys. He was always with the girls, but he wasn't teased by his classmates."

The way the elder César described his son, in a simple but elegant way, was that being muxe was a part of nature, and he didn't try to understand or to question something that was natural. César's father said some other revealing things. He noted that muxes were generally accepted and participated in the main vela in May for San Vicente, but they weren't allowed to dress as women because of the belief that it might be seen as disrespectful or as mocking the saint honored by the vela. He also said that they had held a Mass the day before at the small church downtown. The former priest, Father Pancho, allowed the muxes to have their Mass. When the new priest said the Mass, however, and realized that the men in the church were dressed as women, he felt he'd been duped or misinformed and said that he wouldn't do the Mass for them in the future. I told him I was surprised to hear this because I had spoken with the new priest, Father Luis, recently, and both he and Father Pancho were very accepting of the muxes. The last thing César Sr. said is that people no longer wear gold necklaces and jewelry, not only because it is too expensive, but because they are afraid of being assaulted or knifed.

## GOVERNMENT OFFICIALS' VIEWS

### CARLOS GARCIA BUSTAMANTE, ASSISTANT TO EL PRESIDENTE MUNICIPAL

I went to the presidente municipal's office to see how I could arrange a meeting with him or one of his emissaries and was told that I should check with his *secretario*, or assistant. His office is on the upper floor above the main market. I returned later to see if I could arrange an interview with the assistant and was surprised that the secretario could see me immediately and welcomed me warmly.

Garcia Bustamante was dressed casually in jeans and a plaid shirt. He was intense, not reluctant to speak at all, and he expressed himself well. Garcia Bustamante said that he is concerned that muxes are accepted on a superficial level but still suffer discrimination. Their acceptance is more superficial because many people come from distant places to attend their velas. But on a daily level, the homosexual still suffers, just like anyone else.[6] There are people who discriminate against them and don't accept them. The Church accepts them now because muxes have accepted the Church and asked for its blessing. When they asked to be incorporated into the Church and to have a Mass, the Church had to accept them.

I inquired about the status of women and their role in the family and he said that there are also a lot of misconceptions and misunderstandings relative to the role of women. People come, observe, and arrive at superficial, unfounded conclusions without fully understanding what they see. What they fail to understand is that Zapotec families are very close and united. Women work, not only in the home but also in any way possible to support and advance the family. The woman is very aware that she has to put forth a great deal of effort so that the family prospers as much as possible. Even if a woman is a professional, she works extra hard on behalf of her family. For example, if a woman is employed as a teacher during the day, after school she will do something else in addition to teaching. She might sell something or make and sell jewelry, or whatever.

Like many other respondents, he thought that the Zapotec woman was very industrious, works hard, and sometimes even makes more money than her husband. But if she makes more money, she will not hesitate to support her husband. The woman plays an equal and important role in Juchitán, but it is not a matriarchy. This is something that has been greatly misunderstood. The reality is that there is a division of labor, with the man as the producer of various products. He is the one who catches the fish, cuts the wood, harvests the produce, or prepares the meat or fish for consumption, whereas the woman distributes it in the market. People, therefore, misunderstand because the woman is more visible, but each plays an important and separate role in the division of labor.

Garcia Bustamante added with a great deal of emotion and fanfare that women have always played an important role in supporting the community throughout all phases of Juchitán history, including a famous battle when the Juchiteco troops were on the verge of being soundly defeated by French troops. The women came forth and implored the men to either stand up and fight against the French or take off their *pantalones* (pants) and let the women fight in their place.[7] The men were emboldened, fighting valiantly, and on September 5, 1868, they defeated the French army, the most renowned army in the world at the time.

He also told me that Juchitán faces a number of social problems today. One of the most pressing problems: "We have become a society of consumers rather than producers. Our economy is completely dead with regard to production of cattle or produce. We are consumers, and everything we consume is brought in from nearby places like Salina Cruz. The way the economy is maintained, then, is through the circulation of money within the community."

He continued by saying, "Another major problem is double talk among politicians; they will say something and do something else." He added that it was almost like living in an era in which some people believe that it is better to hide the truth. He elaborated that there was a need to develop the area's natural resources because they are ideally located, bordering Veracruz and having access to the Pacific and the Gulf of Mexico. He felt that outsiders came into Juchitán and exploited the community. There are thousands of vendors in the Plaza Central, for example, who claim to be acting on behalf of the community but they are exploiting it.

I had attended the meeting in Espinal concerning the development of eco-friendly wind energy turbines backed by Spanish investors. I asked if he favored the plan, and he responded,

> I am neither for nor against it. The point is that we don't know because the people who should know are not telling us. The politicians are keeping people in the dark. A situation like this provides an opportunity for *coyotes* [predators] to come, take advantage, and exploit the situation.

He couldn't understand why people get all up in arms over the idea of privatizing Pemex, the nationalized Mexican oil company, and yet they don't say a word about preserving natural resources when it came to the question of using the wind in the area to produce energy. He clearly saw the windy nature of the

Isthmus region as a valuable natural resource that had to be cherished and protected, just like any other valuable natural resource.

Señor Garcia Bustamante acknowledged that excessive alcohol consumption is another major problem in the community. When I asked whether it might be linked to the many parties and festivals that are celebrated each year, he agreed that it is. Another problem is the Juchiteco diet. There is a lot of obesity and diabetes because of a diet that consists of a lot of meat and carbohydrates—largely meat, bread, and other foods made of *masa* (flour). He said that there are also gangs and delinquency in Juchitán, but until recently, there had been very little organized crime controlled by the *narcotraficantes*. It occurs, but it is on an individual level and is not organized. I thanked him for sharing his thoughts on these matters and concluded the interview.

## LICENCIADO JUAN MÁRQUEZ, CONALEP ASSOCIATE DIRECTOR

On another trip, I rushed to the CONALEP vocational technical school hoping to meet with the director (principal). I arrived before the start of school, at 9:00 a.m., and waited for about forty minutes before finally having the opportunity to speak to Juan Márquez, the acting associate director of the school.

As I was waiting in the reception area of the main office, I noticed that the school had a computerized system to check staff and teachers in and out of the school. The automated system was linked to a computer so that when employees placed their thumbs on a computer pad, the computer flashed their photos to check them in and out. The teachers and staff were dressed casually in jeans, slacks, and polo shirts. Only one of the secretaries wore a traditional Zapotec dress. People were friendly, with most of them greeting me with "Buenos días" or asking if I needed any help as they walked by.

I should mention that in small talk with the cab driver on the way to CONALEP, we touched on the topic of muxes. Samuel was a middle-aged man, apparently in his fifties, who was unshaven and had some missing teeth and white stubble in his beard. He said that muxes were accepted in Juchitán, and that Las Intrépidas had had their vela the previous week. When I asked why they were accepted, Samuel responded, "Ahí es donde la mujer gana porque ayudan mucho en la casa, hasta más que las mujeres." (This is where women benefit because they [muxes] help out a lot in the home, even more than the women.)

The CONALEP (Colegio Nacional de Educación Profesional Técnica, or the National School of Professional Technical Education) prepares students for technical trades by providing hands-on training for various jobs. The associate director, Juan Márquez, is a courteous and politically astute man of about forty who was at once warm and reserved in the interview. He said that positions like his were commissioned or subcontracted until permanent personnel were selected. I interpreted this to mean that these were political appointments, that the current staff represented the PRI, and that they would be replaced once COCEI came into power that December.

Juan Márquez is originally from the town of Ixtepec in El Istmo and has been in Juchitán for about fifteen years. I asked whether he felt that the muxes were accepted in Juchitán, and unlike Garcia Bustamante, he responded, "Lo tienen como algo cotidiano; no hay discriminación." (They are part of daily life; there is no discrimination [against them].) They are not mistreated by other youth at CONALEP, he added, because they have *reglamentos* (rules or regulations) regarding behavior, and students are expected to treat each other with dignity and respect. I then asked if they were teased, and he answered, "El choteo es cotidiano." (Joking or teasing is part of the daily routine here [in Juchitán].) The school has some students and teachers who have "that predisposition" [to be muxe]. Unfortunately, the teachers were not there that day. He said that their muxe circle is more *con las mujeres*, meaning that they hung out with the female staff.

The school has a gender-based dress code that requires all students to wear a uniform. Both boys and girls wear golf-type white shirts with the CONALEP logo and their area of study (e.g., Automotriz) inscribed on them. Boys wear black pants and girls wear pleated blue skirts like those worn in Catholic schools. Once students get older, they begin to show their muxe style and dress.

CONALEP has about eight hundred students with four primary areas of study, or technical trades: automobile repair (*automotríz*), computers (*computadoras*), business (*administración*), and public health (*salud pública*). Most muxes are in public health, some in administration, and none in auto repair. They do have girls in auto repair, but only about one every new academic year. Juan Márquez teaches in the area of computers.

Interestingly, he linked the existence of muxes to the Catholic Church because it permits the integration of various social institutions, including the muxes through the velas. The velas and various saints' days are an extension of this practice. When asked about the possibility of having a focus group with students, he said that it would have to be dealt with by submitting a written proposal and specifying the goals and objectives. It would also have to be approved by the administration, various political entities, and someone would have to *respaldar*, or be responsible for it. "It's all very political," he said. "We could be closed if a parent was offended or complained. COCEI could close us or bring about a *bloqueo*." Bloqueo is an increasingly common political practice employed by COCEI and other progressive groups in the area. They block major highways with trucks and buses as a protest tactic.

I quickly realized that having a CONALEP youth focus group on the muxes was a political hot potato and would have to wait for another day. I thanked him for his time and comments and left.

## THE CHURCH AND MUXES

### SANTA CECILIA, PATRON SAINT OF MUSICIANS

After visiting the Casa de la Cultura, where an art exhibit included multiple large sketches of several muxes, including Felina, Biiniza, and Amaranta, I was walking in front of the San Vicente Ferrer Church next door when a car pulled up and parked, and about six or seven men dressed in melon pink shirts got out. They were part of a celebration, so I followed them in to see what was going on. At first I thought it was a baptism because there was a little girl about six months old dressed in a pinkish dress. All but two of the women in her party were dressed in traditional Zapoteca attire.

I decided to stay and discovered that it was not a baptism but a Mass in honor of Santa Cecilia, since November 22 is her saint's day. The same Mass is a ritual rite of passage that recognizes the mayordomos for the current and the following years' velas. Several images, including framed portraits, of Santa Cecilia were located behind the priest and below the altar, which was surrounded by flowers and three large candles. Father Luis said during the sermon that today was the day of Santa Cecilia, the patron saint of musicians. So most of the people in attendance were musicians.

Santa Cecilia was said to have lived in Roman times and was engaged to marry a man named Tiburcio. On the day of her wedding, she decided to forgo the celebration and instead declare her devotion to Christ. She talked her fiancé and his brother into also declaring their devotion to Christ. The three of them went to see the Pope to affirm their commitment. This was a radical move at the time because the Romans believed in pagan gods. As a result, Cecilia was arrested. The Romans attempted to kill her by boiling her in a steam bath, but she survived, so they tried, unsuccessfully, to decapitate her. Eventually, she was killed and was sanctified as a virgin and a martyr. In short, Father Luis explained, she came to be the patron saint of musicians because she was so devoted to Christ that she decided to forgo the celebration of her wedding in order to affirm her faith.

The Mass ended with a *banda* playing "Las Mañanitas," the Mexican birthday song. I had not heard the song played by banda musicians before, and it was very warm and moving. After the Mass, people went up to the altar and embraced each other. It was all very intimate, and I felt like I was part of a family gathering. When I spoke with Father Luis after the Mass, he said that the ceremony for the mayordomos was not conducted properly because the mayordomos for the following year's vela did not attend. When the ceremony is conducted properly, the mayordomos stand on each side of the priest, with the ones for the current year on his right, and those for the upcoming year on his left. The mayordomos from the previous year then move toward the images of Santa Cecilia, take three large candles, and hand them over to the mayordomos for the forthcoming year. In other words, the ceremony didn't work as it should have because the future mayordomos were not present, and they had to use a stand-in for them.

## FATHER LUIS

After the Mass, I stopped Father Luis as he was exiting the back of the church, explained my research purpose, and asked if I could talk to him. He was very cordial and agreed to meet with me immediately, so we went into a room in the rectory to conduct the interview. Father Luis was helpful and cooperative. He looks like he might be about forty, with prematurely gray curly hair, and average height and weight. He is from Oaxaca and has been in the region for some time, but he has been in Juchitán for only about three months.

What struck me most during the interview is that he linked the acceptance of muxes in Juchitán directly to the family, and this was a unique perspective. Zapotecs are very familistic, he explained, so when they have a child that shows feminine tendencies, some families might not accept him initially, but they will eventually incorporate him into the family. Another interesting point he reinforced is the link between the acceptance of the muxes and the economy. Zapotecs are very hardworking, industrious people, especially the women. The women readily incorporate the young muxe child into the family because he is an extra hand that can help with household chores, cooking, and other work that women must do. He stressed that it's not just that they are accepted because they are muxe, but rather that like anyone else, they are accepted because they are part of the family.

His observation was that muxes are generally accepted not just by family members but also by the society at large. I also asked whether muxe children were accepted by their school classmates, and he said yes, although there were some exceptions, as in any other case. Other children or adolescents might tease them, but that is the exception. He shared that when he was a student in the prepa, boys would tease one another about their sexual orientation even though they were straight. He also gave an example of a young two- or three-year-old child he had observed who was already exhibiting feminine tendencies and was accepted by both his family and the community.

When I asked about the acceptance of the muxes in the Church, he said that the Church also accepted them. One important thing he stressed is that Zapotec people are more linked to the Church socially than they are religiously, so the church functions as part of a larger social network. His description sounded like popular religion to me. He gave the example of velas, other fiestas, and church ceremonies like the one today for Santa Cecilia. He underscored the fact that the Church simply serves as part of a larger network of festivities.

Father Luis believes that muxe participation in Church was encouraged several years ago by his predecessor, Father Pancho, who spoke with the muxes and encouraged them to participate. Father Pancho asked them to select a patron saint for their Mass, and surprisingly, they selected the Virgen de la Asunción, whose feast day is celebrated on August 15. He is not sure why they selected La Virgen, but they apparently felt some affinity toward her.

As far as social problems are concerned, Father Luis believes that people have a lot of pride and identified closely with their various groups. He saw no shortage of leaders, as everyone was president of this or that group. I sensed that Father Luis felt there were "Too many chiefs and not enough Indians," although these were not the words he used.[8] He thought this situation was good but sometimes led to intergroup conflicts and antagonisms, so that people were afraid to go into la séptima sección, for example. Here, there were gangs and intergroup conflicts. He mentioned a recent incident in which a man was found with his throat slit, his arms and legs amputated, and a note on the body. He did not elaborate on what the note said, but it appeared to be a warning to others, and someone was taking credit for the murder. Presumably it reflected tension between one section of the city and another. Alcohol and drugs are other problems, as is domestic violence. Father Luis affirmed that he hears about these things in the confessional.

Like Carlos Garcia Bustamante, Father Luis doesn't believe there is an Isthmus matriarchy, although women play an important role in the economy, and this creates the impression that men don't work and lay around sleeping in a hammock all day. The problem is that one never sees the men working because they get up early in the morning to go fishing, cut wood, or work in the fields and are home by 8:00 or 9:00 in the morning. Women control the market and are more visible, selling fish, wood, or other products. He saw their roles more as a division of labor that is interrelated and interdependent. Father Luis expressed this eloquently. I thanked him for his time and for sharing his thoughts and said good-bye.

## FATHER PANCHO

I had interviewed Father Pancho, Father Luis's predecessor, during my first visit to Juchitán. In reflecting on the Mass on the day of the vela, I was surprised not only that the local Catholic Church was so welcoming of the muxes but that they were a part of a Mass, like other groups. This was another example that reflected their acceptance and integration into the community. When I interviewed Father Pancho, who is credited with working to integrate the muxes into the Church, he told me that the muxes were a part of the community and accepted like everyone else. Near the end of the interview, however, he did admonish that sodomy was prohibited, and a sin, making reference to the book of Leviticus. This revealed a contradiction in that while he accepted muxes and held a Mass to bless them, he believed that sodomy was still forbidden in the Bible. In other words, it suggested that he accepted them as God's children but could not accept the practice of sodomy. This is reminiscent of the attitude of early friars like Sahagún who sought to convert the Indians and bring them into the Church but condemned the practice of the abominable sin of sodomy.

## VIEWS OF ORDINARY CITIZENS ON MUXES

The foregoing interviews with teachers, two muxe fathers, a government official, the CONALEP administrator, and two priests have provided views of the acceptance of muxes among some key community members and social notables. The following set of interviews adds the views of ordinary citizens, including younger respondents, students, housewives, visitors to Juchitán, food vendors, and finally, a memorable interview with two muxes from the nearby town of Unión Hidalgo, whom I interviewed while they were surrounded by their relatives on a relaxing Sunday afternoon.

## DAVÍD, THE BODY BUILDER

I've often had to improvise and interview people as the opportunity arises because many interviewees missed their appointments. I found a gym for morning workouts where I met a trainer named Davíd. Davíd is eighteen, about five foot seven, and he obviously works out regularly and is a body builder. He helped me with my workouts, and I was able to talk to him every day and ask questions about the community and attitudes toward muxes, particularly among youth. It may not have seemed like I was interviewing him, but I was. Davíd asked me questions about what I do and why I was studying the muxes. I told him I was writing a book and how many I'd written.

Davíd is the oldest of three children. The middle child is a girl and the youngest a boy. He said that both parents have equal say in the family: "y que ni uno ni el otro manda." He is from la octava sección, and his father sells huaraches in the market; his mother and grandmother also help out in the business. Their puesto is located on the second floor of the mercado at the top of the stairs. It was ironic that they owned it because I had been to that puesto looking unsuccessfully for huaraches.

Davíd is studying at the CONALEP and eventually wants to study *nutrición*. He seems to be calm, self-assured, and confident but pleasant. He wore a shirt one day that read in Spanish on the back, "Self-confidence is the key to success in life," or words to that effect.

According to Davíd, muxes are so generally accepted in Juchitán that you never point your finger at someone disdainfully and say, "Hay va un muxe." (There goes a muxe.) On the other hand, students do tease them at school. He agreed that there were men who have sex with muxes, "pero normalmente es por dinero" (but it's usually for money). Those who do it for money are called mayates. I asked whether there were men who had sex with muxes and were also their partners, or novios. He responded, "A, sí, pero esos sí son tachados. Son bisexuales." (Oh yes, but those people are rejected. They are bisexual.)[9] Davíd told me that he has a good friend who pays to have sex with a muxe, which is rare. He doesn't bring it up to him or point his finger at him, but Davíd doesn't think it's acceptable to do that.

I asked if there was a difference between being gay and being muxe. Like Ricardo and others, he said there was a class difference, so that if you were of a higher class, you would say you were gay, but if you were lower class, you would be a puto, faggot, or muxe. I am not sure he grasped what I meant, but I understood his point, and I decided to keep probing and ask more questions in the next few days.

In a subsequent conversation, Davíd said that mayates who partnered with gays were more *catrines* (dandies), dressing up in a suit and tie and looking really good, whereas those who were with muxes were more working class and more likely to be *marijuanas o pandilleros* (potheads or gangbangers). They had sex with muxes to support their habit. He saw economics as a major motivator for mayates to get involved with muxes, particularly for poor, working-class youth.

When asked if his father would have a hard time accepting a muxe son, he reflected thoughtfully, then said, "Sí sería difícil como cualquiera." (Yes, it would be difficult, just like it would be for anyone else.) Davíd has muxe friends and eventually put me in touch with Mario, who was in fact gay and did not identify as muxe (see chapter 3).

## ROLÁN, ANOTHER PERSONAL TRAINER

On another trip to Juchitán, I went to work out in the morning and learned that Davíd was no longer working at the gym. Rolán, the new trainer at the gym, greeted me and asked whether Davíd had gotten a hold of me. I told him that Davíd had found me at the Hotel Central and thanked him for telling Davíd where I was staying. In my workouts with Rolán, I found that he would answer questions but was not as proactive about coaching me during workouts as Davíd or as forthcoming about his views. As I got to know him, though, I found him to be more responsive.

Rolán is nineteen years old and is studying computer programming at El Tecnológico. His father works for CEMEX, a cement distributor, and his mother is a secretary in the government building. He has fourteen-year-old twin brothers. When asked who controls the household, he said with a wry smile, "En la casa, mi mamá manda. Es por su carácter." (In my house, my mother rules. It's in her nature.) His father respects his mother a great deal and readily defers to her. Rolán has friends who are muxe, but there are no muxes in his family, although he acknowledged that there are many muxes in la séptima sección, where he's from. He doesn't see his father as a machista, although he is strong. His father respects women, and Rolán believes he would eventually accept a son who was muxe.

Rolán has friends who are mayates, and he accepts them. Some just do it for the money, others like it, and some have sex with a lot of different muxes. He added, "El termino [mayate] se usa como para burlar." (The term [mayate] is sometimes used to tease people.) As to why it's more accepted in Juchitán in general and la séptima sección in particular, he wasn't sure, except that, "La gente es muy tolerante, aquí. No juzgan a la gente que es diferente." (People are very tolerant here and don't judge people who are different.) Muxes have more rights and are not as discriminated against as they are elsewhere.

When I probed about the difference between gays and muxes, he said he didn't see any difference but wanted to know what I thought, so I told him what I had heard from a couple of gays I had interviewed. He asked if there was a distinction between a travestí and a muxe, and I said that some men cross-dressed but were not gay. He wanted to know about cultural differences between México and the United States, and I said that the family was more important in México, with more respect for parents. I took his asking me questions as a sign of rapport and respect, but he also seemed genuinely interested. Rolán reinforced the view that muxes were commonly accepted in the poorer and more indigenous sectors of Juchitán.

## LAS TRES AMIGAS

On another occasion, I had gone to Felina's for a scheduled interview with Francisco (Franki), but it was closed when I arrived. I was a bit early, and while I was waiting for my interview, a group of three girls and a boy were also waiting. They asked if I was waiting for Felina, and I told them that I wasn't. They were apparently volunteering for an event on Sunday to promote safe sex in the community and were scheduled to help by passing out condoms in front of the municipal palace.

The young people, three girls and a boy, whom I termed Las Tres Amigas, were horsing around and although I was initially reluctant to engage them, I asked if I could ask them a few questions. They were all fifteen-year-old prepa students and understandably apprehensive at first, wanting to know what the questions were about. I explained that I was a sociologist, that I had been interviewing muxes, and was interested in how they were perceived and treated in Juchitán.

Las Tres Amigas agreed that muxes were accepted but giggled when I asked if they had any friends who were muxes. They said, "Yes," they knew some, and they were accepted. They have friends who are muxe and accepted by their peers. The boy, Carlos, and one of the girls, Rosita, didn't say much. But Carolina, who stood near the front of the group and appeared to be the informal leader and spokesperson, answered most of my questions. Juanita, a girl in the back, seemed especially interested and attentive but was quiet and reticent. The young people were less positive when I mentioned mayates because they were not as accepted as muxes. One thing that concerned them about mayates was that if they had a sexually transmitted disease, they could transmit to it to a woman. Carolina was the most vocal and animated about this.

She volunteered to me that Juanita had a brother who was muxe. Juanita hadn't said much, but I asked how old her brother was. She said that he was twelve. When asked if he was accepted, she said no, not by her father. Her father did not accept him and beat him with the hope that he would change. I wanted to talk more with them, but Franki showed up for his interview (see chapter 3). I was glad to see him but sorry I had to cut this spontaneous youth "focus group" interview short. I thanked Las Tres Amigas for their time and said good-bye.

## MIGUEL, PREPA STUDENT

When I ran into Miguel, he was leaning against a car, relaxing as if he was waiting for someone. He was seventeen, thin, about five foot six and had brown skin and somewhat light eyes. I found him to be personable, articulate, and engaging. He is from la octava sección and proudly told me, "no solamente hablo Zapoteco pero lo canto." (I not only speak Zapoteco, but sing in it.) He acknowledged that the Zapoteco language is starting to be lost in his barrio but is most maintained in la séptima, novena, octava, and quinta. Muxes are very accepted in Juchitán. He doesn't know why they are more accepted in Juchitán but thinks it must be linked to Zapotec culture. Muxes are still widely accepted across different secciones.

Like other young people, he has friends who are muxe. They invite him to their velas, and he goes with them. Muxes get along very well with women and tease you like women, he said. He then made a hissing sound like Zapotec women make when they are teasing someone. Mayates are also accepted.

Uno no va y dice, "Yo soy mayate" pero luego, luego se nota. No lo pueden esconder. El muxe tiene un interés económico. Lo que pasa es que cada muxe tiene dos o tres mayates. Escogen a los más jovencitos, los mas pollitos y les compran este regalito o otra cosa y poco a poco los convencen.

[One doesn't go around saying, "I am a mayate," but it is immediately obvious. Muxes have an economic interest. What happens is that each muxe has two or three mayates. They select the youngest (boys) and most vulnerable ones and they buy them a little gift or something else and little by little they convince them (to have sex).]

Miguel believes that poorer youth are more vulnerable because they have more of an economic interest and need. He gave an example based on what he saw on his soccer team last year. The coach was muxe and had two or three team members that he seduced who were young and poor, and he made them into mayates.

He thought the difference between a muxe and a gay is muxes are more open, out of the closet, and dress like women, whereas gays are still in the closet. He also believes, as did other respondents, that gays are "gente con más recursos de la alta sociedad" (people with more money and from a higher stratum of society).

## LOS COMPADRES: EUGENIO Y JOSÉ LUIS

I was at the plaza downtown one day and decided to improvise and strike up a discussion with two middle-aged men. Eugenio appeared to be in his mid to late fifties and was from Salina Cruz, while José Luis was sixty-two and from Tehuantepec. The latter had a moustache and a stocky build. He looked athletic and was wearing three-quarter-length plastic workout pants, a windbreaker, and a baseball cap. The other one, Eugenio, was of average height and weight, perhaps a bit thin, and was less athletic looking. In talking to them, I found José Luis more urbane and sophisticated than Eugenio.

They were sitting on a bench in the middle of the Plaza Principal in front of the kiosko. I walked up, sat down next to Eugenio, and introduced myself. I told him that I was from California, un profesór y sociólogo. Eugenio leaned over toward José Luis with a puzzled look on his face, held up his hands and asked, "¿Qué es un sociólogo?" José Luis gave a pretty good explanation that a sociologist is a person who studies society and how it affects people. Eugenio works for Pemex, and José Luis is a physical therapist who works with sports injuries.

I asked whether muxes were accepted in El Istmo, and they both responded that muxes are more accepted and open in Juchitán than they are in other places. They are not as open in their towns of Salina Cruz and Tehuantepec. José Luis was more responsive, articulate, and politically correct. When I asked about the muxes, Eugenio said, "O, sí los putos" (Oh yeah, the queers, or faggots).

I found it very interesting that they each have muxes in their respective families. Eugenio has a maternal uncle whose son is muxe. His cousin is a güero and was born with blonde hair and light eyes. He said that the boy lives at home and is generally accepted. His family took in a shaman from Guatemala who is muxe, and he and the boy both live there with his uncle. I am not certain, but it appeared that the shaman was brought in, perhaps to treat the son, but was still living with them. They agreed that muxes are more accepted now than they were in their day. José Luis was born in 1951, and in his day, people were not as open about being gay. José Luis and Eugenio linked it to changing times and modernity, and José Luis said, "Who would have thought back then that men would be wearing earrings or have long hair?"

Neither of them knew how they would react if they had a muxe son. Their children are married and grown up. José Luis has a son who is thirty-three, married, and has children, but speaking frankly, he believes he would have had a hard time accepting it. José Luis said that when his son plays fútbol with his buddies, they engage in homosexual joking among friends, but that's just within their own group.

I asked whether mayates were accepted, and they shook their heads and said, "¡Eso, no!" (No, that's not acceptable!) Eugenio agreed with the prepa students that the problem with them is that "Luego, se acuestan con las mujeres, y transmiten la sida." (Then they turn around and sleep with women and give them AIDS.) I asked if they knew any mayates, and they said that they did. José Luis also confided man to man that on a couple of occasions, when he was very young and crazy, he had had sex with a muxe, assuming the activo role.

Gesturing toward his genitals, he said that once he even hurt his foreskin, and that it was very painful.

Although this was an informal discussion and impromptu encuentro, it went very well. I found these two men to be surprisingly candid, receptive, co-operative, and sincere. I was amazed that they would confide like this with a complete stranger. At the start of the interview, Eugenio asked whether I was Mexicano o Norte Americano. I answered that I was Mexicano but lived in the United States. He seemed to approve but asked whether I spoke English, and I said that I knew it better than Spanish. At the end of the interview, Eugenio asked for my telephone number and e-mail address so that he could contact me in case he ever decided to pay a visit to the United States.

## CRISTEN, THE SECURITY GUARD

I met Cristen, a young man, in front of El Restaurante Internacional, where he works as the security guard. I had greeted him a number of times before but had never stopped to chat. Cristen was wearing dark blue pants; a shirt that looked like a police uniform, with the name of the restaurant above the left pocket; and combat boots.

Cristen was born and raised in Juchitán but attended only secundaria, be-cause he had to work and could not go on to prepa. He got married at age fif-teen, but it didn't work out, and he is now divorced. His father is deceased, and his mother is a housewife, who supports herself with the help of her adult chil-dren. Cristen is nineteen and the youngest of four children. He has a brother who is twenty-one, a sister who is twenty-two, and another brother who is twenty-six or twenty-seven. His father was a *marinero* (sailor) in the Mexican navy and was very machista and a mujeriego (womanizer).

Cristen believes that his parents would have to accept it if they had a child who was muxe. He has two uncles who are muxes on his father's side, so he thinks they would accept a muxe child because there are muxes in the family. He stressed that the family would just want to make sure that the muxe lifestyle was a voluntary choice and that someone else wasn't coercing him into being one.

Cristen added that muxes are widely accepted in Juchitán. They have their own vela, and a lot of people come to the vela from all over the world. There were muxes in his school, and some young people did make fun of them, but they are largely accepted. He has friends who have had sex with muxes. They don't talk about it much, except with their intimate friends. I asked Cristen if he had ever had sex with a muxe, and he said, "Sí, una vez." (Yes, once.) When asked who initiated it, he said he was only fourteen, and that it was mutual. I ended the interview, but I saw and greeted Cristen virtually every day as I walked past the restaurant.

## BETTIE, THE HAIR STYLIST FROM QUINTANA ROO

I approached a woman outside of Felina's who was waiting for a ride. She appeared to be in her twenties, but when I got closer, she looked like she was in her thirties. Bettie was born in Juchitán but has been away for about twelve years. She lives in Quintana Roo and was visiting here. She has three children, two boys and a girl, ages twelve, ten, and two. Bettie is a hair stylist who knows Felina.

With regard to the muxes, she believes they are very much accepted and feels, as many others do, that it is because "they are very hard working and help out a lot in the family. Sometimes they help even more than women." She has not seen any muxes in Quintana Roo. She is sure they exist, but they are much less visible. Bettie said that if she had a muxe child, she would probably be disappointed at first but eventually would have to accept the child because it would be her child and you have to accept them.

## LORENA, LA ELOTERA

I spent a lot of time walking around the principal plaza and stopped one evening to speak to a young woman who was selling elotes (corn on the cob). It was cold and windy, something I hadn't experienced in Juchitán before, so I wore a light jacket for the first time. People were wearing coats and jackets as though they lived in North Dakota or Alaska, especially the kids at CONALEP. Because of the weather, I felt like eating elote.

Lorena is twenty-eight years old and one of three sisters. Her mother has a puesto across the street in the main plaza and also sells elotes, and her father is a chauffeur who works at the presidential palace. She said that muxes are very much accepted in Juchitán and have their vela in November. But people do tease them quite a bit, especially in secundaria and prepa. Lorena has friends who are muxe.

It's pretty common for young men to have sex with muxes, referring to them as mayates. Many mayates also have girlfriends and a muxe on the side. They have relations with the muxes, but they are discreet about it. It's at the velas that you really find out who is with whom. If the girlfriend finds out about the muxe, the relationship will end, because the girls will not put up with it.

I asked Lorena whether she thinks her father would have accepted a muxe child, and she answered, "¿Mi papá? No, porque mi papá es muy machista." (My father? No, he would not accept him because he is very macho.) She felt this would be true especially if he were the only boy, since all of his other children are girls.

## KRISTÁL, JACKI, Y FAMILIA

Realizing that today, Sunday, would be the last day of this particular trip, and I had to leave in the morning, I decided to call Kristál to ask if we could change her interview from tomorrow morning to today. The appointment was scheduled in Juchitán, but she asked if I could come to Unión Hidalgo. I was reluctant to go because it was about thirty-five minutes from Juchitán and because I had been stood up for so many interviews. I didn't want to repeat what had happened the day I went all the way to Tehuantepec only to have an interviewee not show or answer his cell phone.

It was about 2:00 in the afternoon, but I agreed to go. I took a colectivo to El Mercadito and then a green second-class bus to Unión Hidalgo. Kristál assumed I had a cell phone, which I did not, and told me to call her when I got to the terminal and she would come get me. I arrived at about 3:00 p.m. The bus depot is an abandoned dirt parking lot, and there were no phones to be found, so thinking on my feet, I got the idea of asking a moto-taxi driver, who often know muxes, if he knew a muxe named Kristál who owned a bar. He pointed straight ahead and said she was only about four blocks away. I decided to take the moto-taxi and pay the five pesos so that I would be sure to find her house.

The driver directed me to a yellow-colored bar just off the corner, with a red Corona beer sign and emblem painted on the side of the building. Although I could hear Mexican ranchero music from inside the bar, there were two large locks on the gates, and no one was in sight. I repeatedly banged on the middle gate, but no one responded, so I started yelling to see if someone would hear me. It looked like everyone in town knew everyone else, or that Kristál, at least, is well known, because a woman yelled out loudly to me from a house halfway down the block, "¡Está acá!" (She's over here!) I turned and started walking toward the woman and was greeted by two menacing dogs that she promptly calmed. She yelled out that one of the dogs was pregnant and was feeling very protective. "Está atrás" (She's in the back), she said. As I walked around, I was greeted by a young blonde wearing a white blouse and mini jean shorts. I thought it was Kristál, but it was Jacki, and she directed me to Kristál.

I got to the backyard and was greeted by Kristál, her aunt Isabét, uncle Gonzalo, and cousin Nelson, as well as Jacki. They were sitting around an outdoor table drinking beer, eating *botanas* (appetizers), and laughing raucously, the way people laugh when they've been drinking and partying for a long time. I told them that I felt like I'd won the lottery ("¡Me saqué la lotería!") because I had been playing phone tag with both of them for the past few days, and here they were, together! Jacki had in fact not shown for an appointment the previous week.

I had met both of them at a recent vela and gotten their respective telephone numbers, but when I had called Jacki, Kristál had answered. It now all began to make sense because Kristál owns the bar, Jacki works there, and they are childhood friends. I explained my purpose, and when I said I was doing research on the muxes, they laughed and said, "Well, you came to the right place." The aunt jokingly added, "Aquí tenemos de todo—muxes, gay, lesbiana, lo que quiera." (We have a little bit of everything here—muxes, gays, lesbians, whatever you like.) As I turned on my tape to record, Kristál commented, "O, es como la entrevista en que nos juntaron para el documental." (Oh, this is like the interview where they gathered us all for a documentary.)

I have to say at the outset that this interview was a gold mine and became more like a spontaneous focus group session. I was interested in finding out how muxes were accepted by their families and the community, and here they were, not only Jacki but Kristál, her tíos, a primo, all of them in a festive mood, a bit tipsy and more than eager to talk.

Kristál was wearing a jean skirt and a white sleeveless tee shirt. She was sitting down and was quite large, with meaty arms. Her hair was short, dyed bright red and combed straight back in a unisex wet-look style. She was boisterous and very expressive, exactly like the image one would have of a rough-and-tumble woman who runs a bawdy bar. Jacki was quieter and more inebriated. She sat on a deck chair that was low to the ground, sometimes closing her eyes and making an occasional comment, but laughing and joining in the talk. She is darker than Kristál and has short, blonde curly hair. Cousin Nelson looked to be in his mid to late thirties, was clean-shaven, and sat at a rectangular table to the left of Kristál. He was very sociable and served as a sort of intermediary, attempting to explain various things about the community. The aunt, Isabét, was sitting at another small rectangular table across from Kristál. She looked to be about fifty, was dressed in a jean skirt and blouse, and wore glasses. Uncle Gonzalo sat to the left of his wife, and also looked about fifty. He wore a baseball cap and glasses and had a moustache. He was more quiet and reserved but seemed very self-assured. I sat on a chair with Jacki to my immediate left, who in turn sat next to Kristál.

Kristál and Jacki were both born and raised in Unión Hidalgo. I didn't ask, but they looked to be about thirty years old. Kristál's father is in la marina (the navy) and her mother is a housewife. Kristál has known that she was muxe "desde que he sido consciente de razón" (ever since I can remember). When asked how she was treated by her peers, Kristál said she led a very normal childhood, just like anyone else. She lived a normal childhood, that is, until she went to El Norte (the United States) when she was about seventeen or eighteen. When she returned, she started to cut loose and let her hair down. She said this in a very animated, excited, celebratory tone. She had lived in Arizona, and it was there that she had really cut loose. I asked what she did there, and she answered, "We cleaned office buildings at night."

When asked about her first sexual experience, Kristál got all animated and excited and gave me a second look, sort of like saying, "Man, this is going to get interesting." The piñatero had responded in a similar way (see chapter 3). I felt a mixture of excitement and trepidation because I was venturing into something that is very personal and that one does not generally share publicly. It reminded me of the film *Sex, Lies, and Videotape,* because here I was, a perfect stranger, very calmly and coolly prying into their respective sex lives. Although they were initially surprised by the question, they were not at all reluctant to respond. Kristál looked to the side of the house, pointed, and said, "Fué bajo de un gotero." (It was under a rain gutter.) She said this in a very nostalgic way, as though she had pleasant memories of her first sexual experience. She had liked it. She had been twenty, and he had been twenty-eight. Juan Gómez (pseudonym) was someone from the neighborhood, and un hombre.

I continued and asked, "¿Y cómo fue?" The syntax of my question may have been grammatically incorrect. I meant to ask how it had happened to take place, but she took it to literally mean "How was the sex?" She laughed and said, "¡Fué estupendo!" (It was great!) Her first sexual encounter was thus consensual, very positive, and apparently occurred not long after she had returned from Arizona.

Her response also reminded me of Biiniza's first sexual encounter with a high school boy, which she had described as "beautiful."

Jacki's father was an obrero and her mother, a housewife. Her first sexual experience was when she was eleven. The boy was eighteen. When I again asked, "¿Y cómo fue?" they laughed because it sounded like I was asking again whether the sex was good when I was asking how it happened that they had had sex. Jacki then proceeded to illustrate the literal meaning. She got up from her chair, simulated the anal sex position by getting down on her hands and knees and raised her rear end up in the air as if she were the recipient. She then explained that it was by mutual consent and that she had liked it because it was a pleasant experience. But she also related that two boys had raped her at age eleven, which had been a negative, traumatic experience.

When I asked, "¿Y cómo se ve al mayate?" (How are mayates viewed?), they all said, "Bien" (Fine), except for the tía. Kristál's aunt asked me in a challenging tone, "¿Bueno y qué es un mayate? ¿Cómo lo define usted?" (Well, and what is a mayate? How do you define it?) I was taken aback by the question and responded, "I don't know. I'm asking the questions and don't have a definition. How do *you* define it? That's what matters." The sense that I got from the ensuing discussion was that she saw mayates as men who have sex for money, but that there are men who have sex with muxes who don't do it for money, and she wanted to differentiate between them. Nelson interceded and admitted that he had had sex with some muxes, strongly implying that he had had sex with Jacki, and this seemed normal to him.

When asked how muxes are accepted in Unión Hidalgo, they all agreed that it was very common here and that they were accepted. La tía reiterated, "Aquí hay de todo." (We've got everything here.) She mentioned an uncle who is very respectable and not at all effeminate until he's had too much to drink. Then his feminine tendencies come out, but only when he drinks. Isabét added that some people's nature is just that way, although they may try to mask it. "Unos nacen, y otros se hacen." (Some are born that way, and others become that way.) Kristál responded that yes, that might be true, but she was a firm believer that people are born muxe. She also didn't buy the idea that some people turned gay because they were molested. You either were born that way or you weren't.

We talked about the various muxe groups. They said that there are several. The major one is Las Intrépidas, then Baile Conmigo, and another one that had held a vela the previous weekend. Unión Hidalgo has two muxe velas with the major one on July 19. Kristál said that velas are divided by social class, and that the *ricas* (wealthy muxes) had their fancy vela with many dignitaries attending. Interestingly, the larger and better organized vela is the one that the poor muxes host. We socialized for a while, then I thanked them for their time and left, taking a colectivo back to Juchitán.

# 6

# TWO-SPIRIT MUXE ZAPOTEC IDENTITY

Two-Spirit *affirmed their [Native] belonging to cultural traditions by displacing anthropological terms and—notably* berdache—*setting a new basis and method for indigenous knowledge. After the term's proposal, scholars writing from within non-Native intellectual histories tended to understand that* Two-Spirit *replaced* berdache, *but most tended to miss how the term massively shifted the bases of knowledge production by interrupting anthropological authority to define Indigenous truth.*

QWO-LI DRISKILL, CHRIS FINLEY, BRIAN JOSEPH GILLEY,
AND SCOTT LAURIA MORGENSEN (2011, 10)

THE QUOTATION ABOVE refers to a conference held in 1993 and 1994 and two workshops sponsored by the American Anthropological Association and the Wenner-Gren Foundation, which brought together Two-Spirit organizers and anthropologists to reexamine anthropological writing on the berdache. The workshops resulted in the 1997 publication of *Two-Spirit People: Native American Gender Identity, Sexuality, and Spirituality* (Jacobs, Thomas, and Lang 1997). While *Two-Spirit People* brought together academic and Native activists and resulted in non-Native contributors discarding the term "berdache" in favor of "two-spirit," it failed to integrate an indigenous methodology and theory into the work.

Despite *Two-Spirit People* questioning anthropological authority over indigenous people, its format seemed to reproduce it, in that the opening and closing sections highlighted non-Native anthropologists doing academic theory, while most interventions by Two-Spirit people appeared in between or were bracketed as personal narratives rather than as scholarship. (Driskill, Finley, et al. 2011, 13)

While the Two-Spirit People conference failed to establish a clear break with hegemonic Western conceptions of the berdache, it did set the stage for subsequent two-spirit writing and scholarship that sought to decolonize queer and third-gender indigenous research and theory.[1]

In this chapter I explore the concept of two-spirit and the phenomenon of the berdache among North American Native groups. Although the muxes of Juchitán are a unique Zapotec sexual/cultural system, they have more in common with, and might be better understood by examining them within, indigenous traditions rather than through the Western gender binary.

Two-spirit, or "two-spirited," is an English term that refers to gender constructions and roles that occur in many indigenous communities outside the Western gender binary as well as to Native people who are now reclaiming and redefining these roles within their respective communities (Driskill, Justice, et al. 2011, 4). Just as two-spirit shifted the bases of knowledge production by challenging anthropological authority to define indigenous truth, so does the term "muxe" shift the focus of analysis from external nonindigenous traditions to Zapotec conceptions of a third gender that is neither male nor female but muxe, and proudly Zapotec.

Although distinct from two-spirit North American indigenous groups, muxes in El Istmo de Tehuantepec self-identify and are recognized by the community as having a separate and distinct third-gender category and status.[2] In the previous chapter, Florencio Mendoza, the retired Zapotec teacher, described muxes as "una cultura," or as a separate culture. Another Zapotec teacher, José Abél Acevedo, agreed that muxes are accepted by everyone in the society and believes they have ancient origins in Zapotec culture. He and Bettie, a mother and hair stylist, defined "muxe" as a Zapoteco word that means someone who is biologically male but has the social characteristics of a woman. Although biologically male, muxes see themselves and are seen by others as being neither male nor female, but muxe. Finally, muxes identify with women, or lo femenino, and distinguish themselves from gays in that their sexual partners are "hombres," rather than other muxes or gay men.

This discussion seeks to extend the analysis of the findings of this study by placing muxes within a global theoretical context that draws parallels between anthropological writings on the berdache among North American Indian communities and academic and journalistic accounts of the muxe experience. It also addresses the need to link the muxe experience to indigenous configurations of sexual identity and behavior. I argue, in other words, that Zapotecs have developed a particular system of gender categories and lifestyles that, while similar in some respects to two-spirit and other third-gender systems elsewhere, retains it own internal logic and distinctiveness.

## ANTHROPOLOGICAL AND HISTORICAL DESCRIPTIONS OF THE BERDACHE

Faced with gender nonconforming males among numerous Native American communities, early anthropologists settled on the term "berdache," a variation of *bardaje*, which was used by French explorers to signify a boy kept for unnatural purposes (Roscoe 1991, 5). The berdache tradition shaped two streams of academic writing in the twentieth century (Driskill, Finley, et al. 2011, 11). The term was first used in the early part of the twentieth century to examine "deviant" sexual practices, "notably among gender-transitive males who had sexual and domestic relations with men in tribal societies" (2011, 11). Berdaches were first seen as "failed" or incomplete men and women who had weird desires or could not conform to the norms of their gender (Blackwood 1997, 284). Anthropologists in turn extrapolated from the berdache experience in Native American tribes to explain contemporary social roles in society worldwide (Driskill, Finley, et al. 2011, 11).

The status of the berdache was reexamined once again in the 1980s in response to feminist interventions when anthropologists began to call into question conventional constructions of gender and sexuality (Driskill, Finley, et al. 2011, 11). In short, anthropologists like Harriet Whitehead (1981) and Charles Callender and Lee Kochems (1986) focused on the berdache and "became concerned with discovering the reasons why American Indians had 'tolerated' same-sex sexuality and gender variance while Euro-Americans remained hostile, misogynist, and heterosexist" (Driskill, Finley, et al. 2011, 11). This suggests parallels of the view Europeans had of New World sexuality and, specifically, the hostile view Cortés and the friars that accompanied him had of the practice of sodomy (see chapter 2).

Those in the anthropology of the berdache tradition also noted that while berdaches were generally recognized as biological males, they became women in a social sense by assuming the dress and the work of women, and by preferring the tools of the female trades (Callender and Kochems 1986, 169–71). These "gender crossers" often donned women's clothes and assumed female duties like basket weaving and acorn pounding (Kroeber 1925, 46; Fletcher and La Flesche [1911] 1972, 132), or spontaneously adopted female speech patterns (Whitehead 1981, 88). The muxes of Juchitán are similarly "gender crossers," who often dress in women's clothing and assume female voices and duties and/or work that is specifically designated for muxes.

Because the cross-gendering person was anatomically a man and socially a woman, many American Indian groups saw the berdache as a mixed creature, as a "woman-man," part man and part woman, or a third sex or gender (Whitehead 1981, 88). Not surprisingly, the berdaches not only assumed specific roles with specialized duties, but were also often imbued with special powers since they could assume the tasks of men or women. Among the Yokuts, for example, berdaches were corpse handlers, whereas among other groups, they tended to the ill and carried provisions for war parties (Whitehead 1981, 89).

Although the berdache were found among many North American Indian groups, in looking at same-sex relations cross-culturally, anthropologists have also noted the importance of distinguishing between behaviors that are institutionally and normatively accepted and those that may occur spontaneously but are not accepted. In a classic article, Harriet Whitehead observed that "cultural processes (and psychological ones as well) operate in quite different fashion in behaviors that are formally instituted as opposed to those that are spontaneously expressed" (1981, 81–82). Although data on spontaneous same-sex expression are limited, the rate of its expression appears to be independent of its societal acceptance and may be high in places where it is condemned, as in the United States, or low where it is accepted, as among Trobriand Islanders (81).

Societal acceptance, in turn, will undoubtedly influence identity, self-esteem, and interiority. In contrast to the New Guinea belief that "manhood" is contained in semen, so that a boy was believed to become a man through sexual intercourse with older men (Herdt 1984), in the anthropology of the berdache tradition, scholars like Whitehead noted that among many indigenous groups of North America, it was possible for a man to become, in socially important respects, a woman. Male-to-female cross-gendering, which generally took the form of biological males dressing and assuming the tasks of women, has been much more prevalent than female to male cross-gender transitions (Lang 1998, 261) and was frequently reported by early travelers, missionaries, and anthropologists (Whitehead 1981, 85; Katz 1976, 29). According to Whitehead, gender crossing was the practice of the person of one "anatomic sex assuming part or most of the attire, occupation, and social—including marital—status of the opposite sex for an indeterminate period" (1981, 85). There is also evidence that berdaches were highly respected by Indian communities (Greenberg 1986, 180).

Much like muxes, berdaches' most common way of transitioning was through exhibiting behaviors or characteristics of the opposite sex at an early age. Parents and relatives invariably reported observing feminine characteristics in a young boy. Gender-crossing behaviors might also be indicated by dreams or visions. Less common was the practice of a person being taken captive, integrated into the household of a captor, and assuming the status of "wife" socially and sexually (Whitehead 1981, 86).

One of the harshest academic critiques of the berdache tradition is provided by historian Ramón Gutiérrez (2007), who focuses specifically on accounts of American Indian men in the Southwest. Gutiérrez notes that a number of historians and anthropologists were fascinated by the discovery of the berdache and saw it potentially as a path, if not to gay liberation, at least to greater societal tolerance for gender-variant individuals (2007, 19). When Spanish soldiers and missionaries first saw Native American men performing women's work, dressed as women, and offering receptive sexual services to men, they were quick to link this phenomenon to the *bardaje*, a word derived from the Arabic term *berdaj*, which referred to a male prostitute (2007, 20; see the conclusion, this volume).

One of the first accounts was found in the narratives of Alvar Nuñez Cabeza de Vaca, a survivor of the ill-fated Narváez expedition off the Florida coast in 1528. In 1536 he observed that when he came across the three lone survivors of the expedition, "I saw a wicked behavior [*diablura*] and it is that I saw one man married [*casado*] to another, and these are effeminate impotent men. . . . And they go about covered like women, and they perform the tasks of women, and they do not use a bow, and they carry very great loads" (Gutiérrez 2007, 21). After Nuñez Cabeza de Vaca's account was published in Spain, it became the primary source for Francisco López de Gómara's *Historia general de las Indias* ([1552] 1954; see chapter 2, this volume).

After examining evidence on the history of the berdache tradition, Gutiérrez concludes that in México's north and in what was to become the American Southwest, the bardaje was not a culturally celebrated and permissive status that encompassed both the masculine and the feminine but a status of subordination and humiliation that individuals were forced to accept (2007, 26). He adds, "Conquest narratives, travelers' accounts, and ethnographies indicate that the social status of the berdache had meaning primarily in the sociopolitical world of men," and the berdache were said to be under male ownership (27). Gutiérrez concludes by noting that a universal representation of conquest is the victors asserting their virility and dominance by transforming the losers into effeminates (27).

Contrary to Gutiérrez's negative depiction of the anthropology and history of the bardaje tradition, anthropologists have long observed that acceptance of same-sex social and sexual relations was widely reported among North American Indian communities within every type of social and economic organization (Roscoe 1991, 24). According to Will Roscoe, male and female berdaches (women assuming traditional male roles as warriors and chiefs or male work and occupations) have been documented in more than 130 North American tribes across the continent, ranging from Alaska to Florida, including the Pueblo Indians of Arizona, the Acoma, Hopi, Isleta, Laguna, Santa Ana, Santo Domingo, San Felipe, San Juan, Tesuque, and Zuni (1991, 5). Female-to-male berdaches were much less common and reported among a relatively small number of Native American groups (Lang 1998, 261).

In traditional Native societies, moreover, berdaches, like muxes, were accepted, integral, and valued members of their respective communities. European cultures, on the other hand, were incapable of adequately describing or understanding the place of berdaches in Indian society (Blackwood 1997, 285). The Zuni, for example, differentiated between sex and gender identity. Whereas sex was fixed at birth, gender involved an evolution from the original maternal common ground shared by males and females to adult roles (Roscoe 1991, 144).

Among the Zuni, a person's identity was never fixed but was situationally determined, as "[t]he social and religious experiences of both men and women modulated across a range of gender positions and identities" (1991, 144). Since men were technically not permitted to be present at a birth, for example, if a medicine man was summoned to assist at childbirth "he was temporarily referred to as grandmother" (144).

The Zuni *ihamanas*, or boys with female tendencies, underwent the first male initiation rite but not the second. The ihamana was seen as an incomplete, or "unfinished," male who could participate in certain male activities, like kachina dancing, men's work, and even farming, but not warfare and hunting, which were part of the second male initiation (Roscoe 1991, 144). Similarly, he could not undergo certain female rites of passage linked to biological functions he did not possess, but he did learn some women's lore and rituals when he joined female members in observing domestic rites. Thus, "[t]he Ihamana was, in functional terms, a nonwarrior or nonaggressive male, a crafts specialist rather than a primary producer, an individual who combined elements of male and female social, economic, and religious roles" (Roscoe 1991, 145). The mode of dress of the Zuni man-woman, We'wha, for example, was based more on social convention than on personal choice. As an unfinished male, he could not wear male symbols, but he was always recognized by his family and community as a male, as illustrated by the fact that he always wore pants beneath his dress (145).

The response to whether We'wha was viewed as a man or a woman was that, like the muxe, he was "neither." He represented a third-gender status, distinct from the gender status not only of men and women but also of transsexuals or transgender persons. "The man who becomes a woman contributes to society as a woman. But the berdache made unique contributions, as we have seen in the case of We'wha and . . . society [b]enefited by having three, instead of two, genders" (146). Having three genders as a reference point not only increased options geometrically for sexual identity and behavior but challenged the gender binary by making it possible to recognize various combinations of gender traits (146).

Whereas the Western gender binary is based on fixed biological conceptions of gender (Blackwood 1997, 285), the Zuni readily distinguished between being male biologically and "acting like a man." In their worldview, one's status as man, woman, or ihamana was the result of culture, and adopting the traits of more than one gender was a desirable trait for all Zuni. Members of this third gender "were considered an affirmation of humanity's original, pre-gendered unity—representatives of a form of solidarity and wholeness that transcended the division of humans into men and women. The third gender role was one of native North America's most striking social inventions" (Roscoe 1991, 146).

While Western cultures adhered to a sexual/gender dichotomy (Blackwood 1997, 285) and considered nonconforming behavior deviant and unwanted, indigenous cultures were more accepting of gender variations. Sabine Lang's 1998 work, *Men as Women, Women as Men* (translated from the German), for example, offers a comprehensive look at Native American cultures and finds that a third-gender status was institutionalized and that a radical departure between one's biological sex and one's chosen gender role was more readily accepted (Lang 1998, 219). Generally, the woman-man was believed to be "two-spirit" and to have been born with a dual nature; the two-spirit was accepted but such acceptance normally depended on some proof that the individual was in fact a man imbued with feminine tendencies. Proof that the individual was indeed a woman-man had to be demonstrated in tests such as the choice of objects during a berdache test or a dream or vision, and such tests varied from group to group. It was also not uncommon for a boy to be allowed to wait until puberty to decide whether he wanted to assume a feminine gender role. As with the muxes, fathers might attempt to force feminine sons to assume a masculine role, but ultimately the boy's decision to adopt the woman-man status was normally accepted once the child gave proof of his woman-man nature in a culturally accepted way. "Regardless of whether a dream or vision finally supported the change of gender role through a supernatural legitimation, an interest in activities and (often, but by no means always) clothing of the opposite sex often became noticeable during childhood" (219).

Table 1 identifies common characteristics shared by the Native American two-spirit person and the Zapotec muxe third gender. In Juchitán, especially in the poorer and more historically indigenous sections of the city, like la séptima sección, it is not unusual to see boys as young as eight or nine dressed in feminine attire. Similarly, if a boy among the Bella Coola and surrounding tribes demonstrated an unusual skill in performing women's tasks, the parents would conclude that he would prefer to be a girl and begin to dress him in feminine clothing and to treat him like a girl (Lang 1998, 219). Among the Omaha and Ponca, one could identify the *mixu'ga* during childhood because, like muxe children, they were constantly playing with girls (221).

In a small number of tribes, such as the Aleut, Kaniagmiut, Juaneño, Luseño, and probably among the Illinois, Yuma, and Zuni, the family played a significant part in gender role assignment and often assigned the feminine role to a boy shortly after birth. Rather than acquiring the status of woman or even girl, he acquired a unique status, such as *shupan* among the Aleut and Kaniagmiut (Lang 1998, 223). In other tribes, as in certain Zapotec families, the family affected the gender status of a child in that women-men preferably came from certain families or descent groups, as their relatives had supposedly also been women-men (223).

It thus appears that in many tribes, a boy's interest in feminine activities emerged and was often recognized in early childhood. Among the Kato, Pomo, Yuki, and Lassik, for example, men could make baskets without reflecting on their masculinity, but a boy who was a maker of fine baskets was suspected of having opposite-sex gender inclinations (Essene 1942, 65). One of the most interesting phenomenon observed across a number of Native American communities

TABLE 1. Similarities Between Two-Spirit and Muxe Third Gender

| TWO-SPIRIT | MUXE |
|---|---|
| Cross-gender identification in childhood | Cross-gender identification in childhood |
| Help with feminine tasks (acorn pounding, basket weaving) | Help with feminine tasks (household chores) |
| Gender evolution into puberty | Gender evolution into puberty |
| Expert at basket weaving | Excel in embroidery, dress making |
| Transition into third gender through rites of passage, visions, dreams, or tests and rituals | Transition into third gender through velas, quinceañeras |
| Don feminine dress | Don Zapotec feminine dress, makeup, and jewelry |
| Community recognition as incomplete, unfinished male, man-woman, woman-man | Socially recognized as muxe, not man or woman |

is that women-men were widely reported not only to assume feminine tasks but also to equal and often surpass women in the performance of such tasks (Lang 1998, 241). A popular explanation for this view is that women-men were generally perceived to be physically strong. Coalhuiltecan, for example, were highly valued for their strength as load carriers, and the Juaneño *kwit* and the Luseño *cuut* were considered to be especially robust housewives (241). The Zuni also viewed the ihamana as great helpers with household tasks because they did double the amount of work and performed the most physically demanding tasks (241). Muxes in Juchitán are similarly recognized, especially by mothers, for being household helpers, hard workers, and exceptional in the performance of women's tasks.

Not only were women-men recognized for their physical strength but they were also known for being great housewives (Lang 1998, 242). Crow *bate*, for example, were known for having the best and most beautiful tipis and were considered to be experts in handiwork and culinary arts (Simms 1903, 580). Like the muxes, women-men's superiority in handicrafts has been particularly stressed, perhaps because it requires a special talent over and above the diligence required for women's everyday activities (Lang 1998, 242).

Lang attributes the cultural importance placed on having women-men attain perfection in feminine occupations to the fact that there was no ritual to mark the transition to this status. Because there was generally no "public legitimation of his status enacted at a particular point in time, the woman-man had to legitimate his status continually, so that no doubt was cast on him or his status by the community" (246). Given that carrying out of women's tasks was considered the major distinguishing characteristic of the woman-man, perfecting feminine occupations served to legitimate and reinforce the woman-man's special status in the community. In Juchitán, muxes are similarly recognized for their strong work ethic and excellent embroidery skills. One respondent also commented that muxes might surpass women in performing household tasks.

Entrance into the woman-man role varied from society to society, but the putting on of women's clothes generally coincided with entrance into woman-man status, and in societies that stressed the ambivalence of this status, a combination of male and female attire was worn. "Occasionally, such a hybrid costume was also the expression of external influences which, to a great extent, made it impossible for women-men to cross-dress completely" (Lang 1998, 252). This is reminiscent of muxes like Enrique and Mandis, who might assume feminine Zapotec attire but are unable to cross-dress because they work in traditional occupations.

In addition to dressing in feminine clothing and performing feminine tasks, women-men performed most aspects of the feminine role (Lang 1998, 252), including everyday handiwork, artistic handiwork, and the raising of his/her own (adoptive) or relatives' children, the imitation of the feminine voice and intonation, and in a few instances, physiological characteristics like menstruation, pregnancy, and childbirth (252).

Like muxes, women-men sometimes also entered into sexual relationships, usually with men, which ranged from casual contacts to relationships that lasted for years. But women-men did not typically enter into permanent bonds and like the muxes usually lived alone or in their birth family (Lang 1998, 254). Unmarried women-men generally had sexual contacts with numerous men, including married men and fathers, as well as young unmarried single men (255). Similar to muxes, women-men were popular as sexual outlets because they could be visited when the men's wives were unable or not allowed to have sexual intercourse as a result of menstruation, pregnancy, or other taboo conditions. Lang argues, however, that it would be wrong to classify these relationships as homosexual in the Western sense of the word because the men involved, like the mayate, did not perceive themselves as homosexual and led completely heterosexual daily lives. "The women-men likewise did not regard such relationships as homosexual, because they after all did not possess straightforwardly unambiguous masculine gender identity, and their gender status differed from the masculine gender status of their partners" (1998, 255).

The phenomenon of women-men, or berdache, varied considerably across Indian cultures, and the only element held in common by males cited in the literature as berdache is a distinct preference for women's work as opposed to men's work (Lang 1998, 255). All the other dimensions, such as cross-dressing, specialized occupations, or their status as holy or sacred persons, were added to this basic element. Lang compiled a comprehensive table detailing role changes among women-men in one hundred indigenous societies. The most common characteristic found among 90 percent of the tribes was doing women's work, followed by cross-dressing in 84 percent of the tribes. Interestingly, having sex with men was found in only about 33 percent of the cases (256).

This minimal definition of the two-spirit as a person of one physiological sex assuming the status or role of the opposite sex is, according to Lang (1998, 7), more conducive to understanding berdaches within their own cultural traditions than to impose Western standards by labeling the practice as a form of homosexuality or designating it as "transvestism." In short, "the berdache phenomenon basically comprises all of those cases in which males voluntarily performed women's work within the framework of a special, culturally defined gender status" (256).

After an extensive analysis of the gender practices among many tribes, Lang concludes that several cultural patterns are associated with the initiation of males into the woman-man status. The first indication of gender role change was typically manifested in childhood (239). If neither dream nor visions were viewed as essential for a gender role change, and a boy's inclination toward feminine activities was insufficient to justify the transition, he was subjected to a test during puberty to determine whether he was serious about his decision. Second, when visions or dreams were considered central to making the transition, a standardized vision or dream served to legitimate the change in gender role (239). Third, when neither dreams nor visions played a significant cultural role, emphasis was placed on personal inclinations, and the woman-man status was culturally defined, connected to special roles and privileges, and the would-be woman-man ultimately had to decide whether to make the transition. Finally, in some instances, the person's desire to assume the role and generally the clothing of the opposite sex was sufficient to make the transition without requiring dreams, visions, tests, or rituals, but the person had to make a final binding decision at sometime in his life (239).

Like West and Zimmerman (1987), Callender and Kochems (1986) made an important analytical distinction between two gender levels: *gender category* and *gender status*. Although culturally constructed, gender category designates the biologically identified classes consisting of males and females (1986). Gender status, on the other hand, is less directly tied to anatomical differences. At the gender status level, one can be classified as "not-male" without necessarily being classified as female. Male berdaches were not attempting to achieve social recognition as females, since this was impossible, but rather they "were assigned to a particular gender status designated by a special label" (166). Like muxes and hijras, these "not-men" assumed a gender-mixing status that combined attributes of men and women, which differentiated them from women as well as from men (166).

Despite the tendency of Westerners to equate gender crossing with homosexuality, there is no reason to believe that same-sex sexual preference or same-sex object choice behavior itself was used as a basis for reclassifying a person to a gender-crossing status. Whitehead notes, "In contradistinction to occupational and clothing choice, cross-sex erotic choice is never mentioned as one of the indicators of a budding berdache" (1981, 95). Callender and Kochems add that "not-men" limited sexual acts to partners belonging to other gender statuses, men or women, and that it was "intercourse with persons outside their status, rather than homosexual acts per se, that most consistently defined the sexual aspects of the gender-mixing status" (1986, 171–72). Similarly, the gender status of muxes is generally defined by intercourse with persons outside their status, rather than by homosexual acts per se.

## "TALKING BACK":
## TWO-SPIRIT INDIGENOUS IDENTITY

From this overview of two-spirit literature, it is clear that in the 1990s, indigenous people challenged the prevailing gender binary in North America as gay, lesbian, and third-gender persons targeted the anthropology of the berdache and sought to "displace colonial knowledge by making Native knowledge the methodological ground of research by and for Native peoples" (Morgensen

2011, 139). The emergence of two-spirit identity represented a critique not only of the anthropology of the berdache but also of Western notions of gender and sexuality (Driskill, Finley, et al. 2011, 11). Will Roscoe's award-winning book, *The Zuni Man-Woman*, came in response to the anthropology of the berdache and turned the focus of research away from individual identity to indigenous cultural perspectives by arguing that the Zuni ihamana represented a third-gender status, which was "less about sexual identity and more about the cultural categories of indigenous communities" (Driskill, Finley, et al. 2011, 12). Muxe identity is similarly less about sexual identity and more about Zapotec cultural categories and practices. Many respondents in this study indicated that they had muxe relatives and pointed out that families in a number of indigenous neighborhoods in Juchitán were known to speak Zapoteco and have a history of muxes among their relatives. The Intrépidas, in turn, have dedicated themselves to the preservation of their indigenous roots.

Having discussed attempts by two-spirit people to decolonize the anthropology of the berdache, in the next chapter I turn to an examination of contemporary Mexicano/Latino configurations of sexual identity and behavior and their influence on muxe and Zapotec conceptions of gender and sexuality.

# 7

## BEHIND THE MASK

### Unraveling Sex and Gender

HAVING DISCUSSED TWO-SPIRIT IDENTITY and acceptance of a third-gender woman-man status among various North American indigenous groups, in this chapter I turn to a reexamination and comparison of traditional Mexicano/Latino conceptions of gender and sexuality with emergent, modern, and Western object choice configurations. I then address the effects of these two sex/gender systems on traditional muxe and Zapotec conceptions of gender and sexuality. I conclude by recognizing the existence of a new hybrid model that simultaneously reconciles and integrates these seemingly contradictory and conflicting systems.

## MEXICANO/LATINO VERSUS MODERN OBJECT CHOICE SEX/GENDER SYSTEMS

Noting the absence of research on Latino same-sex identity and behavior, Tomás Almaguer contends that Chicano men must negotiate a modern American gay identity with Mexicano-Latino configurations of same-sex identity and behavior (2001, 415). He develops a perspective on Latino gay men by drawing on what he terms the insightful narratives of Chicana lesbians like Cherríe Moraga and perceptive studies of sexuality in México and Latinoamérica carried out by anthropologists like Joseph M. Carrier, Roger N. Lancaster,

Richard Parker, Barry D. Adam, and Clark L. Taylor, who have pointed to the inapplicability of Western European and American categories of sexual meaning for understanding sexuality in Latinoamérica (2001, 416).

According to Clark L. Taylor, for example, sexual roles in México are divided into two basic categories—pasivos and activos (1986, 119). As discussed earlier, pasivos (passives) are those who are insertees in the sexual act, or who have the penis of another man inserted into one of their orifices, usually the anus, whereas activos (actives) are inserters, who place their penises into the orifice of another person. There is also a third, less common category, the *internacionales* (internationals), who are deemed to be somewhat foreign (not like Mexicans) because they take on both of these roles (119).[1]

Peter Fry (1986) and Richard Parker (1986) have similarly examined sexuality among men in Brazil and identified two basic roles, the *bicha* and the macho, or *homem* (Fry 1986, 141). Although both terms refer to biological males, in sexual encounters, the bicha assumes the female, or insertee, role, while the homem assumes the inserter role (141). The bicha metaphorically "eats" the homem, or "real man," while the latter "gives." The same terms are used to describe heterosexual relations, with the male viewed as giving and the female seen as receiving. Ultimately the homem/bicha or activo/pasivo relationship is one of male power and dominance. Bichas are seen as *efeminadas* (effeminate), as many assume traditional female roles and, like the muxes, adopt female pseudonyms or screen names (142). In addition, the bichas and male homosexuality are associated with people on the margins of society and with Afro-Brazilian possession cults in Belém do Pará (143).[2]

According to this line of research, sexual categories and personages in the United States differ from those of the Mexicano and Latino sexual system because they are determined by sexual preference or object choice rather than by power or dominance. In the United States same-sex relations are viewed as homosexual and the opposite as heterosexual, whereas those who have sex with both sexes are categorized as bisexual. The traditional Mexicano/Latino system is different, more nuanced and complex.

While the contemporary Western binary sexual system is divided into discrete sexual categories, in the traditional Mexicano/Latino sexual system, homosexuality is ostensibly defined not by object choice, but rather by the power exerted in the sexual relationship. According to this traditional view, some Mexican and Latino men such as mayates can engage in sex with other men without impugning their masculinity, as long as they retain the dominant activo, or inserter, position in the sexual act. In this sexual system, gay and straight status are thus determined not by object choice but by the respective power of the participants in the sexual act. A person is only considered a maricón (homosexual), a *joto* (queer), or a puto (fag) if he assumes the passive, insertee role in the sexual act (Almaguer 2001, 417). Not only is the active partner, like the mayate, not stigmatized, but he may be recognized as muy macho.

Another important distinction in how male sexuality is manifested in Latinoamérica compared to the United States is where sexual activity takes place. While an overt gay world is common in large cities in the United States, with gay enclaves or gay communities, same-sex activity and interaction in Latinoamérica often takes place in public settings (Taylor 1986, 117). Annick Prieur, for example, claims that much sexual activity in Mexico City takes place in el metro, the underground public transportation system, and in hairdressing parlors (1998, 182).

## CONTEMPORARY ETHNOGRAPHIC
## SEXUALITY STUDIES IN MÉXICO

A number of ethnographic studies that have focused on sexuality among gay and transvestite men in contemporary México are indirectly relevant to the discussion of the muxes. One of the most important of these is Annick Prieur's (1998) ethnographic study *Mema's House, Mexico City: On Transvestites, Queens, and Machos*. The location for the study was the poor barrio of Nezahualcóyotl, a crowded urban area on the outskirts of Mexico City, where a group of young homosexual men meet to do what they cannot do openly at home. Mema, an AIDS educator like Felina and Biiniza, invited Prieur, a Norwegian sociologist, to live and conduct fieldwork in a house he shared with a group of prostitutes and hairdressers, where Prieur could observe their daily life.

Prieur examines how super macho men are able to reconcile their masculine identity with their bisexual conduct by linking machismo and bisexuality. In a reexamination of Octavio Paz and Manuel Ramos's conceptions of machismo and masculinity, Prieur observes that Paz links enacted or symbolic homosexuality in Mexican culture to its practice, noting that

Masculine homosexuality is regarded with a certain indulgence insofar as the active agent is concerned. The passive agent is an abject, degraded being. This ambiguous conception is made very clear in the word games or battles—full of obscene allusions and double meanings—that are so popular in Mexico City. . . . These jibes are full of aggressive sexual allusions; the loser is possessed, is violated, by the winner, and the spectators laugh and sneer at him. Mexican homosexuality is tolerated, then, on condition that it consists in violating a passive agent. (Paz 1985, 39–40)

What is critical in order for the macho male to retain his masculinity and machismo, then, is not to open himself up but to open or rip open (chingar) his opponent, the other, whether the other is female or male (1985, 40).

According to Prieur, "mayate" is a term used by jotas (aka jotos), or gays, to denote men who have sex with other men without being feminine and without seeing themselves as homosexual (1998, 179). As in Juchitán, many mayates are married and most also have sex with women. Although there are no quantitative studies on the subject, Prieur claims, "It is not at all unusual for Mexican men from the working class to have sexual experiences with men, at least during certain periods of their lives" (180).[3]

At the same time, because no one other than the participants or witnesses of the homosexual encounter knows for sure who assumed the active role in the sexual act, such encounters are always treated with great discretion for fear "that a man's masculinity may be perceived as impaired" (Prieur 1998, 207). An example is when one of the jotas, Pancha, did not want her man to come over to Mema's house for fear that her friends would be interested in him. Her man not only came over but slept with Mema, Lupita, and Patricia. What most infuriated Pancha about this encounter was not the infidelity but the fact that "On top of the whole damn thing, they fucked him! So I was embarrassed and didn't want anything more to do with him" (1998, 248). Pancha didn't care that her man had been unfaithful or even "turned over." What bothered her most was that he did this with her friends, and they were now making fun of her, rather than of him, because her man was not macho.

Héctor Carrillo (2002) carried out another pioneering study of sex in Guadalajara, México's second largest city. Carrillo elaborates on the object choice model of sexuality, which is the dominant model in the United States discussed earlier. According to this model, people can be grouped into four categories, two normal and two abnormal, based on object choice (2002, 62). The first category, quadrant 1, hombres heterosexuales (heterosexual men), are men who are exclusively attracted to women and are assumed to be masculine and not homosexual.[4] Carrillo's table similarly includes, in quadrant 4, mujeres hetero-sexuales (heterosexual women), women who are exclusively attracted to men and are assumed to be feminine and not homosexual. Quadrant 3 is homo-sexuales/gays, or men who are exclusively attracted to other men, regardless of whether their partners are masculine or feminine (62). The last category, quad-rant 2 is lesbianas, or women who are attracted exclusively to other women, whether their partners are masculine or feminine. The middle categories be-tween quadrants 1 and 2, and 3 and 4, consists of bisexuals and includes men who are attracted to women and to other men, and women who are attracted to men and to other women.

The object choice model thus includes two criteria: one is biological sex and the other, sexual attraction, or object choice. In this model, biological men can thus be heterosexual, bisexual, or homosexual, regardless of whether they are masculine or feminine or assume the activo or pasivo role in the sexual act (Carrillo 2002, 62). While the bisexual category includes men and women who proclaim their attraction to both men and women, Carrillo argues that this category is different from the hybrid category of "*heterosexuales* who exhibit oc-casional homosexual behaviors" or "from the identities of men and women who identify as 'normal' but who have sex with both men and women" (63).

Carrillo contrasts the Anglo object choice binary model with the prevailing sex and gender model found in Guadalajara and in México as a whole (2002, 38). The sex/gender model includes four major categories, or quadrants, and one intermediary (internacionales) and links biological sex or sex category (male/female) and demeanor (masculine/feminine), or sex status. The two "normal" categories, includes hombres normales (quadrant 1) and mujeres normales (quadrant 4). The first quadrant, hombres normales, encompasses both hege-monic men who are masculine and exclusively attracted to women and mascu-line men who are attracted to men and women, or only to men. The latter are assumed to be inserters in sex with men and are labeled as activos. The second quadrant includes women who have a masculine demeanor and are assumed to reject men, are attracted to women, and are labeled with derogatory terms such as *machorras, manfloras, tortilleras,* or *chancleras.* The third quadrant includes men who are effeminate, assumed to be exclusively attracted to men, and to assume the pasivo, or receptive, partner in sex with other men. They are labeled pejoratively by society as maricones, putos (aka putas), or jotos (2002, 38).

What is significant is that in this model, it is not necessary to know the sex of one's sexual partner in order to determine "normality" (Carrillo 2002, 39).

The model simply assumes that masculine men are attracted to women and that feminine women are attracted to men (Carrillo 2002, 39). It also assumes that men assume a more dominant role in sexuality as the active, inserter partner, while women assume the more passive, receptor role. The second assumption "also validates the notion, often associated with machismo, that the realm of the masculine dominates over the feminine (and by extension that men are superior to women)" (39).

In an insightful study, *Erotic Journeys: Mexican Immigrants and Their Sex Lives*, Gloria González-López (2005) similarly reports that it is not uncommon for self-defined heterosexual immigrant men to have sexual encounters with other men while retaining their identity as normal men. Such sexual encounters are often associated either with sexual play among groups of immigrant men or with the excessive use of alcohol. Mauricio, for example, a twenty-six-year-old man from Mexico City, seemed remorseful when discussing "one-on-one sex" he had with an "attractive woman" he met at a bar, noting, "By the time you realize it, you already kissed them and did everything" (2005, 137). Mauricio also admitted that he and some of his other immigrant friends had had sexual relations with gay men who performed oral sex on them, but he did not penetrate the gay man (137). Similarly, in Juchitán, a number of muxes commented that some sex workers have been attacked at the Cruzero because their partners did not initially realize that they were biological males. González-López concludes that self-identified heterosexual men who have sexual relations with other men (MSM) do not identify as gay as long as they assume the activo role in anal sex and are the recipients of oral sex. "In addition, for self-identified heterosexual MSM who play the insertive role, penetration may become an expression of honor, power, and masculinity" (2005, 137).

## A COMPARISON OF KOTI SOUTH INDIAN AND MUXE ZAPOTEC GENDER/SEXUAL MODELS

In an ethnographic study of the hijras, Gayatri Reddy (2005) discusses how their sexual identity is negotiated in South India. Consistent with the discussion in the previous chapter of two-spirit indigenous identity and third-gender status of women-men found among many North American Indian tribes, Reddy distinguishes between traditional subjectivities, as manifested in *koti* sexual archetypes and modern subjectivities found in modern gay sexual archetypes (2005, 214).

Reddy begins by outlining the koti model of same-sex sexuality that hijras subscribe to, which constitutes the grid against which the emergent gay model is constructed. First, under the traditional koti model, all sexually active adult persons are categorized into one of three identities—*kotis*, *narans*, and *pantis* (2005, 214). The distinction between kotis (hijras) and narans (women) is especially instructive because it parallels the distinction between muxes and mujeres.

"While narans are women—an undifferentiated category based primarily on anatomy and gendered practice, kotis are defined by their public expression and enactment of gendered desire—liking to 'do women's work' and desiring the receptive position in same-sex encounters with other men" (Reddy 2005, 214). As illustrated in table 2, hijras, like muxes, are not mujeres but biological males who like to do women's work, or jobs reserved for them, and to assume the receptor position in same-sex encounters with hombres. Like hombres, pantis (men) in this sex and gender system are partners of either kotis (muxes) or narans (women/mujeres). Similarly, as seen in table 2, hombres can have sex with mujeres or muxes while still being considered hombres normales. Thus, as in the pantis gender-sexual system and among North American indigenous groups, the Zapotec system has three categories of gender and sexual identity—hombres, mujeres, and muxes.

There is a broad range of koti identities, with hijras as a group positioned in a hierarchy of authenticity and respect. According to the hijras, the most important factor in garnering authenticity and respect are kinship, sexual desire (or lack of it), and the amount of visibility and respect in the public sphere. One of the most important aspects of hijra attribution of authenticity and respect is lineage or kinship and "affiliation and social obligation to one of the hijra houses or lineages in the community" (Reddy 2005, 214).

Hijras define themselves in opposition to the *kada-catla* kotis, or *gandus*, who are viewed as licentious and are disparaged (214). Gandus are men who enjoy receptive anal sex and are defined not only by the form of their sexual desire, but by its excess. As a result, gandus are disparaged by all hijras, whether the hijras are asexual or sexually active (215). The condescending attitude of hijras towards gandus is reminiscent of the disparaging way muxes like Enrique and Felix(a) describe sex workers at the cruzeros and antros, as well as travestís who engage in outrageous public sexual displays.

TABLE 2. Koti and Muxe Gender and Sex Categories

| | | | KOTI GENDER AND SEX CATEGORIES | | |
|---|---|---|---|---|---|
| SEXUAL CATEGORIES | GENDER IDENTITY | ATTRACTED TO | SEX ROLE | GENDER ROLES | GENDER STATUS |
| Pantis | Masculine | Women/kotis | Active | Men's work, dress, demeanor | Man |
| Narans | Feminine | Men | Passive | Women's work, dress, demeanor | Woman |
| Kotis | Feminine | Men | Passive | Women's work, dress, demeanor | Third gender, not-man |
| Modern/gay men | Masculine | Men | Alternatively active/passive (aka international) | Men's work, dress, demeanor | Man |

| | | | MUXE GENDER AND SEX CATEGORIES | | |
|---|---|---|---|---|---|
| SEXUAL CATEGORIES | GENDER IDENTITY | ATTRACTED TO | SEX ROLE | GENDER ROLES | GENDER STATUS |
| Hombres | Masculine | Women/Men | Activo | Men's work, dress, demeanor | Man |
| Mujeres | Feminine | Hombres | Pasivo | Women's work, dress, demeanor | Woman |
| Muxes | Feminine | Hombres (masculine), not muxe or gay men | Pasivo | Women's or muxe work, dress, demeanor | Third gender/not-man |
| Modern/gay men | Masculine | Men (straight, gay) | Internacional | Men's work, dress, demeanor | Man |

The subjectivities in the traditional model of koti same-sex desire and identity stand in sharp contrast to emerging subjectivities articulated by self-defined gay individuals in modern India and México. In table 2, this modern classification grid of gay identity in South India and contemporary México is defined largely by sexual object choice. Those who desire sex with members of their same sex are defined as gay, whereas those attracted to the opposite sex are defined as straight. Much like the production of the homosexual/heterosexual medical model in the nineteenth century in the West (Foucault 1990, 43), gay men in modern India define themselves in opposition to the heterosexual population, since their identity is determined by their sexual orientation as opposed to anatomical differences or gendered (feminine) practices (Reddy 2005, 214).[5] Rather than accepting the penetrative/receptor koti/panti model, both partners in this modern same-sex relationship are defined as gay, "a move that elides the focus on public displays of femininity that apparently define 'lower-class' koti identity" (216).

What is perhaps most interesting is that in the breakdown in the koti/panti sexual system, which is based on publicly acknowledged enactments of "female" desires and practices, including being receptors in same-sex sexual practices with pantis, is ultimately linked to modernity. As one self-styled gay spokesman told Reddy, "Those are different, old-fashioned ideas—this koti, panti, and all this top/bottom business. It is not fixed like that. Some like to do this way, some like to do another way. But we all like to go with another man. That is the difference. . . . Here we are all just 'homosexuals' or 'gays,' you know" (216–17).

## GAYS, MUXES, AND ZAPOTEC CULTURE

Although muxes generally assume the pasivo role in sexual relations, it would be erroneous to conclude that they are simply gay men conforming to the traditional Mexican activo/pasivo sexual system. As noted in chapter 3, muxes are generally careful to distinguish themselves from gays, and gays are even more emphatic in distinguishing themselves from muxes.

According to several respondents, gays are more inter and come from a higher economic stratum. Coni noted that gays are more masculine and less visible publicly because they remain in the closet. In contrast, muxes are out, very visible, and often dress in traditional feminine Native attire. It was interesting that she and most Intrépidas linked being muxe not only to being out, but to maintaining Zapotec culture, traditions, and language. She added that most Intrépidas were indigenous and spoke Zapoteco, estimating that some 60 percent of families in Juchitán had one or more family members who were muxe. She also noted that muxes were generally more accepted in the poorer, largely indigenous sections of the city. Fany, like many community respondents, talked about the Zapotec origins of the muxes, while Gabriel saw lots of support for the muxes in la séptima because it is 100 percent Zapotec. Valera also noted that muxes are accepted in la séptima and viewed as a blessing from God. Mayté similarly expressed the view that all muxes were Intrépidas at heart because they had the courage to come out and be open about their sexuality, even if they were not members of the organization. Darina has a sister who is muxe and noted that some families have up to three muxes. Judy added that gays are masculine and not vestidos.

The gay men I interviewed were even more emphatic and quick to differentiate themselves from muxes. Mario, for example, said that muxes worked in female trades, identified as a women, and liked to dress like them, and was also emphatic in saying that he was not muxe but gay because he had never wanted to dress like a woman or to be one. Mario's identity as a gay man was more defined by his sexuality and his object choice preference for sex with other gay men, rather than by assuming feminine tasks or dress. Unlike muxes, Mario also lives with his partner, a gay man.

While muxe identity is not based on religious beliefs and lineage or kinship, like hijra identity, muxe acceptance is more prevalent in poorer, indigenous sectors of the city and appears to be firmly grounded in Zapotec culture. Biiniza was perhaps most eloquent when she expressed that "being muxe is not something you put on and then take off like a dress. It's a way of being that includes not only dressing like a traditional Teca but also maintaining, incorporating, and respecting Zapotec language, customs, and traditions." She added that one of the pressing concerns faced by the Intrépidas is recruiting more members who will represent the organization and maintain their local indigenous language and traditions. A point of contention the Intrépidas have with smaller, rival muxe organizations is that the latter espouse a departure from wearing traditional Zapoteca attire at velas while the Intrépidas are equally resistant and unwilling to dress in modern, professional female apparel.

## QUEER MEXICANO/LATINO INTERVENTIONS AND REJECTION OF IMPERIALIST SEXUALITIES

Just as the two-spirit movement in Canada and the United States presented an indigenous perspective on gender constructions and roles outside the Western gender binary, so have we also witnessed the proliferation of interventions from queer and transgender mestizo Latinoamérica and the rejection of imperialist sexualities, including those of the anthropologists described by Almaguer. José Quiroga, for example, interrogates the idea of the "Gay is Global" movement (2000, 191). Richard Goldstein introduced this notion by noting, "[j]ust as feminism has resonated around the world, gay liberation reverberates across widely different cultures," adding that many gays still suffer persecution globally (quoted in Quiroga 2000, 191). The celebratory tone of articles discussing the acceptance of transsexuals, gays, and lesbians speaks of a global movement that began in New York and has ostensibly been transported around the world to engender a sense of gay pride and identity without borders (Quiroga 2000). A number of Latino scholars have issued a cautionary note, however, calling into question the reductionist celebration of a global quest for a gay/transgender identity.[6]

The concern of third world scholars is that the Stonewall celebration in New York of a modern global movement might become a starting point "for a gradual assimilation of difference within society," as opposed to a celebration of difference itself (Quiroga 2000, 192). The concern, moreover, is that this globally inspired movement might become another example of how American culture is exported for consumption and dissemination as part of an imperialist project that makes it look like the world is "just like us" (193). The Intrépidas in Juchitán, for example, attract thousands of tourists from around the world, including gays who identify with them, yet muxes are aware of those who are pretenders and are simply imitating the muxe mode of dress and lifestyle. The velas are used to publicly celebrate their indigenous muxe identity.

At the 1993 Buenos Aires Marcha de Orgullo (Gay Pride Parade), organizers passed out masks to marchers who did not wish to be recognized but were supportive of the movement (Quiroga 2000). As gay and lesbian organizers gathered in a central plaza, people went into the crowd trying to convince others to join, not as open members of the community, "but as *openly masked* members in support of that community" (2000, 1), in solidarity with a disenfranchised minority. While the closet was an element of the equation, it was only part of a complex cultural relationship between subject and identity. There were obviously Latino men and women who lived in open relationships with partners but who could not "come out" to employers and family members, just as Dalhit, the piñatero, chose not to come out, out of respect for his family. Although there were some whose sexuality was an open secret, and they lived openly in relationships with partners, in such families "the social fabric depended on something that would have been destroyed, had the very notion of homosexuality as identity been put on the dinner table" (2). The organizers also knew it would have been too much to have family exile as the cost of coming out.

In retrospect, the "mask" proved to be a liberatory act because it challenged the relationship "between the visibility of homosexuals and their invisibility in the population at large" (2), simultaneously inverting the categories and "othering" and rendering invisible those who were unmasked. Quiroga's aim in *Tropics of Desire* was to move the discourse from focusing on identity narratives in the United States toward one that questions and blurs the certainties of assumed identities (3).

## TRAVESTÍS, CARNALES, AND THE CARNIVALESQUE

In another analysis of Latino masculinity and transvestism, Ben Sifuentes-Jáuregui describes transvestism as a form of voyeurism that entails a performance of gender (2002). Transvestism is ultimately the performance of gender and what is historically and culturally labeled as femininity and masculinity. But transvestism has different and dialectical meanings for outsiders and insiders. For *an outside viewer*, male transvestism is about representing, occupying, and (re)-creating the figure of the (m)other, whereas for *the transvestic subject* it is about representing, becoming, and (re)-creating the self (2002, 3). "Transvestism signals, a 'crossing' from one gender space to another; on the other hand, it is a travesty or a lie" (4). Significantly, transvestism is a functioning strategy "that deconstructs a specific 'normality' in a gender binary and hierarchy" (4).

Sifuentes-Jáuregui references Manuel Puig's *El beso de la mujer araña* (*The Kiss of the Spider Woman*) as a "dazzling example of gender crossing" (2002, 151). Following the genre of a film script, the story is about two political prisoners, Valentín and Molina, who share a jail cell. Valentín is a Marxist political prisoner charged with antigovernment activities; Molina, an extremely feminine gay man, is accused of "corrupting youth." Puig's goal in *La mujer araña* is to depict sexual culture and demonstrate how a particular type of femininity is capable of both believing in and creating a super macho. Sifuentes-Jáuregui notes, "What interested me was a feminine character who would believe in the existence of a superior man (*macho*), and the first thought I had was that today that character could not be a woman, because a woman nowadays doubts in some manner; at this level, she doubts that the partner who will guide her in everything exists" (2002, 152). For Puig, women are no longer capable of believing in the superior macho because they "doubt" and can no longer sustain or support the ideology of an overpowering patriarchy. On the other hand,

> a homosexual with feminine fixations, indeed, still can defend that ideology (of the superior man), because, since he wishes to be a woman, but cannot perform (*realizar*) the experience of being a woman, he is unable to disabuse himself (*desengañarse*) and continues the deception (or trick) of the illusion that becoming a woman lies in finding a man to guide her and to take care of her; this means finding a father and not a partner. (153)

Interestingly, the purveyor of a patriarchal ideology is not a woman but a hegemonic conception of femininity itself. The conception of femininity is not produced by woman as subject but by the Spanish neuter of lo femenino, a construct held and articulated by a gay man. Ultimately, "Puig is suggesting that the conceptualization of the superior macho happens as a relation or liaison between men, that is, the homosocial" (153), rather than between men and women.

Like distinguished Mexican intellectual Octavio Paz, other scholars have commented on the importance of humor and joking in Mexican culture, particularly the verbal art and aggression often associated with the lower-class Mexican man, or *pelado*. Anthropologist Renato Rosaldo, for example, remarked on the role played by distinctive jokes and banter in Mexican culture, noting that they are also an important component of Chicano culture, as a source of both resistance and positive identity (1989, 150)—a form of joking from which outsiders, particularly ethnographers, are largely excluded.

Paz adds that verbal aggression and bantering is especially prevalent among lower-class Mexican males, saying that it is "significant that Mexican homosexuality is regarded with a certain indulgence as far as the active agent is concerned" (1985, 39), while the passive agent is seen as an abject and degraded being. Sexual activo/pasivo roles are evident in such verbal bantering. "Each of the speakers

tries to humiliate his adversary with verbal traps and ingenious linguistic combinations, and the loser is the person who cannot think of a comeback, who has
to swallow his opponent's jibes" (1985, 39). The loser in these verbal battles becomes symbolically castrated, possessed, and violated, or *chingado*, by the winner
and sneered at and ridiculed by the audience (1985, 40). Homosexuality among
men is thus tolerated to the extent that it consists of the violation of a passive
agent.

Chicano folklorist José Limón has problematized this aggressive sexual banter in his study of homosexual joking and word play among largely working-
class South Texas Mexican men. Turning Paz on his head, Limón (1994) suggests that men who take part in such word play and verbal jibing do not frame
them as aggression or subjugation of one's opponent but as friendly joking and
teasing among friends, or *carnales* (bros). Participants in these folkloric performances see them as "ludic," or spontaneous moments of simply bantering,
*relajando* (playing), or committing chingaderas (screwing around).

Limón describes a scene where a group of working-class men, considered
discards of capitalist cattle ranching by the dominant society, are drinking beer
and barbecuing fajitas and other local delicacies on a rusty grill, in a dry and
desolate piece of land one of them owns, which they jokingly refer to as his
ranchito. Limón describes a humorous encounter between two of these men,
Simón, a construction worker known as el Mickey Mouse because of his large
ears, and Jaime, nicknamed el Midnight because he is very dark.

> Simón takes Jaime's hand as if to shake it but instead yanks it down and firmly
> holds it over his own genital area even as he responds to Jaime's "¿Cómo estás?"
> with a loud, "¡Pos, chinga ahora me siento a toda madre, gracias!" (Well fuck,
> now I feel pretty great, thank you!"). There is more laughter, which only intensi-
> fies when "Midnight" in turn actually grabs and begins to squeeze "el Mickey's"
> genitals. (1994, 126)

The two men eventually come to their knees, embracing as they tumble, laughing raucously, onto the ground.

Limón challenges pejorative and aggressive depiction of traditional Mexican male joking patterns and machismo by characterizing joking among these
South Texas carnales as an example of what Foucault calls "discourses of power"
(Limón 1994, 97–98). Like Paredes and Rosaldo, Limón proposes that such joking and banter in Mexican culture serve both as a source of positive identity and

a form of resistance to domination (125). The Mexican, particularly the lower-class Mexican male, for example, extends the term "chingar" beyond sexual violation to social violation, as when they comment, "Me chingaron en el jale" (They screwed me at work) or "Nos chingaron los politicos" (We got screwed by the politicians). They also refer to the dominant Chicano and Anglo upper classes as *los chingones* (the big screwers) (132). In this sense, Limón sees such homoerotic behavior and joking not simply as expressions of latent anxieties about homosexuality but as a way of "reversing the sociosexual idiom of *chingar* as practiced by *los chingones* that continually violates the well-being and dignity of these working-class men" (132).

Limón also notes that the seemingly aggressive idiom of sexual and social violation is introduced and reframed not as aggression but as play among friends. "Through interactionally produced play, through artistic creativity which does not deny the existence of aggression but inverts its negativity, the aggression of the world is transformed into mock aggression, mock fighting" (133). In the end, Limón interprets the symbolism associated with meat, body, and language as examples of what Mikhail Bakhtin termed the unofficial language of the Middle Ages, the folk culture of grotesque realism, or the carnivalesque (Bakhtin 1984, 24). Limón sees all these cultural practices, including meat taken from the internal stomach-centered parts of the animal, the concern with the body, and the grotesque joking as examples of degradation, an important component of the carnivalesque (1994, 138). But this is not degradation in the top-down bourgeois sense intended by Ramos and Paz.

> Degradation here means coming down to earth, the contact with earth as an element that swallows up and gives birth at the same time. To degrade is to bury, to sow, and to kill simultaneously, in order to bring forth something more and better. To degrade also means to concern oneself with the lower stratum of the body, the life of the belly and the reproductive organs; it therefore relates to acts of defecation and copulation, conception, pregnancy, and birth. . . . [I]t has not only a destructive, negative aspect, but also a regenerating one. (Bakhtin 1984, 21)

In an essay, "Guto's Performance," anthropologist Roger N. Lancaster (1997) also affirms the importance of humor and word play in Latino cultures by vividly describing the transvestism of everyday life in Nicaragua. When Aida, Guto's sister, arrived home proudly displaying a new blouse, a distinctively feminine garment that was soft to the touch, she summoned family members to come and admire it. At that moment, her shirtless teenage brother, watching television in the living room, made a broad gesture, wrapping himself in the soft garment and engaging in a fifteen- to twenty-minute transvestic performance that took the anthropologist by surprise. What was most surprising was how other family members readily joined in to support and applaud Guto's performance.

Lancaster was unclear in how to interpret Guto's performance and the response from the audience. Was it an attempt to assess Lancaster's own sexual preference, which was ambiguous? Was Guto mocking women or celebrating them? Was the performance designed to mask homosexual flirtation or a way of getting rid of such desires? Was the audience making fun of *cochones* (queers) or suspending prevailing prejudices against them by celebrating them? (1997, 11).

Although Guto's ritual performance illustrates the transvestism of everyday life, it is also linked to the ritualistic transvestic performances that are part of carnaval, or "festival of disguises" (19). Many of these everyday performances are in the spirit of carnaval. Some persons perform their role with great flair and adornment; others are simply men in plain dresses. Yet, all performers are greeted with the familiar moniker "queer" (20).

Lancaster describes carnaval as "the Revolt of the Queers," in the sense that the festival of masks plays on the lapses, contradictions, and ambiguities in the prevailing sexual culture. And a great deal of "its 'gay ambivalence' plays off reverses of the usual valences associated with queers, homosexuality, effeminacy, and desire" (20).

But carnaval also extends beyond gender and sexuality. Though associated with ritual reversals in the performance of gender and sexuality, like the bantering among the South Texas carnales described by Limón, carnaval also addresses questions of race, ethnicity, and class (Lancaster 1997, 20). For example, peach-colored masks with rosy cheeks and pencil moustaches mimic the Spanish gentry and expose the colonial history of carnaval.

Indians take on the color, wear the face, mimic the dances—and thereby mime the powers—of white Spaniard rulers. More modern Carnival images likewise traffic in depictions of class, administrative, or neocolonial power. Images include a transvestic whiteface jazzercise class, whited-coated physicians with vaudevillian implements, bankers, politicians, *internacionalistas*. (20)

In short, carnaval offers the opportunity to recall, interrogate, and play with systems of domination (20), but at the same time, it is much more. According to Bakhtin, carnaval, like the muxe velas, celebrates "temporary liberation from the prevailing truth and from the established order" (1984, 10) and suspends all the hierarchies and norms that govern them. It allows for gay ambiguity and a proliferation of crossover desires that embrace not only the social and political world, but also the physical and natural world, as humans are able to take on animal forms, and people morph into fantastic creatures. In fact, there is a sense in which "transvestic" becomes "panvestic" as social distinctions are blurred and the contours of the body are extended and tested (Lancaster 1997, 21).

Bakhtin's discussion of the celebration of carnaval's capacity for metamorphosis is relevant here as is his conception of the sensibility of the mask:

> The mask is connected with the joy of change and reincarnation, with gay relativity and with the merry negation of uniformity and similarity; it rejects conformity to oneself. The mask is related to transition, metamorphoses, the violation of natural boundaries, to mockery and familiar nicknames. It contains the playful element in life; it is based on a peculiar interrelation of reality and image, characteristics of the most ancient rituals and spectacles. (1984, 39–40)

Without endorsing Marjorie Garber's provocative claim that transvestism lies at the origin of culture, Lancaster concludes that transvestism is implicit in any gender system and is undoubtedly necessary for gender to exist. In other words, the sort of manipulating, learning, and play that underlies a successful transvestic performance also goes into other cultural practices, and "where there is gender, there must also be transvestism" (1997, 28).

Carnaval and the velas in Juchitán are associated with the changing of the seasons and the harvest, and with images of bodily life, fertility, and abundance (Bakhtin 1984, 19). But carnaval is not associated with any feast of the Church, and in Europe, México, and Latinoamérica it comes immediately before Lent, usually in February or early March, depending on when Easter falls. It comprises parades, public celebrations in the streets, and combines elements of a circus and the use of masks or other disguises. People often dress up in costumes and other masquerades during the celebration, overturning daily societal norms. There is a sense in which carnaval is a year-round celebration in Juchitán, as there are literally dozens of festivals such as velas throughout the year that resemble carnaval (Holzer 1997, 79).

Although one can readily distinguish between the transvestites of carnaval in Nicaragua and muxes, there is undoubtedly an important transvestic component to los muxes. Camelia, la Tejana, shared that she does not normally dress up like a woman, although for her, Enrique, Anilú, and other muxes, this was the ultimate fantasy. She added that dressing up like a woman is not easy and not everyone can pull it off. Miano Borruso similarly described the long and difficult process of getting a man to dress and act like a woman. On a historical trip she made to the city of Huatulco, Oaxaca, with Kike, she spent several hours observing a group of locas (muxes) getting dressed up and preparing for a transvestite show and beauty pageant. The Italian anthropologist vividly describes the complicated ritual it took to transform a group of men into women, in addition to their taking female hormones to enlarge their breasts, broaden their hips, and accentuate their waistline (2002, 151).

As she observed the locas preparing, Borruso discovered a wide assortment of paraphernalia, objects, and tricks that facilitated the metamorphosis, such as coloring the hair for those who needed it, a very long bath to open the pores, the application of makeup that took more than two hours—pencil for the lips, creams, powders, and perfumes. In addition, there were numerous tricks for applying makeup so that one's face would look longer, ways to increase one's bust size with foam cups or a sock, and other techniques for producing the desired illusion (2002, 149). One of the most curious tricks for creating a more elongated nose was to take the stick from a Tootsie Roll pop, cut it to the length of one's thumb, double it, color it black, and place it in one's nose (152).

Transforming into lo femenino is demanding, and it is just as difficult to maintain the illusion, since "it is not natural for a man to act and conduct himself in a feminine manner" (Miano Borruso 2002, 168). It is therefore necessary for muxes to actively do gender, to be taught or trained to act and talk in a feminine manner, with gestures that presumably make a woman attractive. In fact, Borruso likens the process of assuming the identity of another gender to assuming a role in a theatrical production, which

> presupone el dominio de una serie de saberes que componen el universo femenino. Para las vestidas es un rito que se renueva cotidianamente. Salir de la casa para ir al mercado o a una fiesta demanda un trabajo previo y laboroso que sobre su cuerpo y una reafirmación, a los ojos de los otros y a través del la mirada de los otros de su identidad femenina. (2002, 168)
>
> [requires mastering a knowledge set that composes the feminine universe. For the muxes who dress up, it is a ritual that is renewed daily. To go out from one's house to the market or to a fiesta requires a great deal of effort and preparation of

one's body, and a reaffirmation of one's feminine identity in the eyes of others as reflected in their gaze.]

The older and more experienced locas train those who are just entering this lifestyle, as was the case with Franki, who was being mentored by Roque and Anilú. Naomy and Mitzary, two of the younger muxes, related how some of the older Intrépidas, like Felina and Biiniza, had been important role models for them and, specifically, how Mandis had taught a group of fledging muxes to dance the traditional Zapotec dances, carrying themselves and their skirts with presencia, as women do.

But there is always a danger that a bad imitation of the feminine might make one look ridiculous. Kike, for example, a self-proclaimed travestí with the feminine persona of Kika, La Performancera, dressed up like a woman daily between the ages of eighteen and twenty-one, but now he limits his transvestic performances. At the Huatulco travestí beauty contest and show, Kika was very nervous because it had been some time since her last performance, yet she made a sensational entrance and carried off an impressive show. In a demonstration strangely reminiscent of Guto's transvestic performance,

> La entrada de Kike fue sensacional, de caché. Este tronco de mujer se deslizaba como una pantera entre mesas-manos-besos-albures-insultos-ofrecimientos-sarcasmos-deseos, cruzando el salón de cabo a rabo en un triunfal exhibicionismo. (Miano Borruso 2002, 152)
> [Kike's entrance was sensational, memorable. Her feminine torso glided like a panther between tables-hands-kisses-jokes-insults-propositions-sarcasms-desires, moving across the dance floor in a triumph of exhibitionism.]

Although the participants in the event were *jovencitas* (young women) of humble origins from all parts of the Republic, the audience was diverse, including laborers; *lancheros*, or boatmen (known for being raucous and gross); teachers; tourists; artists and musicians; and politicians of diverse genders and sexual orientations.

Kika worked hard to suck in her stomach as she displayed her runway walk, strutting gracefully and crossing one leg in front of the other as if defying the laws of gravity, but during a brief lapse, a lanchero insulted her with derogatory and sarcastic comments about her physique. Kika responded with an *ahí te va* (up yours) and let loose with an unrelenting verbal assault, reminiscent of the aggressive lower-class Mexican male banter and word play described by Paz, Rosaldo, Limón, and others, that "left the poor bastard speechless" (Miano Borruso 2002, 153).

Miano Borruso concludes from her fieldwork that although one may die a loca, there comes a time in one's life when the body will no longer have the flexibility or energy to maintain the daily ritual of keeping up the illusion and, at that point, will only dress up as a woman on special occasions like the velas. Camelia, la Tejana, dressed up only during the Intrépida Vela, for example, while Coni commented that now, as she gets older, she has a more relaxed attitude about taking hormones and keeping up appearances. "What's the point?" she wonders.

Muxes are generally careful to put on a convincing and authentic rendition of lo femenino, so that they are not embarrassed or perceived as a poor imitation. Kike remarked in wonder, "There is nothing like the original," after he saw Miano Borruso emerge after only twenty minutes, bathed, dressed, made up, and doused with perfume (2002, 168). In some instances, muxe femininity is not simply a bad imitation but an attempt to invert gender categories and present an exaggerated, grotesque, and caricatured treatment that is neither man nor woman. Feminine exaggeration is also used to gain the upper hand in sexual seduction and brings into question whether in active/pasivo roles, muxes are in fact pasivos.

Si el hombre heterosexual, el macho, que toda loca de este grupo aspira a conquistar, "quiere engañarse," es decir, no quiere asumir conscientemente su homosexualidad latente o sus prácticas homosexuales y necesita la imagen de una mujer para excitarse: "Ahí te va, con toda exageración, hasta el ridículo y lo chusco, tal vez, lo que *yo* gay veo en las mujeres, y con esta ficción compartida, yo loca, te conquisto a ti, macho." (168)

[If a macho heterosexual man, which every loca in this group aspires to seduce, wants to delude himself, that is, if he doesn't want to consciously acknowledge his homosexuality or latent homosexual practices and needs the image of a woman to get aroused: "Here it is, with all its exaggeration, including the ridiculous and grotesque, perhaps, what I, as gay, see in women, and with this shared fiction I, as loca, am able to seduce you, a macho."]

And so the fine art of seduction becomes an essential component of the muxe lifestyle, as does maintaining the illusion of lo femenino, even when it is manifested in an extreme and grotesque manner. For the muxes, like other Tecos and Tecas, la vida is a perpetual fiesta, or carnaval, where you don a feminine carnivalesque mask to preserve the illusion. In short, through the act of seduction, the muxe reaches for the feminine persona to gain the upper hand, and in the process, simultaneously unmasks the unsuspecting macho. Ironically, despite assuming the pasivo role in sexual encounters, the feminine muxe in fact works actively to seduce or *echarse* (screw) el macho (chingar), while he attempts to hide his latent homosexuality behind the mask of the activo role with all the external trappings of hegemonic macho masculinity.

## TOWARD A THEORY OF MUXE HYBRIDITY, GENDER, AND SEXUALITY

Although the pioneers of homoerotic anthropology, like Carrier (1976), Taylor (1986), Alonso and Koreck (1993), and Almaguer (2001), pointed to the need to focus on local sexual systems and avoid ethnocentrism, "their texts show a rather lax use of terms like homosexual, homosexuality, gay, and heterosexuality" (Núñez Noriega 2014, 168). These authors, for instance, "speak of 'heterosexual' men, an identity category that is virtually unknown in Mexican culture, and whose very inclusion in these studies betrays an inadequate problematization of sex/gender ideologies and identities in work on homoerotic experiences in Mexico" (Núñez Noriega 2014, 168).

While most muxes distinguish themselves from homosexuals and gays, they are not impervious to the larger Mexican gay universe. Carrillo, for example, points to the existence of sexual hybridity and the coexistence of older gender-based conceptions of sexuality and emergent object choice interpretations, resulting in a proliferation of seemingly contradictory interpretations based on competing logics, which are not seen as contradictory or incompatible. While it would be problematic to see muxes simply as gay men, neither are they altogether dissimilar from some Mexican gay men, and in this sense, I propose, as illustrated in figure 7, that they too occupy a hybrid space within the larger universe of Mexican conceptions of gender, sexuality, and homoerotic experiences.

On the surface, at least, muxe sexuality may appear similar to that of many Mexican gay-identified men, like the jotas in Prieur's book. There are certainly gay men throughout México who are similar to muxes in maintaining gender-based interpretations of sexuality and gendered sexual roles, becoming vestidas,

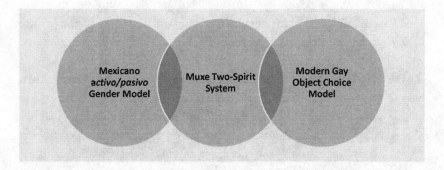

FIGURE 7.  Hybridity model

adopting a feminine persona, or assuming the pasivo role during sexual intercourse. Also, like the muxes, these gendered gay men seek partners who are masculine, hombres, or even "hombres hombres," a term designating them as real
heterosexual men, rather than gay men posing as hombres.

But the findings of this study suggest that muxes are able to maintain a sex-
ual/gender hybridity that allows them to adopt seemingly contradictory perceptions of sexuality that extend beyond the hybridity identified by Carrillo. While
most muxes are pasivos, seek hombres as sexual partners, and are not attracted
to or sexually involved with other muxes or with women, a few like Armando,
Enrique, and Huicho have engaged in bisexual behaviors. Enrique, Huicho, and
Ino have also been married to women and have children, and a few, like Kika,
do not assume the pasivo role. Muxes are also generally careful to distinguish
themselves from gays, and gays are even more emphatic in distancing themselves from muxes. This is particularly true of the younger muxes I interviewed
(under twenty-five years old), like Naomy, who have a high regard for the traditional muxe lifestyle and want to preserve it.

More current and nuanced literature on Mexican homoerotic behavior has
also challenged the pasivo/activo paradigm as the sole reference for interpreting
male same-sex desires and suggested a hybrid model that reconciles seemingly
contradictory conceptions of male sexuality (Carrillo 2002; Laguarda 2010;
Núñez Noriega 2014; Parrini Roses 2007; Quiroga 2000; Sifuentes-Jáuregui
2002). In a recent ethnographic study, Guillermo Núñez Noriega (2014), for
example, demonstrates how masculinities in the Sonoran mountain region are
constructed in such a way that men are able to adhere to traditional patriarchal

masculinity while enjoying male-to-male intimacy and affection. Some of the muxes like Huicho and Kike retain elements of aggressive Mexican masculinity and machismo, while maintaining their identity as muxes, and even cross-dressing.

The results of a study of a men's Mexican prison by Rodrigo Parrini Roses also questions the traditional gender-based Mexican pasivo/activo binary, invoking a much more complex, fluid, and nonhierarchical conception of sexuality, gender, and power. An older travestí prisoner, La Paz provided the key to a fuller understanding of the transience of gender and sexuality when she remarked that "'Lo puto lo tenía en el culo,' pero le podía dar 'unos madrazos' al quien se le cruzara en el camino" ("The faggot in me is in my rear end," but he could still "beat the shit out of anyone" who crossed his path; Parrini Roses 2007, book jacket). The statement provided insights into gender fluidity in a prison setting:

> Nos señaló cómo funcionaba el orden carcelario, al menos en el ámbito del género y la sexualidad. Ella anunciaba un mapa de identidades y posiciones que nos fue muy difícil de desentrañar. No había jerarquías estríctas ni posiciones fijas y estables. (Parrini Roses 2007, book jacket)
> [This pointed to how the prison order functions, at least in the area of gender and sexuality. She showed us a map of identities and positions that was difficult for us to disentangle. There were no strict hierarchies or fixed, stable positions.]

The overlapping nature of sexual and gender categories is captured by La Paz's statement that despite being gay, she was still a cabrón. In fact, "*Lo puto* goes through her body to *lo cabrón*" (book jacket). She remains in an intermediate zone, a permanent transitive status between puto and cabrón that is neither solely gay nor solely macho but both at the same time and consecutively. La Paz is at once hombre y mujer, masculino y femenino.

Coincidentally, Huicho invoked almost the exact phrase when he declared, "Lo puto lo tengo por atrás. De frente soy muy macho" (The fag in me is in my rear end. Up front I'm very macho). He added that being muxe was a reflection of his gender and sexuality that in no way detracted from his being a man and "muy macho." Like La Paz, being muxe didn't make him any less of a man, or passive.

In sum, muxes maintain a sexual/gender hybridity that allows them to adopt seemingly contradictory perceptions of gender and sexuality. They expand this model beyond the gay experience because, although exposed to the traditional Mexican sexual system and the modern object choice binary, they represent an indigenous two-spirit system, which allows for a hybrid third gender.

John Tutino has noted that the people of Juchitán have been remarkably successful in maintaining a community that is proudly Zapotec, and "they continue to resist with remarkable tenacity and notable successes the encroaching powers of the Mexican state and the national culture it promotes" (1993, 41). The muxe Zapotec sexual/gender system is not solely the result of war, conquest, and subordination but one that is endemic to many indigenous societies and cultures. This study found that being muxe is less about contemporary identity politics and more about the retention of gender categories in indigenous communities.

# CONCLUSION

## Lessons from the Field

---

*My use of personal experience serves as a vehicle for making the quality and intensity of the rage in Ilongot grief more readily accessible to readers than certain more detached modes of composition. At the same time, by invoking personal experience as an analytical category one risks easy dismissal.*

RENATO ROSALDO (1989, 11)

I N A CLASSIC STUDY of "Grief and a Headhunter's Rage," Renato Rosaldo inserts himself into the discussion by addressing how his wife's tragic and untimely death during his field research informed his understanding of Ilongot headhunting as a response to bereavement. Rosaldo noted, "Despite the risks involved, as the ethnographer, I must enter the discussion at this point to elucidate certain issues of method" (1989, 7).

In this concluding chapter, I too must abandon the mantle of objectivity, neutrality, and detachment and enter the discussion by presenting my personal experiences and reflections on my role as a researcher and an outsider in Juchitán. Specifically, I address the primary issues, foibles, and concerns that arose in the course of the fieldwork. The first issue has been of recurrent interest to ethnographers and central to the two-spirit peoples' critique of the anthropology of the berdache. It centers on problems, questions, and dilemmas that arise when social scientists undertake ethnographic research in a community and culture that is very different and subordinate to their own. Before elaborating on my reflections, I begin with the problems encountered by anthropologist Beverly Newbold Chiñas (2002) during her study of Isthmus Zapotecs.

In the preface to her book, Chiñas describes the unwelcome reception she received from local residents when she embarked on her fieldwork in the Isthmus and started asking questions at the local mercado, noting that at first,

[p]eople apparently assumed that I was a curious *turista* (tourist) who would soon disappear. When that did not occur . . . people began to display increasing curiosity about my motives. . . . The word went around (without my knowledge at this point) that I was a spy . . . for the government sent in to gather information for the purpose of increasing taxes! It was not long before a few women refused to answer my questions. More women joined them. In a very few days the general attitude of the market place was hostile. (2002, xii)

Hostility against Chiñas persisted, and eventually the armed guard at the market asked whether she had permission to ask questions. When she produced a letter from the presidente municipal, the guard threw it on the floor, saying that it was worthless because a new president was now in office, and she would have to obtain his permission (xii). Chiñas tried to weather the storm and continued to go into the market with a forced smile, but she was just as doggedly attacked by another elderly señora who mounted the center of her puesto and began a long and loud tirade against the gringa (xii).

While I am sympathetic and can relate to the problems reported by Chiñas, my experience as a researcher in the field was quite different and much more positive. As noted earlier, I too arrived in Juchitán "uninvited, unannounced, and unexpected," but I felt welcomed and remained relatively unperturbed throughout my stay. I walked through the market and around the central plaza daily, unaware that I might be viewed with hostility as a foreigner.

According to Andrés Henestrosa, in Juchitán "foreign" refers to "all that is not from the Isthmus" (1993a, 129). Despite my status, I possessed cultural capital as a Mexicano who was fully fluent in Spanish, and unlike Chiñas, I did not have trouble understanding the Spanish spoken by Natives.[1] In fact, I strongly identified with the muxes, who seamlessly went from Spanish to Zapoteco or interlaced their Spanish with Zapoteco terms and idioms in a way that was strangely reminiscent of how Chicanos, or U.S. Mexicans, code switch while effortlessly navigating between English and Spanish.[2]

In addition to being Mexicano and fluent in Spanish, the fact that I was an educated and mature person provided certain advantages in a society that tends to accord a great deal of respect to elders. Finally, being a man, or hombre, was undoubtedly a plus in establishing rapport with the muxes, who are generally responsive to men.

## SAHAGÚN: FATHER OF MODERN ETHNOGRAPHY

In addressing the insider/outsider controversy, it should be noted that the issue of how the researcher's insider/outsider status affects ethnographic and historical research is not new and can be traced to the pre-Conquest chronicles of Sahagún and his aides, who authored the *Florentine Codex*, as well as to a couple of post-Conquest Nahua, mestizo, and Spanish historians.

J. Jorge Klor de Alva maintains that the Sahaguntine project played a critical role in the rise of modern anthropology and what is today referred to as fieldwork (Klor de Alva 1988, 31). Describing Sahagún as the first modern ethnographer, Klor de Alva notes that

> Sahagún's questions, like those of some modern ethnographers in the tradition of Franz Boas and his students, had to be couched in terms that led the informant to examine himself and his culture in a way that (1) made him see himself as both in and outside of it, and (2) made him willing and capable of divulging the results of his reflection on himself and his world. (39)

While modern ethnography generally expects this inquiry to occur in a non-coercive setting, the ideal is often compromised, as it was in Sahagún's time, by the unequal and asymmetrical relationship that typically exists between ethnographer and informant (1988, 39).

According to noted Nahua scholar Pete Sigal, even when the informants are indigenous and mestizo authors, as in colonial México, the issue remains. Diego Muñoz Camargo, for example, a late sixteenth-century historian who at least identified with his Nahua world, failed to assume an indigenous identity and focused much more attention on the Spaniards (Sigal 2011, 184). While Muñoz Camargo did not identify as a Tlaxcalan, he nonetheless wrote from the vantage point of that community, but he wrote exclusively in the Spanish language and used the word "bardaje" (berdache), a term with Arabic origins, to describe "a cross-dressing, cross-gender figure" (184). Muñoz Camargo noted that while the Tlaxcalans did not punish bardajes, they denigrated them and considered them to be effeminate.

Unlike Muñoz Camargo, Fernando de Alva Ixtlilxóchitl (1891), identified closely with his mestizo indigenous roots, his noble Texcoco lineage, and with indigenous societies. He was proud of his heritage and history, writing that "both the Toltecs and the people of Texcoco outlawed sodomy with the punishment of death" (quoted in Sigal 2011, 184). According to Sigal, these diverse Nahua, mestizo, and Spanish chroniclers produced a unique genre in which the presence or absence of ritualized sodomy was inextricably linked to the discourse on sodomy. "Those who argued for the fundamental corruption of the indigenous population by endemic sodomy tended to mark the conquest as a valid enterprise. Those who argued that sodomy was rare and punished tended to stress that the conquerors were too savage in their treatment of the indigenous populations" (185).

## INSIDERS AND OUTSIDERS

A parallel and recurrent question in the extant literature on Chicanas/os has been to ask who is qualified to conduct research in subordinated communities. Is the study of subordinated groups their exclusive domain or is it open to anyone interested in the field? Are insiders too close to the phenomenon under study to be detached and objective observers? Is an insider/outsider, such as a Mexicano who is not Zapoteco or from the Isthmus, qualified to carry out research on the muxes? Is being an insider or an outsider a choice or an ascribed status?

In an article on the "Colonizer/Colonized," Sofia Villenas describes herself as a "'native' ethnographer, a first-generation Chicana born in Los Angeles of immigrant parents from Ecuador" (Villenas 1996, 712). For Villenas, being a "Chicana" and "native ethnographer" are determined by her position as a Latina from Los Angeles who identifies as Chicana rather than by being a person of Mexican origin living in the United States. While Villenas tried to reconcile her relationship with the Latino community as a privileged insider, she found herself having to resist being coopted by the dominant English-speaking community where she was doing her research and becoming complicit in the dominant discourse, which sought to problematize Latino family education and child rearing (Villenas 1996, 729), her subjects of study.

Rather than suggesting that insiders have monopolistic access to knowledge about their own communities, Américo Paredes, a distinguished folklorist, believes it is more important to address how ethnographic methods can be improved in working with minority groups and correctly observed that, in the end, "[t]he advantages and disadvantages of using 'ethnics' as ethnographers is not an immediate issue here, if the ethnics are to receive the same kind of training that has been received by their mentors in the past" (1977, 2). For Paredes the issue is thus not having to choose between insiders and outsiders but determining whether ethnographers are knowledgeable about and understand the communities they study.

Paredes also observed that social scientists who have studied Mexican communities often appear to be oblivious to the fact that Mexicanos love to put strangers on and fail to distinguish between factual information and joking or other types of folkloric performance by their "native" respondents (8). He cautions ethnographers to be leery of the native "trickster," to "always be aware of the informant as a potential performer of folklore," and to have an independent knowledge of the culture and folklore of the people they are studying (27).

At times "the informant may select the ethnographer rather than the other way around" (19). In any Mexican community, a certain number of natives will have a better knowledge of English than the ethnographer has of Spanish and will appear to be more articulate than their counterparts. It is precisely these more acculturated individuals, or cultural brokers, who are likely to assume the role of informant. They are likely to be the better performers, jokers, and gifted role players in the community. The ultimate danger, of course, is not only that these individuals may be the deviants or exceptions in the community, but also that "the informant may go out of his way to tell the ethnographer what he [or she] thinks the ethnographer wants to hear" (Paredes 1977, 20).

After reviewing relevant literature on research in minority communities, noted sociologist Maxine Baca Zinn presents two critiques of research in minority communities. The first is conceptual and maintains that inappropriate assumptions and frameworks have all too often produced distorted descriptions of minority group life. The second is political, stressing that "the relationship between social researchers and the people they study has been unequal at best and exploitative at worst" (1979, 209). She contends that researchers take information and advance themselves professionally, while minority communities receive little or nothing in return for their time or the information they provide. She also suggests that far more attention has been given to ethical and conceptual problems than to methodological problems, and, in particular, that very little is known about unique problems and challenges faced by minorities conducting field research in their own communities (209).[3]

In reflecting on her own field research in New Mexico, Baca Zinn turns to the unique ethical, methodological, and political problems faced by minority researchers. One is that although Chicanas/os are insiders because they are Chicana/o, they are also typically outsiders relative to the groups they study, or "insider/outsiders." An additional problem is the lack of reciprocity in the research enterprise. She tried to overcome this by participating in the day-to-day lives of her respondents and attempted to develop relationships of mutual exchange and reciprocity (215).

The issue of insiders/outsiders is indirectly addressed in Renato Rosaldo's (1989) poignant chapter on headhunting and bereavement among the Ilongots, an isolated preliterate group in the Philippines perhaps best known for their practice of ritualized headhunting. As a Chicano from Arizona, Rosaldo was obviously an outsider conducting field research on an indigenous group with its own unique language, culture, and customs. He and his wife, Michele, had studied them for nearly fourteen years and had written several articles and a book. But it was not until a tragic incident occurred that he was able to question and seriously reexamine his previous understanding of grief in ritualized headhunting.

Michele was walking along a trail with two Native companions when she lost her balance, fell down a sixty-five-foot precipice into a swollen river, and drowned. Prior to his wife's tragic death, Rosaldo had dismissed as simplistic the one-line statement made by older Ilongots that they took heads to "throw away the grief" they felt during bereavement. He had searched unsuccessfully for a thick description, deeper, truer, more elaborate explanations in various social theories. It wasn't until he experienced the uncontrollable rage that accompanied his own bereavement after a personal, inexplicable loss that he began to understand what his respondents had previously described so vividly and simply—he cuts heads to "throw away the anger of his bereavement" (1989, 1).

Before Rosaldo could do anthropology again, he had to reposition himself emotionally as both subject and object in writing. He finally concluded that personal experience can function as an effective vehicle "for making the quality and intensity of rage in Ilongot grief more accessible to readers than certain modes of composition." He saw his essay as at once "an act of mourning, a personal report, and a critical analysis of anthropological method" (1989, 11).

Several lessons can be taken from Rosaldo's essay. One is to recognize the tendency to describe our observations in field research as detached, objective, neutral, impersonal descriptions of a reality devoid of feeling and emotion. The second is to recognize the importance of the cultural force of emotions in conducting field research and how much of our understanding in the social sciences is based on cognitive, rather than on an affective, understanding of the other. Outsiders can effectively conduct research in minority communities if they learn the language and the nuances of the culture, and draw on the cultural force of emotions derived from the experiences they may share with respondents.

While it is possible to gain cross-cultural understanding in cultures that are radically different from our own, Rosaldo also cautions against adopting facile understandings of universal human nature. Although the prior death of Rosaldo's brother and the subsequent death of his wife allowed him to immediately recognize the experience of rage, it would be a mistake to see the cultural experiences as the same. He notes that "Ilongot anger and my own may overlap, like two circles, partially overlaid and partially separate. They are not identical" (1989, 10).

Like Villenas, Baca Zinn, Paredes, and Rosaldo, I too discovered that despite my ostensible insider/outsider status and the warm reception I received, to a certain extent I conducted the research with cultural blinders on and encountered limitations as a non-Zapotec outsider.

## THE COMMODIFICATION OF MUXES

One constant frustration I encountered early on in the research was the number of people who were not showing up for interviews, several of them multiple times. Anilú, as well as other Juchitecos, dismissed the problem by simply saying that people there were muy informal or not very punctual. Despite these explanations, my frustration was evidenced in my field journal:

> I was supposed to meet with "Mayté" at 2:30 p.m. in front of Felina's Hair Salon. I called to confirm this morning. Unfortunately, she did not show up and I waited for about an hour. The Spanish woman who owns the Hotel Centrál, and others had told me that "la gente aquí es muy informal," meaning that people here are not very punctual. I am finding that to be frustratingly true.

The problem peaked after an initial attempt to interview Héctor Contreras, the father of a muxe, in the neighboring town of San Blas. Héctor had suggested I meet him at the bus terminal in the nearby town of Tehuantepec (Tehua) on a Sunday morning between 8:00 and 9:00 a.m. Tehua is next to San Blas and about thirty minutes from Juchitán, and I had to take a bus early that morning. I called Héctor after I arrived, but he never showed or picked up his cell phone, as I tried unsuccessfully to reach him for several hours. I again noted in my field journal,

> I was frankly disappointed that I was stood up by señor Contreras. I am very responsible and punctual and wondered how someone could be so irresponsible. Why would you make an appointment? Make someone go to quite a bit of trouble and expense and then turn off your cell phone? It struck me as odd from the start that he wanted me to call him that early in the morning after I arrived in Tehua.

Roque was the first person to alert me to another possible explanation for the "no shows" when he warned that some muxes now charged for interviews. He didn't believe in doing this. The issue of charging for interviews came up again with Naomy, a twenty-four-year-old Intrépida, who agreed with Roque by saying that she didn't believe it was right to charge for interviews.

> If someone has a genuine interest in learning about me and my culture, I believe that I have a moral obligation to speak to them and to share my experience with them. It has to come from the heart. Now if the person subsequently feels like giving me something, that's another story.

Naomy shared a story about a young Italian woman who was interested in the muxes and came and stayed at the same place I was staying, el Hotel Centrál. She served as the woman's informal tour guide, took her all over town and even to the beach at a nearby community. They developed a close bond and friendship. The Italian woman later gave her some money, which she used to buy *zapatillos* (shoes) for the vela.

Kike was the first person to bring up paying for an interview directly, and we actually negotiated payment prior to beginning his interview. When he asked me about a *contribución* (donation), I explained that I didn't have a budget to pay for interviews, and it would have to come out of pocket. After some bartering, as one might do in purchasing a pair of huaraches in the market, we agreed on three hundred pesos (about twenty-eight U.S. dollars at the time) as a fee, or "contribution." Kike showed me his cast and explained that he was needy and hurting financially because he'd broken his wrist and hadn't been able to work for several weeks. I joked with him afterward, saying that I felt "compromised" or cheapened because I had to pay for the interview. He laughed as he took my money.

Another muxe who requested a fee for the interview was Coni. Coni had given me her number, and I had spoken to her several times by telephone, but she was very evasive about setting up an interview and stood me up once. When I finally went to her house looking for her, she apologized and explained that most muxes were now getting paid for interviews. She elaborated by saying that people were coming to Juchitán from all over the world, and they all paid. The Japanese, Dutch, Greeks, Canadians, and other groups paid between five hundred and one thousand pesos per interview (forty-five to ninety U.S. dollars at the time). The Japanese were the most recent visitors who had paid but there had also been Canadian and Dutch teams recently who had also paid. The Canadians, for example, made a date to interview a group of muxes and paid for dinner for all of them. The dinner cost more than three thousand pesos (about two hundred and eighty U.S. dollars at the time). Coni also confided that the year Mística was the Intrépida queen, the Japanese had paid for the entire event and that it was something like forty or fifty thousand pesos (four thousand or five thousand U.S. dollars), supposedly because they filmed her. Coni added that people in Juchitán were generally feeling exploited by foreigners and outsiders and that some of the Tecas in the market were now also insisting that tourists pay them something, even for taking their picture. Garcia Bustamante also mentioned outsider exploitation in my interview with him.

One of the most interesting things Coni shared at the conclusion of her interview was that some of the muchachas were also feeling exploited internally because a couple of the leaders of the group had become brokers, putting themselves in charge of arranging meetings between foreign visitors and large groups of muxes.[4] This reminded me of the *contratistas*, or *enganchadores*, who rounded up farmworkers to work for farmers and got paid as contractors or brokers.[5] Coni added that las muchachas were also feeling exploited because the person who arranged meetings typically got paid a substantial sum, and rather than sharing the money with other muxes, she simply gave them a token amount, saying something like, "Here, buy yourself a beer or refresco."

During one of my last visits to Juchitán, another muxe, Gabriel, affirmed that the growing split between Intrépida leaders and rank-and-file members had to do with the distribution of payments. He referred to a recent visit by a foreign group for which one of the muxes' leaders had acted as a broker and arranged a meeting with a group of muchachas (muxes). Each person was paid a nominal sum, something like one hundred pesos, and people later learned that the leader had pocketed most of the money. Gabriel also confided that there was another minor *ruptura* (split) among Las Intrépidas. He said, for example, that every year they went door to door asking for donations for the Intrépida Vela. Apparently the prior year, two or three of the leaders had organized people and gone door to door asking for donations without telling anyone. Eventually, when the others found out what had happened, they got very upset, so there is tension in the group.

Kike acknowledged that the muxe experience has been commodified and blamed it on foreigners who came and paid them for interviews. I noted in my field journal:

> Every time I am around Kike and Coni at Kike's Salon they mention the issue of getting paid for interviews. Kike said yesterday that it wasn't their fault because it was *los extranjeros que vinieron, nos entrevistaron, y luego nos preguntaron, cuanto es?* [foreigners came, interviewed us, and then asked us, how much is it? It wasn't our fault that it got commodified because they [the foreigners] started it.]

I gained two insights from these experiences. First, there was clearly a hierarchy among the Intrépidas, and some of the leaders had set themselves up as brokers or liaisons between foreign groups, interested in making documentaries or videos, and the rank-and-file members. The second and more significant one was that being muxe, especially an Intrépida, had become a hot commodity, which was being sold in the open marketplace to the highest bidder. While the Intrépida leadership tended to downplay the significance of internal divisions within the group and with several emerging rival splinter groups, it appears that the split might also be related to issues such as commodification and the selling of the muxe experience as well.[6]

This became more evident both in interviews with younger muxes, who elaborated on two rupturas from the Intrépidas, and in a pamphlet published in Juchitán by a prominent muxe (Bartolo Marcial 2010). The ruptura first arose from the group Vela Santa Cruz Baila Conmigo, comprising youth in la séptima sección, which I have identified as a poor, indigenous, working-class neighborhood. The second ruptura came from another group, La Vela Muxe Gula' sa', who protested the hegemonic order that had emerged among the leaders and matriarchs who had gained control of the Intrépida Vela in recent years (Bartolo Marcial 2010, 84). Specifically, they were protesting the economic profit realized by the muxe vela through sponsorship by a leading beer company, which resulted in higher registration fees being assessed on participants. The result was a vela that was not accessible to the community at large and that was restricted to attendance by the middle class, and foreigners, who pay in euros and come to see "folklore." The third ruptura, by the group Vela Muxe, centered around the new group's lack of interest in reviving nostalgia for a time past or in cross-dressing as indigenous Juchitecas for visiting strangers (84). Instead, they wanted to establish a new postmodern muxe community by wearing high fashion attire.

Although I do not feel that my findings were compromised because I had to pay for some of my interviews, the commodification of the muxe experience has important implications for academic research on third-gender persons and for how muxes are depicted in academic and journalistic accounts. One implication and danger is that the muxe experience may be packaged and marketed like other products, resulting in stereotypical, romanticized, and essentialized conceptions of them.[7] Another, related, and perhaps more significant implication is that some of the muxe leaders may themselves become knowledge brokers who can package, shape, and define the muxe experience for outsiders. In retrospect, I came to the realization that interviews with the older Intrépida leadership may have given me a different perspective from those of rank-and-file members (Paredes 1977, 19).

## THE INTRÉPIDAS: HARBORERS OF ZAPOTEC CULTURE AND TRADITIONS

Many of the participants in this study are directly or indirectly affiliated with Las Auténticas Intrépidas Buscadoras del Peligro, whose name, The Authentic, Fearless Seekers of Danger, reveals characteristics of their assumed identity. Members must be "audacious and fearless seekers of danger" and openly embrace the muxe label and lifestyle. Internally, they also distinguish between genuine muxes who adhere to a certain code of conduct and pretenders who simply mimic the muxe lifestyle, like Alex, whom I met outside the church prior to a Mass. Alex is an openly gay young man who was born in Juchitán but was taken to the United States at the age of four. He was making a return trip to the vela and attending the muxe Mass, and he was excited to be dressed like a muxe for the first time. For him, dressing up like a Teca was like a rite of passage back to his roots, the acting out of a fantasy, but cross-dressing didn't make him muxe.

Biiniza pointed out that Intrépidas particularly want to protect Zapotec traditions and dress and that many accomplished members have forsaken pursuing advanced degrees or going into professions because they require using contemporary gendered clothing. Yet, while many of the Intrépidas sought to retain traditional Zapoteca dress, traditions, and language, they were also aware of the need to recruit younger muxes to carry on their cultural traditions.

Naomy, a designer of traditional Zapoteca clothing, described herself and her friends Mitzary and Jade as part of the new, younger generation of muxes. She saw herself as "una chica trans," who had taken hormones from age fourteen to eighteen but stopped because they made her feel somewhat bipolar. She and her friends are coming up the ranks and will take the place of the older generation. The Intrépida organization just completed forty years of service, and some of the members will obviously need to be replaced. Naomy has not been a queen, but she was one of five muxes who had the honor of representing *las difuntas*, or those who had died, at the recent vela. I was shocked and saddened when she mentioned parenthetically that Roque had recently died and was one of the difuntas who had been honored, as I had grown close to him and considered him a friend.

This new generation of muxes has been mentored and influenced by older Intrépidas like Amaranta and Kike, who have shared much about their social activism. Kike has been like a *madrina*, or godmother, as well as a mentor helping Naomy become a socia in Las Intrépidas. We spoke about Mandis, another difunta, who taught her and other muxes like Mitzary, who manages a huipil puesto at the mercado, how to dance the traditional *son* and how to carry themselves like women. She added that Amaranta, the politician, "me ha influido mucho en el activismo social" (has influenced me a great deal relative to social activism) and that she now goes into the schools and gives workshops on health, safe sex, and AIDS awareness. She sees condoms "as being like a parachute that you wear and [that] protects you as you traverse the world. We teach them everything about different types of diseases." Naomy volunteers but in the future wants to establish "una asociación civil de nuevas identidades" (an organization of New Identities).

Interestingly, the third ruptura, by the younger group Vela Muxe, centered on their desire to establish a postmodern muxe community and wear high fashion clothing instead of Zapoteca attire, yet high fashion dress at velas that was too revealing was seen by some muxe, like Enrique and Felixa, as disrespectful, especially to older muxes, because it violated the traditional muxe femenino persona.

The Intrépidas' mission of creating greater awareness through health education of the dangers of unprotected sex has been successful in making connections with young muxes and other young people in the community who promote their message. I found that young people like Las Tres Amigas not only promoted the message of safe sexual practices, accepted muxes as an integral part of their community, and even had muxe relatives, but also went a step further in disapproving of mayates, who might carry sexually transmitted diseases and infect girlfriends and wives.

## LESSONS FROM THE FIELD

The primary goal of this research was to study and interview the muxes of Juchitán. In the process of conducting the research, I learned that although fluent in Spanish and bicultural, I was unwittingly an outsider, who was neither indigenous nor fluent in the local language and culture. I also came to understand that as a linguistically challenged mestizo, my ability to understand the depth, complexity, and nuance of the people and culture I was studying was affected.

In retrospect, I am aware of several instances when these cultural blinders may have affected my research. The first occurred when I was trying to arrange an interview with Francisco (Franki), who was in the midst of making the transition from being a closeted and confused gay man to adopting a full-fledged identity as a muxe. The second example was the impromptu focus group with two muxes from Unión Hidalgo, Kristál and Jacki. The third is about opposing views of time and punctuality in the United States versus Juchitán. And the final example was the result of an informal *plática* (conversation) I had with César, a muxe father, that made me question my approach to interviews by scheduling formal appointments.

As mentioned in chapter 3, when Roque and I arrived at Franki's house, his older sister wanted to know who I was and why I wanted to speak with him. She initially refused to allow me to speak with him until Roque intervened on my behalf. Perhaps more important than what Roque actually said to gain her confidence was that a member of the community and resident of her barrio, Cheguigo, spoke to her in Zapoteco, endorsed me, and reassured her that no harm would come to her brother.

As I reflect on this incident, it is clear that even though I spoke fluent Spanish, I remained an outsider who did not fully understand the local culture or language. My outsider status made Franki's sister much more suspicious, protective, and hesitant to allow access to her younger brother. I am grateful to Roque for taking me to Franki's house and especially for intervening on my behalf.

The second example was also a test of my language fluency, in a humorous twist that may have yielded the most intimate information I got in interviews, with a pair of muxe respondents, Jacki and Kristál, and several members of Kristál's family. The interview took place on a Sunday afternoon in Kristál's backyard and evolved into a rich, informative, spontaneous focus group session rather than a formal interview. Two things are directly relevant to the discussion. First, although impromptu, it proved to be an excellent experience, not only because I spoke with two muxes at the same time, but also because it gave me a firsthand look at how muxes are treated and accepted by the family. This was a significant turning point in the research because these two muxes allowed me to enter their world and their family's world, and because I chose to do the interview on their terms rather than mine. I was reluctantly willing to be more flexible, to take the half-hour bus trip to Unión Hidalgo, and to come into their space, their world, on their terms, and at their convenience.

The interview reminded me of Paredes's critique of Anglo ethnographers who claim to be fluent in Spanish but, like small children and parrots, know little of what they speak (Paredes 1977, 3), as well as his reference to tricksters. I found that I was translating my questions literally from English into Spanish in my head rather than contextualizing or paraphrasing them. When I asked Kristál and then Jacki about their first sexual experience, they were initially surprised by the question, "¿Y cómo fue?" but were not at all reluctant to respond, and in retrospect, they were obviously teasing, or playing with me like Native tricksters. The syntax of my question was grammatically incorrect, as I meant to ask how the sex happened to take place, but they took it to mean, "How was the sex?" Like an insider trickster who was putting me on, Jacki laughed and said, "¡Fue estupendo!" (It was great!)

I had a similar experience when I asked Dalhit "¿Cómo se ven los mayates?" or how were mayates viewed by people in Juchitán. It sounded to him like

"How do they look?" (in appearance). He laughed and said that muxes dressed their mayates well and that "se ven bien" (they look good); "se ven muy guapos" (they look really handsome).

Another example of my cultural blinders is the frustration I often experienced when I scheduled appointments and people failed to keep them. In retrospect, my field notes convey my Western orientation and attitude toward time and punctuality, which was at odds with the more relaxed and informal indigenous conception of time. It made me recall an old Spanish *dicho* (saying), "Hay más tiempo que vida," which captures the Zapotec view of time. The saying, literally, is, "There is more time than life," implying that we should focus on living and enjoying life for the moment rather than worrying or planning for a future that may never come.

I also had an epiphany of sorts about time, planning, and keeping appointments after I attended a muxe vela and spoke to César, the mayordomo's father. When asked if he accepted having a muxe child, he responded, "Así nació" (That's how he was born). "Of course, I accept him, what else could I do." The words were spoken elegantly, without reproach, and in a matter-of-fact way. He described being muxe as being part of nature, and he didn't try to understand or question something that was natural. The simplicity of his words profoundly conveyed a father's acceptance of a muxe son. I came to the epiphany that sometimes the richest research data and insights are gleaned not from formal recorded interviews but from situations that are totally spontaneous and unplanned. As I noted in my field notes,

> [t]alking with César senior was the highlight of the evening. In fact, it made me rethink the wisdom of conducting formal interviews, since sometimes the richest information and insights occur in informal, spontaneous moments like this, with very little planning or forethought in a setting without much fanfare [or an appointment].

Relative to paying for interviews, I realized that over and beyond the issue of money, and despite my best intentions, I may have misinterpreted muxe requests for payment for their time and information. Rather than being surprised that some people expected to be paid for interviews, I should have seen this as an extension of the enterprising nature of Juchitecos, who are hardworking, often work long hours, and may work at more than one job. Both the teacher, José Abél Acevedo, and the official, Garcia Bustamante, commented to me that it was not unusual for women to work at one job during the day and take a second job in the evening. Among my sample of muxes, more than a third held more than one job.

# POSTSCRIPT

In his discussion of the Balinese cockfight, anthropologist Clifford Geertz says that the Balinese response to people who are not part of their life, including ethnographers, is to ignore them and to treat them as "nonpersons" or "invisible" (1973, 412). When he and his wife arrived in the small village of approximately five hundred persons to study the group, they were so consistently ignored that they began to wonder whether they were in fact real. It wasn't until some ten days later, after attending a Balinese cockfight (which was illegal), that the relationship with the natives took a dramatic turn. In the midst of the third match,

> a truck full of policemen armed with machine guns roared up. Amid great screeching cries of "pulisi! pulisi!" from the crowd, the policemen jumped out, and, sprinting into the center of the ring, began to swing their guns around like gangsters in a motion picture. . . . People raced down the road, disappeared head-first over walls, scrambled under platforms, folded themselves behind wicker screens, scuttled up coconut trees. Cocks armed with steel spurs sharp enough to cut off a finger . . . were running wildly around. (1973, 414–15)

After the chase, Geertz and his wife ended up at village chief's house. When the police arrived, they questioned the chief, but he denied any involvement, although he had not only attended but arranged the cockfight. When the police then proceeded to interrogate Geertz and his wife, asking what two White persons were doing at this illicit event, their host leaped onto his feet and jumped to their defense, giving astonishing detail about how they were American professors who had every right to be there because they had been cleared by the government and were in the village to conduct research and write a book about the culture (1973, 415).

The next day the world changed dramatically for Geertz and his wife. They were no longer invisible, suddenly becoming the focus of attention and the object of an outpouring of warmth and affection from villagers. People asked them over and over again about the incident, why they ran and didn't simply use their status as researchers to explain why they were at the fight, and teasing them about how funny they looked as they ran from the police (416). Geertz concludes by observing, "In Bali to be teased is to be accepted."

Despite geographic and cultural differences between Bali and Oaxacan Zapotec society, there is a very real sense in which I also came to understand and appreciate that among the muxes of Juchitán, to be teased also is to be accepted. Like Geertz, I was shocked that Roque came to my defense when Franki's sister questioned my motives and legitimacy. I also felt accepted when I was subjected to good-natured kidding by Jacki, Kristál, and her family for my inappropriate and awkward use of certain words and phrases. Even Roque's alerting me that some muxes expected payment for interviews, and Kike and Coni directly and boldly asking me for payment, could now be viewed as indirect forms of acceptance.

My findings are consistent with those of scholars like Villenas, Paredes, Baca Zinn, and others who have pointed to the typically unequal and hierarchical relationship between the colonizing researcher and colonized, subordinate communities. Baca Zinn points to the political nature of the research relationship, "which has been unequal at best and exploitative at worst" (1979, 209). She tried to combat this tendency by attempting to establish reciprocal relationships of mutual help and trust with her respondents.

My relationship with people was also initially unequal and hierarchical. Payment for interviews was a nominal way for respondents to attempt to equalize or at least to minimize the unequal nature of the relationship between the researcher and the community. Although I only paid about a third of the respondents, I also understand that people may have thought it culturally rude to openly refuse to be interviewed. Not showing up may have been a more polite, indirect, and less intrusive way of declining.

When I returned from one of the research trips, I obtained funding from the university so I would be prepared to pay for future interviews. Finally, I appreciated the contacts and information my personal trainer, Davíd, had provided. When he admired my Nike shoes and I discovered that we wore the same size, I reciprocated his help by purchasing a pair of black Nike running shoes and personally delivered them to him on a subsequent trip. The fact that he admired them during our workouts and then asked for them was a form of acceptance because it followed a Mexican tradition in which things that are admired by friends or acquaintances are often immediately offered as gifts. I have also become Facebook friends with several study participants, including Biiniza, Naomy, and Davíd. Prior to my last visit, Davíd asked me for another pair of Nike shoes on Facebook and even attached a photo of the shoes, so I brought him a fancy pair of white and green Nike running shoes.

In closing, if Eugenio, one of the compadres I interviewed in the plaza, who had asked for my phone number and e-mail, were to call or visit, I would happily host him in the United States in an effort to reciprocate in a small way the attention and personal courtesies that Juchitecos/as and the muxes extended to me.

# APPENDIX A

## MUXE RESPONDENTS

| NAME/ MUXE NAME* | AGE | OCCUPATION | PINTADA (WEARS MAKEUP AND/OR JEWELRY) | VESTIDA (WEARS WOMEN'S ATTIRE) | INTERNACIONAL (OR INTER) |
|---|---|---|---|---|---|
| | | | 19 (37%) | 24 (46%) | 6 (12%) |
| Ángel 1 | 52 | Businessperson | X | | |
| Ángel 2 | 22 | Student, information technology | X | | |
| Ángel Rolán | 23 | CPA student | X | | X |
| Anilú | 52 | Accountant | X | | |
| Amaranta | 35 | Politician, activist, merchant | | X | |
| Armando | 27 | Photographer, instructor | | | X |

*continued*

*(continued)*

| NAME/ MUXE NAME* | AGE | OCCUPATION | PINTADA (WEARS MAKEUP AND/OR JEWELRY) | VESTIDA (WEARS WOMEN'S ATTIRE) | INTERNACIONAL (OR INTER) |
|---|---|---|---|---|---|
| | | | 19 (37%) | 24 (46%) | 6 (12%) |
| Becky | 30s | Performance artist | | X | X |
| Berenise | 40 | Prepa administrator | X | | |
| Biiniza | 35 | Consultant/sex educator | | X | |
| Camelia | Early 50s | Teacher, activist | X | | |
| César | 25 | Decorations maker | | | |
| Chuchín | 31 | Beer garden owner | X | | |
| Coni | 39 | Decorations maker | | X | |
| Darina | 24 | Seamstress | | X | |
| Diana | 29 | Seamstress, huipil designer | | X | |
| Dulce | 22 | Flower vendor | | X | |
| Enrique | 24 | Politician | X | | |
| Estrellita | 31 | Huipil designer | | X | |
| Fany | 45 | Seamstress | | X | |
| Felina | 40 | Hair salon owner, director of health services, Juchitán | | X | |

*(continued)*

| NAME/ MUXE NAME* | AGE | OCCUPATION | *PINTADA* (WEARS MAKEUP AND/OR JEWELRY) | *VESTIDA* (WEARS WOMEN'S ATTIRE) | *INTERNACIONAL* (OR INTER) |
|---|---|---|---|---|---|
| | | | 19 (37%) | 24 (46%) | 6 (12%) |
| Felix(a)[†] | 42 | Teacher | | | |
| Ferni | 24 | Accounting student | | | |
| Francis | 55 | Hair salon owner | X | | |
| Franki | 23 | Decorations maker | X | | X |
| Gabriel | 40 | Computer teacher, computer salesperson | | | |
| Ingrid Nicole | 21 | Sex worker | | X | |
| Isaac | 21 | Student, architecture | | X | |
| Huicho | 50 | Executive chef | | | X |
| Ino | 53 | Businessperson (small business) | X | | |
| Jade | 22 | Salesperson (mercado), traditional clothing | | X | |
| Jacki | 30 | Barmaid | | X | |
| Jessica Leilana | 40 | Nurse | X | | |

*continued*

(*continued*)

| NAME/ MUXE NAME* | AGE | OCCUPATION | PINTADA (WEARS MAKEUP AND/OR JEWELRY) | VESTIDA (WEARS WOMEN'S ATTIRE) | INTERNACIONAL (OR INTER) |
|---|---|---|---|---|---|
| | | | 19 (37%) | 24 (46%) | 6 (12%) |
| Johnny | 53 | Dressmaker, decorations maker | X | | |
| Judy | 20 | Chef's assistant | | X | |
| Kike/ Kika† | 48 | Hair salon owner, Performance artist | | | |
| Kristál | 30 | Bar owner | | X | |
| Leonel | 65 | Waiter | X | | |
| Mandis | 70 | Government worker, Office of Tourism | X | | |
| María Fernanda | 35 | Domestic worker | | X | |
| Marian | 40s | Performance artist, sex worker | | X | X |
| Mayté | 28 | Clothing designer, former sex worker in DF | | X | |
| Mitzary | 19 | Huipil vendor, businessperson | | X | |
| Mística | 32 | Cosmetics salesperson | | X | |
| Naomy | 24 | Huipil designer, consultant/sex educator | | X | |

*(continued)*

| NAME/ MUXE NAME* | AGE | OCCUPATION | PINTADA (WEARS MAKEUP AND/OR JEWELRY) | VESTIDA (WEARS WOMEN'S ATTIRE) | INTERNACIONAL (OR INTER) |
|---|---|---|---|---|---|
| | | | 19 (37%) | 24 (46%) | 6 (12%) |
| Omar | 65 | Businessperson | X | | |
| Ricardo/ Támara | 30 | Medic | X | | |
| Romi | 25 | Student, physical education | | | |
| Roque | 53 | Hair stylist | X | | |
| Sofia† | 25 | Teacher, physical education | | | |
| Tifani | 21 | Vendor, huaraches and sandals | | X | |
| Valera | 39 | Dressmaker, traditional dresses | X | | |
| Yovana | 39 | Event planner | | X | |

*Pseudonyms or "artistic" names adopted by muxes
†Transformancera/vestida only for velas

# APPENDIX B

## MUXE OCCUPATIONS

| PROFESSIONAL/ WHITE COLLAR 26 (40%) | SELF-EMPLOYED/ MUXE TRADES 26 (41%) | SERVICE OCCUPATIONS 7 (11%) | STUDENTS 5 (8%) |
|---|---|---|---|
| Accountant | Clothing designer | Bar maid | Accounting |
| Administrator, prepa | Salesperson, traditional clothing | Chef's assistant | Architecture |
| Bar owner (2) | Cosmetics salesperson | Executive chef | CPA |
| Businessperson (4) | Decorations maker (4) | Huarache, sandals vendor | Physical education |
| Computer salesperson | Dressmaker (2) | Sex worker (2) | Technology |
| Consultant/sex educator (3) | Domestic worker | Waiter | |

*continued*

*(continued)*

| PROFESSIONAL/ WHITE COLLAR | SELF- EMPLOYED/ MUXE TRADES | SERVICE OCCUPATIONS | STUDENTS |
|---|---|---|---|
| 26 (40%) | 26 (41%) | 7 (11%) | 5 (8%) |
| Government worker | Event planner | | |
| Hair salon owner (3) | Flower vendor | | |
| Medic | Hair stylists (4) | | |
| Nurse | Huipil designer (3) | | |
| Photographer | Huipil vendor | | |
| Politician (2) | Performance artist (3) | | |
| Teacher (5) | Seamstress (3) | | |

NOTE Occupations total 64 because some muxes had more than one. Percentages total 101 percent because of rounding.

# APPENDIX C

## GAY, LESBIANA, AND MAYATE RESPONDENTS

| NAME | AGE | OCCUPATION | SELF-IDENTIFICATION |
|---|---|---|---|
| Armando | 27 | Photographer | Gay |
| Dalhit | 28 | Piñata vendor | Gay |
| Jesús | 36 | Huipil designer | Gay hombre |
| Julie | 40 | Hair stylist | Gay |
| José | 16 | Student | Gay |
| Marcos | 22 | Waiter | Gay |
| Mario | 24 | Photographer | Gay |
| Chano | 37 | Physical education teacher | Lesbiana hombre |
| Carlitos | 35 | House painter | Lesbiana hombre |
| Virgen | 47 | Huarache maker | Lesbiana hombre |
| Javier | 19 | Student | Mayate |
| Pedro | 24 | Carpenter | Mayate |
| Wilmer | 22 | Restaurant worker | Mayate |
| Edgar | 25 | Moto-taxi driver | Mayate |
| Juan | 28 | Truck driver | Mayate |

# APPENDIX D

## COMMUNITY RESPONDENTS

| NAME | OCCUPATION | AGE | INTERVIEW LOCATION | FROM |
|---|---|---|---|---|
| Anél | Evaluator for Nonprofit | 30 | Bus depot, Juchitán | Espinal |
| Ángel | Farmer | 73 | Kiosk in plaza | San Dionísis del Mar |
| Bettie | Bread vendor | 30s | At Regada de Frutas | Quintana Roo |
| Brenda | Young mother, housewife | 30 | At Regada de Frutas | Juchitán |
| Carlos | Prepa student | 15 | In front of Felina's hair salon | Juchitán |
| Carlos García Bustamante | Assistant to mayor of Juchitán | 50s | City hall | Juchitán |
| Carolina | Prepa student | 15 | In front of Felina's hair salon | Juchitán |
| Cecilia | Bread vendor | 34 | In front of Felina's hair salon | Juchitán |

*continued*

(*continued*)

| NAME | OCCUPATION | AGE | INTERVIEW LOCATION | FROM |
|------|-----------|-----|---------------------|------|
| César Sr. | Security guard, beer factory | 52 | Vela | Juchitán |
| Concha Mendoza | Housewife | 65 | Bus station, Oaxaca city | Espinal |
| Cristen | Security guard | 19 | In front of restaurant | Juchitán |
| Davíd | Personal trainer | 19 | Gym | Juchitán |
| Diego | Prepa student, baseball player | 17 | Bus to Oaxaca city | Salina Cruz |
| Eugenio | Pemex oil rig worker | Mid-50s | Kiosk in plaza | Salina Cruz |
| Father Francisco (Pancho) | Priest | Mid-50s | Church rectory | Puebla |
| Father Luis | Priest | Early 40s | Church rectory | Juchitán |
| Florencio Mendoza | Retired teacher/farmer | 65 | Bus station, Oaxaca city | Espinal |
| Señora Griselda | Retired nurse | 65 | Bus depot, Juchitán | Juchitán; left 35 years ago |
| Héctor Contreras | Muxe father, farmer | 50 | Home | Tehuantepec |
| Irasema | Retail clerk | Mid-30s | Telephone store | Chiapas; in Juchitán for 30 years |
| Isabét | Kristál's aunt | 50 | Kristál's backyard | Unión Hidalgo |
| Ismael | Vela visitor | Mid-20s | Puesto at vela | Juchitán |

*(continued)*

| NAME | OCCUPATION | AGE | INTERVIEW LOCATION | FROM |
|------|-----------|-----|--------------------|------|
| José Abél Acevedo | Teacher | 52 | Bus to Juchitán | Small nearby town |
| José Luis | Physical therapist | 62 | Kiosk in plaza | Tehuantepec |
| Juan | Taxi driver | 45 | Muxe vela | Juchitán |
| Juan Márquez | Associate director, CONALEP | 40 | CONALEP school office | Ixtepec |
| Juanita | Prepa student | 15 | In front of Felina's hair salon | Juchitán |
| Julio | Vela visitor | Mid-30s | Puesto at vela | Chiapas |
| Lorena | Vendor, corn on the cob | 28 | Plaza | Juchitán |
| Lupe | Omar's aunt | 70 | Omar's home | Out of town |
| Marcos | Waiter | 21 | Restaurant | Juchitán |
| María Mendoza | Teacher | 32 | Bus station, Oaxaca city | Espinal |
| Maribel | Food vendor | Mid-40s | Plaza | Tehuantepec |
| Miguel | Prepa student | 17 | Downtown street | Juchitán |
| Nanci | Muxe mother | 50 | Home | Juchitán |
| Nelson | Kristál's cousin | Mid-30s | Kristál's backyard | Unión Hidalgo |
| Nun | Teacher | 50s | Bus station, Oaxaca city | Oaxaca city |
| Victor Gonzáles Perez | Director, Casa de la Cultura | 42 | Casa de la Cultura | Juchitán |
| René | Hotel clerk | 29 | Hotel | Juchitán |

*continued*

*(continued)*

| NAME | OCCUPATION | AGE | INTERVIEW LOCATION | FROM |
| --- | --- | --- | --- | --- |
| Rogelio | Moto-taxi driver | Mid-30s | Moto-taxi | Small nearby town |
| Rolán | Personal trainer, student | 19 | Gym | Juchitán |
| Rosaura | Housewife | 60s | Bus station, Oaxaca city | Juchitán |
| Rosita | Prepa student | 15 | In front of Felina's hair salon | Juchitán |
| Sandra | Vela visitor | 20 | At Regada de Frutas | Salina Cruz |
| Sergio | College student | 21 | Bus to Juchitán | Town near Juchitán |
| Socorro | Citizen | Early 30s | Municipal auditorium | Espinal |
| Samuel | Taxi driver | 50s | Cab | Juchitán |
| Verónica | School/hospital administrator | 45 | Bus to Juchitán | Juchitán |
| Virgilio | Farmer | 65 | Municipal auditorium | Espinal |

# NOTES

## PREFACE

1. Muxe is pronounced "moo-shey."
2. Regarding my interest in gender and Mexican masculinity, see Mirandé (1997); Mirandé and Enríquez (1979).
3. For a discussion of transgender terms and concepts, see Stryker (2008, 1–29); Beemyn and Rankin (2011).
4. My translation of e-mail message from Biiniza. Spanish-to-English translations throughout the text are mine unless otherwise noted.
5. Scott Hernández provided technical assistance in preparing high-resolution images for the book. I would also like to thank the anonymous reviewers who commented and made valuable suggestions for revising the manuscript.

## INTRODUCTION

1. Most of the description of Saint Vincent Ferrer's life is taken from Our Lady of the Rosary Library (2013) and Amo (2014).
2. Frida Kahlo's mother was from Oaxaca, and Frida often donned Zapotec costumes, especially in self-portraits and in paintings by Diego Rivera (DeMott 2006, 9). A photo at an exhibit, *Frida's Photographs*, that came to Long Beach,

California, in 2014, for example, shows her dressed as a Juchiteca arriving at the airport in New York.

3. "La zapoteca se puede definir como una sociedad mercantil clásica en términos marxistas. En especial las mujeres producen un excedente bastante fuerte que les permite no solamente ser autónomas económicamente, sino también costear buena parte de la estructura festiva e invertir en su negocio y oro."

4. Although Isthmus women appear to have considerable power and influence in the home and in the marketplace, they are not as well represented in the political arena. In Howard Campbell's discussion of indigenous leadership, he notes three prerequisites for being a political leader in COCEI (Coalición Obrera, Campesina, Estudiantil del Istmo): birth in Juchitán or to Juchiteco parents, fluency in Zapoteco, and knowledge of local history and customs. Although there are no women on the political commission, in a secondary group of political activists, a few females have played key leadership roles in the movement (Campbell 1993, 220).

5. For example, the Sociedad del Señor de la Piedad has been passed on from generation to generation by descendants of el señor Manuel Cristóbal López, who passed an image of El Señor de la Piedad on the eve of his death to his son Felipe López in 1768 (Jiménez López 2005, 65).

6. The Zapoteco name for Juchitán is Xabizende.

7. Gonzalo Jiménez López (2015, 15) contends that the mother culture of the Zapotecs was Olmeca, which originated around the coast of the Gulf of Mexico. The Olmecas divided into two groups, with one moving toward Campeche and Yucatán, and the other toward the valleys of México and Morelos (15). They remained there for many years, and perhaps because they were unable to adapt to the climate or were used to living off coastal fishing, they decided to return, establishing themselves south of Alvarado, Veracruz, and founding a community called Mixtequilla, from which the name Mixtec is derived (15).

8. For an excellent discussion of the battle of Guiengola, see Flannery and Marcus (1983, 316).

9. Areyzaga estimated the population of Tehuantepec at about one hundred thousand, although this may be exaggerated because it was an aggregate of separate wards or barrio communities (Zeitlin 2005, 41).

10. The justice's name is sometimes spelled Avellán.

11. For a discussion of Isthmus of Tehuantepec insurgency against Spain, see Mecott Francisco (2002).

# CHAPTER 1

1. "Un hombre de aproximadamente 30 años, de mediana estatura, con cierta disposición a la gordura, pero bien proporcionado aún, lo que se acentuaba favorablemente con un pantalón negro de buen corte y una camisa blanca entallada . . . igualmente los elegantes zapatos italianos que traía puestos. La única diferencia con respeto a los demás hombres eran la joyas de oro macizo que llevaba en el cuello, las muñecas y los dedos. . . . El joven mayordomo era tratado con tanto respeto, con tanta cortesía y deferencia, y él daba la impresión de una autoridad tan natural e indolente. . . . En esta sociedad él evidentemente tenía un lugar aceptado, sin restricción alguna" (Bennholdt-Thomsen, 1997, 280).

2. Juchitán is divided into nine secciones that are distinct neighborhoods, or barrios, with unique characteristics.

3. All the names used in this study are either fictional or the feminized nicknames adopted by the muxes.

4. In a short photo journal published on the muxes in 2010, Bartolo Marcial notes that there has been a great expansion of muxe velas in the region recently, resulting in the emergence of at least six splinter groups, or *rupturas*, from Las Intrépidas. The first was Vela Santa Cruz Baila Conmigo, founded by a lawyer, Ulisses Toledo Santiago, and it consists of a group of muxes from a barrio in the seventh section of the city who were considered too young to participate in the Intrépida Vela (Bartolo Marcial 2010, 83). This group's celebration is held on December 28, with a regada that includes their Barbie dolls. As members of the group from séptima sección matured, it evolved into a rival organization with its own vela and regada, which is celebrated on El Día de los Santos Inocentes. The second splinter group was La Vela Muxe Gula' sa' por la diversidad sexual, who were responding to the commercialization and increased cost of the Intrépida Vela, which resulted in limited access of the community at large. The sponsors of this group were primarily middle-class women and heterosexual couples (84). The third group, Vela Muxe, is made up of muxes de la séptima who are self-identified postmodernists and who seek to present themselves in modern high fashion clothing (84).

5. Historian Howard Campbell suggests that muxes are very active in Juchitán political life but that Las Intrépidas has tended to favor the PRI over COCEI

(1994, 238–39). Another reason for Intrépida support of the PRI is the organizational ability and influence of a wealthy muxe who is a *priísta* (PRI member or supporter) and has attracted a large number of muxes to the party (239).

6. The first sociedad in Juchitán, as noted in the introduction, appears to have been Sociedad del Señor de la Piedad, which seems to have been passed on across generations in various families. The first written record is dated January 15, 1818, in which a relative of the Manuel Cristóbal López family was said to have inherited an image of El Señor de la Piedad in 1768 (Jiménez López, 2005, 65). The first community-wide sociedad, or association, in Juchitán was established by a group of elite, intellectual leaders who came together on January 9, 1916, at the municipal palace and created La Sociedad del Casino Juchiteco. The goal was to form an association to promote cultural endeavors within a cultural context of peace and respect (58).

7. "La Vela Traditional es una sociedad integrada con socios. La estructura de la vela incluye el presidente, tesorero, secretario, *diputado gola* (ancianos), *guvana gola* (la mujer). La sociedad busca y nombra a los nuevos mayordomos. La mesa directiva se renueva cada año.

   Los mayordomos pueden ser entrantes o salientes. El saliente es el actual. La Mesa busca a las capitanas, la reina, y las princesas. El mayordomo está encardado de organizar la fiesta con la mesa directiva. El mayordomo asume como el cincuenta porciento de los gastos y como cincuenta porciento es de la sociedad. La Reina tiene su puesto, tiene su banda, compra su vestido. Manda a hacer su estandarte."

8. These are necessarily estimates, which fluctuate with the rate of exchange between the Mexican peso and the dollar. In the early phases of my research, the peso was at a rate of approximately 12 to 1. More recently, the exchange rate has been about 16.5 to 1. This makes it look like the cost of the vela is decreasing, but for Juchitecos, it is the same, since they earn pesos, and salaries do not increase when the peso is devalued.

9. I subsequently interviewed Darina I (see chapter 3).

10. A colectivo is an inexpensive taxi that is shared by several passengers. These are not large cars (compacts), but cab drivers often fit five passengers in them, two in the front passenger seat and three in the back, which makes for a tight fit. People obviously do not use seat belts.

11. Interview with cab driver, Juan (2011).

# CHAPTER 2

1. See Gutmann (1996) and Mirandé (1997) for an overview and a critique of this literature.

2. Howard Campbell notes that while there is "a refreshing degree of tolerance of homosexuality in Isthmus Zapotec society," traces of homophobia are also present (Campbell 1993, 230; 1994, 239).

3. In his *Obras Históricas*, Alva Ixtlilxóchitl presents a somewhat different but consistent description, noting that a number of sins, including sodomy, were punished by death.

4. "La Muger, que con otra Muger tenía deleitaciones carnales, a las quales llamaban Patlache, que quiere decir: Incuba, morían ambas por ello."

5. "El Hombre que se vestía hábitos de Muger; moría ahorcado; y lo mismo la Muger, que se ponía hábitos de Hombre."

6. "Se dan muchísimo a la carnalidad, así con hombres como con mujeres, sin pena ni vergüenza." López de Gómara adds that in other areas, such as Pánuco (Veracruz), sodomy was not punished and was practiced publicly ([1552] 1954, 2:404).

7. In the original quotation, there is no comma after the phrase translated as "He is a corrupt person."

8. Crompton notes, for example, that in Catalonia in 1597, about one-fourth of the cases tried in the Inquisition were for sodomy (Crompton 1978, 72).

9. *Cuiloni* has been translated as *puto* (faggot) and refers to the man who has been penetrated during sexual intercourse with another man (Sigal 2011, 111).

# CHAPTER 3

1. West and Zimmerman (2009, 113) note that today, "'doing gender' often appears in print without acknowledgment of its source, and some scholars (such as Judith Butler) play on our wording (*Undoing Gender*) without ever citing our work." See Butler (1990, 2004).

2. Researchers have examined trans lives and experiences in various contexts, but space limitations preclude an extensive discussion of this literature. See, for example, Beemyn and Rankin (2011), Irwin (2002), Meadow (2010), and Stryker (2008).

3. In an excellent ethnographic study, Reddy (2005, 2) generally rejects the view of hijras as the quintessential third sex and suggests that this view "ultimately might be a disservice to the complexity of their lives and their embeddedness within the social fabric of India" (4).

4. Gagné, Tewksbury, and McGaughey (1997) employ the term "transgenderists" as a broad umbrella to include transsexuals, fetish and nonfetish cross-dressers, drag queens, and other identity labels. "Transgenderist" appears to be an outdated and offensive term, however, and it is not used in the mainstream literature today. Catherine Connell (2010, 33) argues that "transgender" has generally replaced the term "transsexual," which is used "specifically to refer to people who have had or desire surgical and medical procedures that will match their sex to their gender" (2010, 33). David Valentine's (2007) book, *Imagining Transgender: An Ethnography of a Category*, provides an excellent analysis of transgender terminology and complex gender and sexual identities.

5. There have been isolated incidents of violence against muxes. See Vélez Ascencio (2009) regarding the alleged murder of a muxe sex worker.

6. The names I use for the respondents are either feminized muxe names or pseudonyms. Thirty-six of fifty-two muxes had feminized names.

7. I also encountered seven men who identified as gay rather than muxe (see appendix C). One of these men, Armando, a twenty-seven-year-old photographer, defied classification and is listed as both muxe and gay. I met him at the Tirada de Ollas on a trip to Juchitán. He was sitting at the puesto for the Intrépida queen, dressed in ordinary male attire, and was interacting with several muxes and other guests of the queen. Armando indicated that he had dated women and hoped to get married to a woman someday, but he confessed that he did not know if he could be faithful to a woman. When I pressed him on whether he was muxe or gay, he was thoughtful and reflective, saying that it was a very good question. He responded that he guessed he was gay because he never wanted to dress like a woman, although unlike other gay men, he clearly identified with and supported Las Intrépidas.

8. Two other men who identified as muxe, Ino and Valera, also engaged in bisexual behavior and were in fact married to women at one point, but they did not identify as bisexual. Valera, for example, reported that his mother had forced him to get married, and that the marriage had lasted only two months. Ino's father beat him severely for being muxe and also forced him to marry. Although Ino has three children and has engaged in bisexual behavior, he does not identify as bisexual as a preference.

9. Depending on the context, he refers to himself as Felix or Felixa. I have used Felixa and masculine pronouns throughout most of this interview to reflect how he chose to refer to himself at the time.

10. The cruzero is literally where two highways intersect, the Pan American Highway and another highway that goes to Espinal.

11. San Pedro Comitancillo is a town and municipality in Oaxaca, in southwestern Mexico. It is part of the Tehuantepec District in the western Istmo region.

12. Another muxe I interviewed, Huicho, also claimed to be the original founder, but he was kidding, since he had been in his teens when the group was founded.

13. Mario clarified that "antro" is a generic name for a place that is a combination bar and music venue.

14. I was glad that I gained enough trust in my relationship with Dalhit that he was willing to share his story. When I told him that he would not be identified in the study and that he could pick whatever name he wanted, he seemed to delight in having the opportunity to assume a stage name, like the muxes.

15. My intent was to ask how society viewed mayates, but it came out sounding more like "How do mayates look?"

16. The sequestering or kidnapping of people for ransom is, unfortunately, a common occurrence in México today, but fearing them in the context of an academic research study was humorous.

17. Literally, *machorra* refers to a sterile female animal.

18. Juan was acting strangely, like he was high on something, so about three-quarters of the way through the interview, I asked him politely if he took drugs, and he said, "I take inhalants."

19. For a discussion of the medical model of transsexuality and transgenderism, see Irving (2013).

20. Annick Prieur (1998) also does not use the term "transgender" in her excellent study of "Transvestites, Queens, and Machos" in Mexico City, which analyzes the relationship between effeminate homosexuals who are mostly transvestites and their partners, who are masculine-looking bisexual men (see chapter 7).

## CHAPTER 4

1. However, not all parents see having a muxe child as a blessing. An Intrépida told of one muchacha who did not like to discuss her personal life because it was very painful, and she always broke down when she talked about it. Her

mother had raised her as *un hombrecito* (a little man), not as muxe. "Su mamá se impresionó cuando lo vió vestido de enaguas y se murió. Es muy triste. Tuvo un infarto." Her mother had apparently been so overwhelmed when she saw her son dressed as a woman, in a traditional Teca skirt and blouse, that she had reportedly had a heart attack and died.

2. I attended one of the games at the park across from the Casa de la Cultura. It was a great gathering of the community, with a lot of good-natured fun, but everyone was competitive, including family members and children who rooted for the muxes. The atmosphere at the event reminded me of a Little League baseball game. Most of the muxes who played were younger, but Huicho played and was also the coach.

3. Guamúchiles are native to the central coast of México, with pea-like fruit that tastes like coconut.

4. I noticed that even in public schools, all children wore uniforms.

5. Prieur (1998, 182) notes that many sexual encounters in Mexico City actually take place discreetly in crowded public places like el metro, noting that "The *jotas* brag about their exploits, and tell me that they also have tried oral and even anal sex in the crowd."

6. Meaning he is very conscientious about having safe sex and protecting himself from HIV and AIDS.

7. This is an important concept theoretically, which I need to integrate.

8. A couple of the younger Intrépidas observed that although Huicho and Kike are more masculine muxes, they become more feminine with mayates, or masculine partners.

9. I found it interesting that although Mayté had worked as a sex worker in Mexico City, she was not employed as a sex worker in Juchitán. This supported Felina's view that sex workers were outsiders.

## CHAPTER 5

1. Guayaberas are a type of shirt worn in tropical climates in México, Cuba, Puerto Rico, and the Philippines. Those made without a collar are called Filipinas because it is a style worn in the Philippines.

2. San Blas Atempa is a historic town where Porfirio Díaz's troops defeated the French army on September 5, 1866. The troops were predominantly Zapotec

Indians from Juchitán, Unión Hidalgo, and San Blas Atempa (see this volume's introduction).

3. This town is not only historic but is also known for the large number of moto-taxis because there are few cars and virtually everyone gets around in these motorized vehicles.

4. It is similar to a BA in medicine or health sciences, perhaps like a paramedic, but it is a college degree.

5. It is customary for the older women to initiate the velas and to do the first dance.

6. I noticed that Garcia Bustamante and a few other people sometimes used the word "muxe," "gay," and "homosexual" interchangeably, whereas muxes and gays in Juchitán are careful to distinguish themselves from one another.

7. The film *Blossoms of Fire* also depicts the important role played by women in history and in Zapotec resistance. One of the women in the film described how the women stood at the top of the river and used handmade slingshots to fling rocks at the French troops.

8. This reminded me of the meeting that I had recently attended in Espinal on the wind turbines project in which they had a panel of about twenty dignitaries representing various federal, state, and local agencies.

9. *Tachado* is the term represented by the symbol X over a word, like "stamped out" or "Say no to drugs." I took it to mean rejected.

# CHAPTER 6

1. See, for example, Roscoe (1991); Driskill (2005); Driskill, Finley, et al. (2011); and Driskill, Justice, et al. (2011).

2. Winston Halapua has similarly identified indigenous *moana* values and worldviews expressed by certain Pacific Islander groups. The Tongan *leiti*, the Samoan *fa'afafine*, and the *mahu* in Tahiti and French Polynesia are biological males who manifest feminine identities in a number of ways (Halapua 2006, 26). Moana, the Polynesian word for "ocean with diverse waves" offers an invitation to launch into its depths to reveal a wide network of human relationships that challenges the Western gender binary. Halapua references the leiti, fa'afafine, mahu, and other biological males who express feminine gender identities and are accepted in Polynesian communities (26). He notes that the

use of their indigenous language is a deliberate attempt to use language in a way that expresses Native values, interconnectedness, and spirituality.

## CHAPTER 7

1. In his research on sexuality in Guadalajara, Héctor Carrillo found that the term "internacional" is falling "into disuse among *homosexuales* as they increasingly identify with object choice categories that imply less of a need for the category" (2002, 63).
2. Parker notes, however, that traditional same sex roles have undergone significant change with the development of the scientific, or medical, model of homosexuality that emerged during the late nineteenth and early twentieth centuries and with the creation of three new categories of sexual thought in Brazil—heterosexual, bisexual, and homosexual (1986, 158).
3. Mema, for example, estimated that about 63 percent of the men in her immediate neighborhood had had sex with a man at some point in their lives (Prieur 1998, 180), either with him or someone he knew, although these data are undoubtedly exaggerated given that Mema regarded himself as a "great seducer."
4. The discussion of these categories (quadrants) is a synthesis of information provided by Carrillo (2002, 38, 62).
5. According to Foucault, the category "homosexual" was created in 1870 in a famous article by Carl Westphal. Previously, "[h]omosexuality appeared as one of the forms of sexuality when it was transposed from the practice of sodomy onto a kind of interior androgyny, a hermaphrodism of the soul" (1990, 43). While the sodomite had been a temporary and episodic condition, the homosexual was now converted into a species.
6. These writers represent a Mexican mestizo worldview that is distinct from the indigenous Zapotec culture and worldview.

## CONCLUSION

1. Chiñas remarks, "The Isthmus dialect of Spanish is so heavily laced with Zapotec intonation and phraseology that I initially found it difficult to understand" (2002, xi).

2. I am using the word "Chicana/o" to refer to persons of Mexican origin who are "living in the United States on a relatively permanent basis, regardless of place of birth or citizenship status" (Mirandé 1985, 241n1). The term had negative connotations in the past but emerged as a symbol of ethnic pride and political consciousness during the Chicano Movement in the 1960s and 1970s.

3. To my knowledge the extant literature on the muxes has been mostly conducted by outsiders. Chiñas (2002), as noted, is an American anthropologist originally from Nebraska, who studied the Isthmus Zapotecs and devoted a scant four pages near the end of her book to the muxes. A team of German anthropologists headed by Bennholdt-Thomsen (1997) similarly focused mostly on women in Zapotec society. Only the penultimate chapter of their book is devoted to the muxes. Deceased Italian anthropologist Marinella Miano Borruso, born to an upper middle-class family in Napoli, with a physician father and an ethnologist, writer mother (DeMott 2006, 157), also carried out field research on Isthmus Zapotec society and wrote her dissertation on the Isthmus. Her out-of-print book *Hombre, mujer y muxé en el Istmo de Tehuantepec* (2002) focuses on the life history of a Zapotec woman from birth to death. Despite her privileged background, Miano Borruso declared herself a communist and a feminist at an early age, obtained a PhD in anthropology from México's National University (DeMott 2006, 157), and spent several years doing fieldwork in Juchitán. She appears to have been highly regarded by the muxes. Kike/a spoke fondly of Miano Borruso and Anilú also talked about hanging out with the Italian anthropologist, describing her as "muy jotera" and as attending many Intrépida events and loving to hang out with muxes. The only other account is a short photo journal of Las Intrépidas, *Las otras hijas de San Vicente*, published in Oaxaca by Elí Valentín Bartolo Marcial in 2010.

4. Coni wouldn't reveal any names, but you wouldn't have to be very observant to realize who some of these leaders might be.

5. Enganchador means a third person who hires someone on behalf of an employer, but the word is derived from *gancho*, which literally means "hook," so an enganchador is someone who "hooks" people into work.

6. See chapter 1, note 4, for a discussion of these splinter groups.

7. There have been numerous documentaries carried out on the muxes of Juchitán. One of the best of these is Alejandra Islas's (2005) *Muxes: Auténticas, intrépidas, buscadoras del peligro*. Another is Patricio Henríquez's (2003) *Juchitán Queer Paradise*.

# REFERENCES

Almaguer, Tomás. 2001. "Chicano Men: A Cartography of Homosexual Identity and Behavior." In *Men's Lives*, 5th ed., edited by Michael S. Kimmel and Michael A. Messner, 415–28. Boston: Allyn and Bacon. Originally published in 1991 in *Differences* 3, no. 2 (1991): 75–100.

Alonso, Ana Maria, and Maria Teresa Koreck. 1993. "Silences: 'Hispanics,' AIDS, and Sexual Practices." In *The Lesbian and Gay Studies Reader*, edited by Henry Abelove, Michèle Aina Barale, and David M. Halperin, 110–26. New York: Routledge.

Alva Ixtlilxóchitl, Fernando de. 1891. *Obras históricas*. México, DF: Secretaria de Fomento. Written between 1610 and 1640.

———. 2012. *Historia de la nación Chichimeca*. Barcelona: Linkgua.

Amo, P. Ángel. 2014. "Vicente Ferrer, Santo," Catholic.net, Presbítero, 5 de abril. http://es.catholic.net/santoral/articulo.php?id=361.

Archivo General de Indias (AGI). 1660. "Motines y alborotos de indios: Tehuantepec, Nexapa e Iztepec." Archivo General de Indias (AGI), ES.41091.AGI/29.6.24.1//PATRONATO,230A,R.2.

———. 1662. "Audencia de Mexico: Pacificación de indios: Oaxaca." Archivo General de Indias (AGI), ES.41091.AGI/29.6.24.2//PATRONATO,230B,R.14.

Baca Zinn, Maxine. 1979. "Field Research in Minority Communities: Ethical, Methodological and Political Observations by an Insider." *Social Problems* 27 (2): 209–19.

Bakhtin, Mikhail. 1984. *Rabelais and His World*. Translated by Hélène Iswolsky. Bloomington: Indiana University Press. First published 1968 by MIT Press.

Balderston, Daniel, and José Quiroga. 2005. *Sexualidades en disputa: Homosexualidades, literatura, y medios de comunicación en América latina*. Buenos Aires: Universidad de Buenos Aires.

Barrios C., Roberto, and Constantino López Matus. 1987. *El Itsmo de Tehuantepec en la encrucijada de la historia de México*. México, DF: s.n.

Bartolo Marcial, Elí Valentín. 2010. *Las otras hijas de San Vicente*. Oaxaca: Carteles Editores-Gráfica de Oaxaca.

Beemyn, Genny, and Susan Rankin. 2011. *The Lives of Transgender People*. New York: Columbia University Press.

Bennholdt-Thomsen, Veronika, coordinadora. 1997. *Juchitán, la ciudad de las mujeres*. Oaxaca: Instituto Oaxaqueño de Las Culturas.

———. 2005. "A Matriarchal Society in the age of Globalization: Juchitán/Southern Mexico." Paper presented at Societies of Peace, 2nd World Congress of Matriarchal Studies, San Marcos and Austin, Texas, September 29–30—October 1–2.

Binford, Leigh, and Howard Campbell. 1993. Introduction to *Zapotec Struggles: Histories, Politics, and Representations from Juchitán, Oaxaca*, edited by Howard Campbell, Leigh Binford, Miguel Bartolomé, and Alicia Barabas, 1–21. Washington, DC: Smithsonian Institution Press.

Blacker, Irwin R., and Harry M. Rosen. 1962. *Conquest: Dispatches of Cortes from the New World*. New York: Grosset and Dunlap.

Blackwood, Evelyn. 1997. "Native American Genders and Sexualities: Beyond Anthropological Models and Misrepresentations." In *Two-Spirit People: Native American Gender Identity, Sexuality, and Spirituality*, edited by Sue-Ellen Jacobs, Wesley Thomas, and Sabine Lang, 284–94. Urbana: University of Illinois.

Booth, Charles. 1902. *Life and Labour of the People in London*. London: Macmillan.

Brandeis Raushenbush, Paul. 2013. "Pope Francis On Gays: Who Am I To Judge Them?" *Huffington Post*, Religion, July 29.

Brown, Lester B., ed. 1997. *Two-Spirit People: American Indian Lesbian Women and Gay Men*. New York: Harrington Press.

Burgoa, Francisco de. [1674] 1934. *Geográfica descripción*. 2 vols. México, DF: Talleres Gráficos de la Nación. Publicaciones del Archivo General de la Nación.

Butler, Judith. 1990. *Gender Trouble: Feminism and the Subversion of Identity*. New York: Routledge.

———. 2004. *Undoing Gender*. New York: Routledge.

Callender, Charles, and Lee M. Kochems. 1986. "Men and Not-Men: Male Gender-Mixing Statuses and Homosexuality." In *The Many Faces of Homosexuality: Anthropological Approaches to Homosexual Behavior*, edited by Evelyn Blackwood, 165–78. New York: Harrington Park Press.

Campbell, Howard. 1993. "Class Struggle, Ethnopolitics, and Cultural Revivalism in Juchitán. In *Zapotec Struggles: Histories, Politics, and Representations from Juchitán, Oaxaca*, edited by Howard Campbell, Leigh Binford, Miguel Bartolomé, and Alicia Barabas, 213–31. Washington, DC: Smithsonian Institution Press.

Campbell, Howard. 1994. *Zapotec Renaissance: Ethnic Politics and Cultural Revivalism in Southern Mexico*. Albuquerque: University of New Mexico.

Campbell, Howard, Leigh Binford, Miguel Bartolomé, and Alicia Barabas, eds. 1993. *Zapotec Struggles: Histories, Politics, and Representations from Juchitán, Oaxaca*. Poetry translated by Nathaniel Tarn. Washington DC: Smithsonian Institution Press.

Carrier, Joseph M. 1976. "Cultural Factors Affecting Urban Mexican Male Homosexual Behavior." *Archives of Sexual Behavior* 5 (2): 103–124.

Carrillo, Héctor. 2002. *The Night Is Young: Sexuality in Mexico in the Time of AIDS*. Chicago: University of Chicago Press.

Caso, Alfonso. 1958. *The Aztecs, People of the Sun*. Norman: University of Oklahoma Press.

CBS News. 2013. "Mexico's Indigenous 'Muxes' Defy Gender Norms." *CBS News*, June 29. http://www.cbsnews.com/pictures/mexicos-indigenous-muxes-defy-gender-norms/.

Chiñas, Beverly Newbold. 2002. *The Isthmus Zapotecs: A Matrifocal Culture of Mexico*. Mason, OH: Cengage Learning.

Cieza de León, Pedro. 1984. *La crónica del Perú*. Edición de Manuel Ballesteros. Madrid: Historia 16.

Connell, Catherine. 2010. "Doing, Undoing, or Redoing Gender?: Learning from the Workplace Experiences of Transpeople." *Gender and Society* 24 (1): 31–55.

Connell, Raewyn. 2009. "Accountable Conduct: 'Doing Gender' in Transsexual and Political Retrospect." *Gender and Society* 23 (1): 104–11.

Cornelius, Wayne. 1982. "Interviewing Undocumented Immigrants: Methodological Reflections Based on Fieldwork in Mexico and the U.S." *International Migration Review* 16 (2): 378–411.

Crompton, Louis. 1978. "Gay Genocide: From Leviticus to Hitler." In *The Gay Academic*, edited by Louie Crew, 67–91. Palm Springs, CA: ETC.

Dalton Palomo, Margarita. 2010. *Mujeres: Género e identidad en el Istmo de Tehuantepec, Oaxaca*. México, DF: Centro de Investigaciones y Estudios Superiores en Antropología Social.

Davis, Kathy, Mary Evans, and Judith Lorber. 2006. *Handbook of Gender and Women's Studies*. London: Sage.

de la Cruz, Victor. 1993. "Social Scientists Confronted with Juchitán (Incidents of an Unequal Relationship)." In *Zapotec Struggles: Histories, Politics, and Representations from Juchitán, Oaxaca*, edited by Howard Campbell, Leigh Binford, Miguel Bartolomé, and Alicia Barabas, 143–46. Washington, DC: Smithsonian Institution Press.

DeMott, Tom. 2006. *Into the Hearts of the Amazons: In Search of a Modern Matriarchy*. Madison: University of Wisconsin Press.

Deutsch, Francine. 2007. "Undoing Gender." *Gender and Society* 21 (1): 106–27.

Díaz del Castillo, Bernal. 2008. *The History of the Conquest of New Spain*. Edited by David Carrasco. Albuquerque: University of New Mexico Press.

Díaz-Polanco, Héctor, and Carlos Manzo, comps. 1992. *Documentos sobre las rebeliones indias de Tehuantepec y Nexapa, 1660–1661*. México, DF: Centro de Investigaciones y Estudios Superiores en Antropología Social.

Driskill, Qwo-Li. 2005. *Walking with Ghosts*. Cambridge: Salt.

Driskill, Qwo-Li, Chris Finley, Brian Joseph Gilley, and Scott Lauria Morgensen. 2011. *Queer Indigenous Studies: Critical Interventions in Theory, Politics, and Literature*. Tucson: University of Arizona Press.

Driskill, Qwo-Li, Daniel Heath Justice, Deborah Miranda, and Lisa Tatonetti. 2011. *Sovereign Erotics: A Collection of Two-Spirit Literature*. Tucson: University of Arizona Press.

Durán, Diego. 1967. *Historia de las indias de Nueva España e islas de la tierra firme*. México, DF: Editorial Porrúa.

Emerson, Robert M., ed. 2001. *Contemporary Field Research: Perspectives and Formulations*. 2nd ed. Prospect Heights, IL: Waveland Press.

Essene, Frank. 1942. "Culture Element Distributions: XXI. Round Valley." *Anthropological Records* 8 (1): 1–97.

Flannery, Kent V., and Joyce Marcus, eds. 1983. *The Cloud People: Divergent Evolution of the Zapotec and Mixtec Civilizations*. New York: Academic Press.

Fletcher, Alice C., and Frances La Flesche. (1911) 1972. *The Omaha Tribe*. Lincoln: University of Nebraska Press.

Foucault, Michel. 1990. *The History of Sexuality*. Vol. 1, *An Introduction*. Translated from the French by Robert Hurley. New York: Vintage. First English translation published 1978 by Random House.

Fry, Peter. 1986. "Male Homosexuality and Spirit Possession in Brazil." In *The Many Faces of Homosexuality: Anthropological Approaches to Homosexual Behavior*, edited by Evelyn Blackwood, 137–53. New York: Harrington Park Press.

Gage, Eleni N. 2009. "Oaxaca's Alternate Lifestyle Scene." *Travel + Leisure*, April 30. http://www.travelandleisure.com/articles/stepping-out.

Gagné, Patricia, Richard Tewksbury, and Deanna McGaughey. 1997. "Coming Out and Crossing Over: Identity Formation and Proclamation in a Transgender Community." *Gender and Society* 11 (4): 478–508.

Garfinkel, Harold. 1967. *Studies in Ethnomethodology*. Englewood Cliffs, NJ: Prentice-Hall.

ge zeta. 2009. "Muxes (Mushes)." *Gaycolectivo* (blog), 7 de febrero. http://gay colectivo.blogspot.com/2009/02/muxes-mushes.html.

Geertz, Clifford. 1973. *The Interpretation of Cultures*. New York: Basic Books.

Giebeler, Cornelia. 1997. "'La Presencia': Importancia del traje en Juchitán." In *Juchitán, la ciudad de las mujeres*, edited by Veronika Bennholdt-Thomsen, coordinadora, 241–58. Oaxaca: Instituto Oaxaqueño de las Culturas.

Goffman, Erving. 1959. *Presentation of Self in Everyday Life*. New York: Doubleday.

González Licón, Ernesto. 1990. *Los zapotecas y mixtecas: Tres mil años de civilización precolombina*. México: Consejo Nacional para la Cultura y las Artes; Milan: Jaca Book.

González-López, Gloria. 2005. *Erotic Journeys: Mexican Immigrants and Their Sex Lives*. Berkeley: University of California Press.

Greenberg, David F. 1986. "Why Was the Berdache Ridiculed?" In *The Many Faces of Homosexuality: Anthropological Approaches to Homosexual Behavior*, edited by Evelyn Blackwood, 179–89. New York: Harrington Park Press.

Gutiérrez, Ramón A. 2007. "Warfare, Homosexuality, and Gender Status Among American Indian Men in the Southwest." In *Long Before Stonewall: Histories of Same-Sex Sexuality in Early America*, edited by Thomas A. Foster, 19–31. New York: New York University Press.

Gutmann, Matthew C. 1996. *The Meanings of Macho: Being a Man in Mexico City*. Berkeley: University of California Press.

Halapua, Winston. 2006. "Moana Waves: Oceania and Homosexuality." In *Other Voices, Other Worlds: The Global Church Speaks Out on Homosexuality*, edited by Terry Brown, 26–39. New York: Church Publishing.

Henestrosa, Andrés. 1993a. "The Forms of Sexual Life in Juchitán." In *Zapotec Struggles: Histories, Politics, and Representations from Juchitán, Oaxaca*, edited by Howard Campbell, Leigh Binford, Miguel Bartolomé, and Alicia Barabas, 129–31. Washington, DC: Smithsonian Institution Press.

————. 1993b. "The Foundation of Juchitán." In *Zapotec Struggles: Histories, Politics, and Representations from Juchitán, Oaxaca*, edited by Howard Campbell, Leigh Binford, Miguel Bartolomé, and Alicia Barabas, 39–40. Washington, DC: Smithsonian Institution Press.

Henríquez, Patricio, dir. 2003. *Juchitán Queer Paradise*. DVD. New York: Filmakers Library.

Herdt, Gilbert H., ed. 1984. *Ritualized Homosexuality in Melanesia*. Berkeley: University of California Press.

Hirsch, Jennifer S. 2003. *A Courtship after Marriage: Sexuality and Love in Mexican Transnational Families*. Berkeley: University of California Press.

Holzer, Brigitte. 1997. "Economía de fiestas, fiestas como economía." In *Juchitán, la ciudad de las mujeres*, edited by Veronika Bennholdt-Thomsen, coordinadora, 79–96. Oaxaca: Instituto Oaxaqueño de las Culturas.

Irving, Dan. 2013. "Normalized Transgressions: Legitimizing the Transsexual Body as Productive." In *The Transgender Studies Reader 2*, edited by Susan Stryker and Aren Z. Aizura, 15–29. New York: Routledge.

Irwin, Jude. 2002. "Discrimination Against Gay Men, Lesbians, and Transgender People Working in Education." *Journal of Gay and Lesbian Social Services* 14 (2): 65–77.

Islas, Alejandra, dir. 2005. *Muxes: Auténticas, intrépidas, buscadoras de peligro*. DVD. México, DF: Instituto Mexicano de Cinematografía.

Jacobs, Sue-Ellen, Wesley Thomas, and Sabine Lang, eds. 1997. *Two-Spirit People: Native American Gender Identity, Sexuality, and Spirituality*. Urbana: University of Illinois.

Jiménez López, Gonzalo. 2005. *Juchitán: Testimonios de un pasado mágico*. Oaxaca: CONACULTA.

————. 2015. *Historia de Juchitán*. Oaxaca: Diamante.

Johnson, Reed. 2013. "Rumor, Legend and a Tabloid Report Sparked 'Camelia la Tejana.'" *Los Angeles Times*, Entertainment, March 16. http://articles.latimes .com/2013/mar/16/entertainment/la-et-cm-camelia-la-tejana-narco-opera-20130317.

Joyce, Arthur A. 2010. *Mixtecs, Zapotecs, and Chatinos: Ancient Peoples of Southern Mexico*. Malden, MA: Wiley-Blackwell.

Jurik, Nancy C., and Cynthia Siemsen. 2009. "'Doing Gender' as Canon or Agenda: A Symposium on West and Zimmerman." *Gender and Society* 23 (1): 72–75.

Karim, Mohosinul. 2013. "Hijras Now a Separate Gender." *Dhaka Tribune*, November 11. http://www.dhakatribune.com/bangladesh/2013/nov/11/hijras-now -separate-gender.

Katz, Jonathan. 1976. *Gay American History: Lesbians and Gay Men in the U.S.A.—A Documentary*. New York: Crowell.

Keller, Judith. 2007. *Graciela Iturbide, Juchitán*. Los Angeles: J. Paul Getty Museum.

Kemper, Robert V., and Anya Peterson Royce, eds. 2002. *Chronicling Cultures: Long-Term Research in Anthropology*. Walnut Creek: CA: Altamira Press.

Kimball, Geoffrey. 1993. "Aztec Homosexuality: The Textual Evidence." *Journal of Homosexuality* 26 (1): 7–21.

Kitzinger, Celia. 2009. "Doing Gender: A Conversation Analytic Perspective." *Gender and Society* 23 (1): 94–98.

Klor de Alva, J. Jorge. 1988. "Sahagún and the Birth of Modern Ethnography: Representing, Confessing, and Inscribing the Native Other." In *The Work of Bernardino de Sahagún: Pioneer Ethnographer of Sixteenth-Century Aztec Mexico*, vol. 2 of *Studies on Culture and Society*, edited by J. Jorge Klor de Alva, H. B. Nicholson, and Eloise Quiñones Keber, 31–52. Austin: University of Texas Press.

Klor de Alva, J. Jorge, H. B. Nicholson, and Eloise Quiñones Keber, eds. 1988. *The Works of Bernardino de Sahagún: Pioneer Ethnographer of Sixteenth-Century Aztec Mexico*. Vol. 2 of *Studies on Culture and Society*. Austin: University of Texas Press.

Kroeber, Alfred L. 1925. *Handbook of the Indians of California*. U.S. BAE Bulletin No. 78. Washington, DC: GPO.

Lacey, Marc. 2008. "A Lifestyle Distinct: The Muxe of Mexico." *New York Times*, December 6.

Laguarda, Rodrigo. 2010. *Ser gay en la ciudad de México: Lucha de representaciones y apropración de una identidad, 1968–1982*. México, DF: Centro de Investigaciones y Estudios Superiores en Antropología Social.

Lancaster, Roger N. 1988. "Subject Honor and Object Shame: The Construction of Male Homosexuality and Stigma in Nicaragua." *Ethnology* 27:111–25.

———. 1997. "Guto's Performance: Notes on the Transvestism of Everyday Life." In *Sex and Sexuality in Latin America*, edited by Daniel Balderston and Donna J. Guy, 9–32. New York: New York University Press.

Lang, Sabine. 1998. *Men as Women, Women as Men: Changing Gender in Native American Cultures*. Translated from the German by John L. Vantine. Austin: University of Texas Press.

León-Portilla, Miguel. 1969. *Pre-Columbian Literatures of Mexico*. Translated from the Spanish by Grace Lobanov and the author. Norman: University of Oklahoma Press.

Lewis, Laura A. 2007. "From Sodomy to Superstition: The Active Pathic and Bodily Transgressions in New Spain." *Ethnohistory* 54 (1): 129–57.

Limón, José E. 1994. "Carne, Carnales, and the Carnivalesque." In *Dancing with the Devil*, edited by José E. Limón, 123–40. Madison: University of Wisconsin Press.

López Austin, Alfredo. 1988. *The Human Body and Ideology: Concepts of the Ancient Nahuas*. 2 vols. Translated by Thelma Ortiz de Montellano and Bernard R. Ortiz de Montellano. Salt Lake City: University of Utah Press.

———. 1997. *Tamoanchan, Tlalocan: Places of the Mist*. Translated by Bernard R. Ortiz de Montellano and Thelma Ortiz de Montellano. Niwot: University Press of Colorado.

López de Gómara, Francisco. [1552] 1954. *Historia general de las Indias: "Hispania vitrix," cuya segunda parte corresponde a la conquista de Méjico*. 2 vols. Modernización del texto antiguo por Pilar Guibelalde. Barcelona: Editorial Iberia.

Lorber, Judith. 2005. *Breaking the Bowls: Degendering and Feminist Change*. New York: Norton.

———. 2006. "A World without Gender?" In *Handbook of Gender and Women's Studies*, edited by Kathy Davis, Mary Evans, and Judith Lorber, 469–74. London: Sage.

Lucal, Betsy. 1999. "What It Means to Be Gendered Me: Life on the Boundaries of a Dichotomous Gender System." *Gender and Society* 13 (6): 781–97.

Madsen, William. 1964. *Mexican-Americans of South Texas*. New York: Holt, Rinehart and Winston.

Malinowski, Bronislaw. 1922. *Argonauts of the Western Pacific: An Account of Native Enterprise and Adventure in the Archipelagoes of Melanesian New Guinea*. London: Routledge.

Manalansan, Martin F. 2003. *Global Divas: Filipino Gay Men in the Diaspora*. Durham, NC: Duke University Press.

Manso de Contreras, Cristóbal. 1987. *La rebelión de Tehuantepec*. Juchitán, Oaxaca: Ayuntamiento Popular de Juchitán.

Martin, Patricia Yancey. 2003. "'Said and Done' versus 'Saying and Doing': Gendering Practices, Practicing Gender at Work." *Gender and Society* 17 (3): 342–66.

Martínez López, Aurelio. 1966. *Historia de la intervención francesa en el estado de Oaxaca*. México, DF: s.n.

Meadow, Tey. 2010. "'A Rose is a Rose': On Producing Legal Gender Classifications." *Gender and Society* 24 (6): 814–37.

Mecott Francisco, Mario. 2002. *Tehuantepec insurgente*. Oaxaca: CONACULTA.

Menjívar, Cecilia. 2000. *Fragmented Ties: Salvadoran Immigrant Networks in America*. Berkeley: University of California Press.

Miano, Marinella, and Águeda Gómez Suárez. 2009. "Géneros, sexualidad y etnia vs. globalización. El caso de los *muxe* entre los zapotecos del Istmo, Oax." *Etnicsexualidad*. http://etnicsexualidad.webs.uvigo.es/wp-content/uploads/2009/12/Ponencia_Bahia_Brasil.pdf.

Miano Borruso, Marinella. 2002. *Hombre, mujer y muxé en el Istmo de Tehuantepec.* México, DF: Plaza y Valdés.

Mirandé, Alfredo. 1982. "Sociology of Chicanos or Chicano Sociology?" *Pacific Sociological Review* 25 (4): 495–508.

———. 1985. *The Chicano Experience.* Notre Dame, IN: University of Notre Dame Press.

———. 1997. *Hombres y Machos: Masculinity and Latino Culture.* Boulder, CO: Westview Press.

Mirandé, Alfredo, and Evangelina Enríquez. 1979. *La Chicana: The Mexican-American Woman.* Chicago, IL: University of Chicago Press, 1979.

Morgensen, Scott Lauria. 2011. "Unsettling Queer Politics." In *Queer Indigenous Studies: Critical Interventions in Theory, Politics, and Literature*, edited by Qwo-Li Driskill, Chris Finley, Brian Joseph Gilley, and Scott Lauria Morgensen, 132–52. Tucson: University of Arizona Press.

Nanda, Serena. 1999. *Neither Man nor Woman: The Hijras of India.* Belmont, CA: Wadsworth.

Núñez Noriega, Guillermo. 2014. *Just Between Us: An Ethnography of Male Identity and Intimacy in Rural Communities in Northern Mexico.* Tucson: University of Arizona Press.

Ochoa, Marcia. 2014. *Queen for a Day: Transformistas, Beauty Queens, and the Performance of Femininity in Venezuela.* Durham, NC: Duke University Press.

Ortner, Sherry B., and Harriet Whitehead, eds. 1981. *Sexual Meanings, the Cultural Construction of Gender and Sexuality.* Cambridge: Cambridge University Press.

Our Lady of the Rosary Library. 2013. "St. Vincent Ferrer (1350–1419)." Lives of the Saints. http://www.olrl.org/lives/ferrer.shtml.

Paredes, Américo. 1977. "On Ethnographic Work Among Minority Groups: A Folklorist's Perspective." *New Scholar* 6 (Fall and Spring): 1–33.

Parker, Richard. 1986. "Masculinity, Femininity, and Homosexuality: On the Anthropological Interpretation of Sexual Meanings in Brazil." In *The Many Faces of Homosexuality: Anthropological Approaches to Homosexual Behavior*, edited by Evelyn Blackwood, 155–63. New York: Harrington Parks Press.

Parrini Roses, Rodrigo. 2007. *Panópticos y laberintos: Subjetivación, deseo, y corporalidad en una cárcel de hombres.* México, DF: El Colegio de México.

Paz, Octavio. 1985. *The Labyrinth of Solitude*. Translated from the Spanish by Lysander Kemp. New York: Grove Press. First published 1961.

Peña, Manuel. 1991. "Class, Gender and Machismo: The 'Treacherous Woman' Folklore of Mexican Male Workers." *Gender and Society* 5 (1): 30–46.

Pickett, Velma. 2013. *Vocabulario zapoteco del Istmo*. México, DF: Instituto Lingüístico de Verano.

Poniatowska, Elena. 1989. "El hombre del pito dulce" ("The Man with the Sweet Penis"). Translated by Cynthia Steele and Adriana Navarro. In *Juchitán de las Mujeres*, 11. México, DF: Ediciones Toledo.

———. 1993. "Juchitán, a Town of Women." In *Zapotec Struggles: Histories, Politics, and Representations from Juchitán, Oaxaca*, edited by Howard Campbell, Leigh Binford, Miguel Bartolomé, and Alicia Barabas, 133–35. Washington, DC: Smithsonian Institution Press.

Prieur, Annick. 1998. *Mema's House, Mexico City: On Transvestites, Queens, and Machos*. Chicago: University of Chicago Press.

Quiroga, José. 2000. *Tropics of Desire: Interventions from Queer Latino America*. New York: New York University Press.

———. 2005. *Cuban Palimpsests*. Minneapolis: University of Minnesota Press.

Reddy, Gayatri. 2005. *With Respect to Sex: Negotiating Hijra Identity in South India*. Chicago: University of Chicago Press.

Reinhart, Albert. 1912. "St. Vincent Ferrer." In *The Catholic Encyclopedia*. Vol. 15. New York: Appleton. Retrieved from New Advent, May 20, 2016. http://www .newadvent.org/cathen/15437a.htm.

Risman, Barbara J. 2009. "From Doing to Undoing: Gender as We Know It." *Gender and Society* 23 (1): 81–84.

Rogers, Mary F. 1992. "They All Were Passing: Agnes, Garfinkel, and Company." *Gender and Society* 6 (2): 169–91.

Rojas, Basilio. 1964. *La rebelión de Tehuantepec*. México, DF: Sociedad Mexicana de Geografía y Estadística.

Romano-V, Octavio I. 1970. "Social Science, Objectivity, and the Chicanos." *El Grito* 4 (Fall): 4–16.

Rosaldo, Renato. 1989. *Culture and Truth*. Boston: Beacon Press.

Roscoe, Will. 1991. *The Zuni Man-Woman*. Albuquerque: University of New Mexico Press.

Rosenfeld, Dana. 2009. "Heteronormativity and Homonormativity as Practical and Moral Resources." *Gender and Society* 23 (5): 617–38.

Royce, Anya Peterson. 1975. *Prestigio y afiliación en una comunidad urbana: Juchitán, Oaxaca*. México, DF: Instituto Nacional Indigenista. Reprinted 1990 in

Colleción Precencias by Dirección General de Publicaciones del Consejo Nacional Para la Cultura y las Artes/INA.

———. 1982. *Ethnic Identity: Strategies of Diversity*. Bloomington: Indiana University Press.

Rubel, Arthur J. 1966. *Across the Tracks: Mexican Americans in a Texas City*. Austin: University of Texas Press.

Rubin, Jeffrey W. 1997. *Decentering the Regime: Ethnicity, Radicalism, and Democracy in Juchitán, Mexico*. Durham, NC: Duke University Press.

Rymph, David. 1974. *Cross-Sex Behavior in an Isthmus Zapotec Village*. Paper presented at the annual meeting of the American Anthropological Association, Mexico City.

Sahagún, Bernardino de. 1961. *Florentine Codex: General History of the Things of New Spain*. Book 10. Translated by Charles E. Dibble and Arthur J. O. Anderson. Santa Fe, NM: School of American Research. Written between 1540 and 1585.

Schilt, Kristen. 2006. "Just One of the Guys? How Transmen Make Gender Visible at Work." *Gender and Society* 20 (4): 465–90.

Schroeder, Susan, ed. 2011. *The Conquest All Over Again: Nahuas and Zapotecs Thinking, Writing, and Painting Spanish Colonialism*. Portland, OR: Sussex Academic Press.

Sifuentes-Jáuregui, Ben. 2002. *Transvestism, Masculinity, and Latin American Literature*. New York: Palgrave.

Sigal, Pete, ed. 2003. *Infamous Desire: Male Homosexuality in Colonial Latin America*. Chicago: University of Chicago Press.

———. 2007. "Queer Nahuatl: Sahagún's Faggots and Sodomites, Lesbians and Hermaphrodites." *Ethnohistory* 54 (1): 9–34.

———. 2011. *The Flower and the Scorpion: Sexuality and Ritual in Early Nahua Culture*. Durham, NC: Duke University Press.

Simms, S. C. 1903. "Crow Indian Hermaphrodites." *American Anthropologist* 5: 580–81.

Smith, Robert Courtney. 2006. *Mexican New York: Transnational Lives of New Immigrants*. Berkeley: University of California Press.

Stores, Bruce. 2009. *The Isthmus: Stories from Mexico's Past, 1495–1995*. New York: iUniverse, 2009.

Strauss, Anselm. 1987. *Qualitative Analysis for Social Scientists*. New York: Cambridge University Press.

Stryker, Susan. 2008. *Transgender History*. Berkeley: Seal Press.

Stryker, Susan, and Aren Z. Aizura, eds. 2013. *The Transgender Studies Reader 2*. New York: Routledge.

Taylor, Clark L. 1986. "Mexican Male Homosexual Interaction in Public Contexts." In *The Many Faces of Homosexuality: Anthropological Approaches to Homosexual Behavior*, edited by Evelyn Blackwood, 117–36. New York: Harrington Park Press.

Torquemada, Juan de. [1723] 1943. *Monarquía Indiana*. Vol. 2. 2nd ed. México, DF: Salvador Chávez Hayhoe.

Tortorici, Zeb. 2007. "'Heran Todos Putos': Sodomitical Subcultures and Disordered Desire in Early Colonial Mexico." *Ethnohistory* 54 (1): 35–67.

Towle, Evan B., and Lynn M. Morgan. 2006. "Romancing the Transgender Native: Rethinking the Use of the 'Third Gender' Concept." In *The Transgender Studies Reader*, edited by Susan Stryker and Stephen Whittle, 666–84. New York: Routledge.

Trexler, Richard C. 1995. *Sex and Conquest: Gendered Violence, Political Order, and the European Conquest of the Americas*. Ithaca, NY: Cornell University Press.

Tutino, John. 1993. "Ethnic Resistance: Juchitán in Mexican History." In *Zapotec Struggles: Histories, Politics, and Representations from Juchitán, Oaxaca*, edited by Howard Campbell, Leigh Binford, Miguel Bartolomé, and Alicia Barabas, 41–61. Washington, DC: Smithsonian Institution Press.

Vaillant, George C. 1975. *Aztecs of Mexico: Origin, Rise, and Fall of the Aztec Nation*. New ed., revised by Suzannah B. Vaillant. London: Penguin.

Valentine, David. 2007. *Imagining Transgender: An Ethnography of a Category*. Durham, NC: Duke University Press.

Velázquez, Marina Meneses. 1997. "El camino de ser mujer en Juchitán." In *Juchitán, la ciudad de las mujeres*, edited by Veronika Bennholdt-Thomsen, coordinadora, 99–125. Oaxaca: Instituto Oaxaqueño de las Culturas.

Vélez Ascencio, Octavio. 2009. "Exigen esclarecer muerte de joven *muxe* en Juchitán." *La Jornada*, March 14, 25.

Villenas, Sofia. 1996. "The Colonizer/Colonized Chicana Ethnographer: Identity, Marginalization, and Co-optation in the Field." *Harvard Educational Review* 66 (4): 711–31.

Warren, Carol A. B., and Tracy Xavia Karner. 2015. *Discovering Qualitative Methods: Ethnography, Interviews, Documents, and Images*. 3rd ed. New York: Oxford University Press.

Weems, Mickey. 2011. "San Vicente." *Qualia Folk*, December 8. http://www.qualia folk.com/2011/12/08/san-vicente/.

West, Candace C., and Don H. Zimmerman. 1987. "Doing Gender." *Gender and Society* 1 (2): 125–51.

———. 2009. "Accounting for Doing Gender." *Gender and Society* 23 (1): 111–22.

Whitehead, Harriet. 1981. "The Bow and the Burden Strap: A New Look at Institutionalized Homosexuality in Native North America." In *Sexual Meanings: The Cultural Construction of Gender and Sexuality*, edited by Sherry B. Ortner and Harriet Whitehead, 89–115. Cambridge: Cambridge University Press.

Williams, W. L. 1986. *The Spirit and the Flesh: Sexual Diversity in American Indian Culture*. Boston: Beacon.

Wood, Stephanie. 2003. *Transcending Conquest: Nahua Views of Spanish Colonial Mexico*. Norman: University of Oklahoma Press.

Zeitlin, Judith Francis. 2005. *Cultural Politics in Colonial Tehuantepec: Community and State Among the Isthmus Zapotec, 1500–1750*. Stanford, CA: Stanford University Press.

Zermeño, Sergio. 1993. "COCEI: Narodniks of Southern Mexico?" In *Zapotec Struggles: Histories, Politics, and Representations from Juchitán, Oaxaca*, edited by Howard Campbell, Leigh Binford, Miguel Bartolomé, and Alicia Barabas, 191–202. Washington, DC: Smithsonian Institution Press.

# INDEX

# ABOUT THE AUTHOR

A native of Mexico City and the father of three children, **Alfredo Mirandé** is Distinguished Professor of sociology and past chair of ethnic studies at the University of California, Riverside, and has also taught at Texas Tech University School of Law. After earning a BS in social science from Illinois State University and MA and PhD degrees in sociology from the University of Nebraska, he received a juris doctorate (JD) from Stanford University. Mirandé was the recipient of Ford Foundation and Rockefeller Foundation Postdoctoral Fellowships.

Professor Mirandé's teaching and research interests are in Chicano sociology, gender and masculinity, constitutional law, civil rights, and law, race, class, and gender. He is the author of *The Age of Crisis* (Harper & Row); *La Chicana: The Mexican American Woman* (University of Chicago Press); *The Chicano Experience* (University of Notre Dame Press); *Gringo Justice* (University of Notre Dame Press); *Hombres y Machos: Masculinity and Latino Culture* (Westview Press); *The Stanford Law Chronicles: Doin' Time on the Farm* (University of Notre Dame Press); *Rascuache Lawyer: Toward a Theory of Ordinary Litigation* (University of Arizona Press); and *Jalos USA: Transnational Community and Identity* (University of Notre Dame Press). He has published widely in sociology, Chicano studies, ethnic studies, and law.

Dr. Mirandé is a full-time teacher and researcher and has a limited, largely pro bono, law practice specializing in criminal law and employment discrimination.